THE PROJECTS

D1132623

THE PROJECTS

Gang and Non-Gang Families in East Los Angeles

JAMES DIEGO VIGIL

Foreword by Thomas S. Weisner

UNIVERSITY OF TEXAS PRESS, AUSTIN

COPYRIGHT © 2007 BY THE UNIVERSITY OF TEXAS PRESS

All rights reserved

Printed in the United States of America

First edition, 2007

Requests for permission to reproduce material from this work
should be sent to:
  Permissions
  University of Texas Press
  P.O. Box 7819
  Austin, TX 78713-7819
  www.utexas.edu/utpress/about/bpermission.html

∞ The paper used in this book meets the minimum requirements
of ANSI/NISO z39.48-1992 (R1997) (Permanence of Paper).

LIBRARY OF CONGRESS CATALOGING-IN-PUBLICATION DATA
Vigil, James Diego, 1938–
The projects : gang and non-gang families in East Los Angeles /
James Diego Vigil ; foreword by Thomas S. Weisner. — 1st ed.
      p.   cm.
Includes bibliographical references (p.   ) and index.
ISBN 978-0-292-71730-5 (cloth : alk. paper)
ISBN 978-0-292-71731-2 (pbk. : alk. paper)
1. Gangs—California—Los Angeles.   2. Gang members—Family
relationships—California—Los Angeles.   3. Poor families—California—Los
Angeles.   4. Public housing—California—Los Angeles.   5. Pico Gardens (Los
Angeles, Calif.)—Social conditions.   6. Los Angeles (Calif.)—Social conditions.
I. Title.
HV6439.U7L785   2007
364.106′60979494—dc22   2007024575

This book is dedicated to
Father Gregory J. Boyle, S.J.,
the human beacon light
and clarion call
for what our nation needs
to combat gangs.

CONTENTS

FOREWORD BY THOMAS S. WEISNER   ix

PREFACE   xiii

ONE.   Introduction   1

TWO.   Rationale and Methods   20

THREE.   A History of the Cuatro Flats Barrio Gang   39

FOUR.   The Gang Subculture: Change and Continuity   54

FIVE.   The Pico Gardens Clique   71

SIX.   A Gang Life   94

SEVEN.   Cholas in the World of Gangs   106

EIGHT.   Why Children Either Avoid or Affiliate with Gangs   126

NINE.   Families Not Involved with Gangs   141

TEN.   A Closer Look at Gang-Affiliated Families   158

ELEVEN.   Gang Prevention and Intervention Strategies over Time   177

TWELVE.   Conclusion and Recommendations   195

REFERENCES   213

INDEX   227

FOREWORD

The next time you read about gang violence, or proposals to do something about gangs and the neighborhoods they inhabit, you will bring an enriched frame of mind and understanding to the topic after reading Diego Vigil's book. *The Projects* brings gangs and families to life; it is a holistic study in the best sense. You will think of gang members not simply as individuals in isolation, but as struggling families and children embedded in their socio-cultural setting, with a sense of how they think, feel, and experience their world. *The Projects* provides evidence across levels of analysis, from structural conditions in the United States and in Los Angeles, to neighborhood and housing project circumstances, to family and school contexts, and—last but not least—to the everyday practices of families and gang members themselves.

The topics covered in Vigil's book move from the physical settings, to local history, to local gang and family subcultures, to a case study of one gang member and his family, to the stories of girls and young mothers in this world (the research team identifies three types of female gangs and gang members, and describes the very frequent sexual abuse and drug/alcohol abuse in their early experience), to important descriptions of the lives of non-gang families, along with a comparison of families embedded in the gang world. The book offers a conceptual overview of the factors pushing and pulling youth, a history of prevention/intervention efforts, and a con-cluding set of policy recommendations.

Vigil offers many compelling examples of everyday activities and rou-tines of gang members and their families. Whatever the structural and neighborhood circumstances that beset these youth and their families, the everyday activities they engage in matter a great deal because they are the proximal, immediate conditions with which youth and parents live. The book describes goals and values; the resources available; the tasks that have to get done; the social relationships and people within these settings; the emotions and motivations brought to the settings or activated by being in them; and the degree of stability and persistence over time (often, across three or more generations) of gang and family circumstances. Gangs provide some semblance of a shared "peer family" and security, however unhealthy and "warped," as Vigil says, these groups might have become for youth.

The depiction of families that managed to make it without much gang involvement is a particularly valuable feature of Vigil's work. Families without gang involvement are better off, have fewer children and more social capital, and are less troubled in many ways. Vigil describes the daily lives and parental monitoring strategies of families that are physically in the projects but not of the gangs' world. Some of the practices of these parents include: sustaining a predictable family routine, being present and available, engaging in monitoring and surveillance efforts, fostering a sense of family pride, making use of community services and programs, engaging in education, maintaining a focus on successful models, and offering affection plus strictness, as well as just getting out of the projects and participating in the wider world. Vigil comments that these strategies may seem "deceivingly simple," yet they are powerful in mitigating gang, neighborhood, and structural influences. These kinds of practices are largely absent in the families of gang members. Vigil comments that families with high gang involvement not only had no set mealtimes in which families would sit down together, but did not even have a pot on the stove or any food in the house to eat. Often there was no schedule or family activity routine at all.

Vigil also is careful to describe the wide range of variation among gang members and their families. He unpackages the categories "gang member" and "gang family," and in this way brings us closer to understanding the complexity of these categories. These families and communities are multiply marginalized, and have been across several generations. Vigil describes families according to their conventionality and their degree of parental and kin control. Youth are not inevitably drawn into gangs; individual differences affect how children respond. Some are pushed into gangs; some are pulled away from them by other forces; some have their paths interrupted by family members or outside interventions; and some families can and do influence their children's gang participation.

The exposure to chronic stress, danger, insecurity, and violence is difficult to overcome in the projects. Vigil comments that, these days, "the bullets whizzing around are marked 'For Whom It May Concern.'" Jeffrey Kling also describes the relief of mothers who get out of dangerous project housing, and away from "bullets [that] got no name." And Xavier Briggs, Susan Popkin, Tama Leventhal, and Gretchen Weismann describe the relief girls feel once they have moved away from the constant fear and harassment they experienced in housing project neighborhoods.

Vigil's work also stands out for its psychocultural perspective, particularly in its use of case materials. Vigil provides emotional depth in many of his accounts. His research provides evidence regarding sexuality (which Vigil describes as sometimes constituting frank abuse of females by males), violence, the needs for belonging and "twisted" kinds of intimacy, protection, early childbearing, and hyper-masculinity. Gang members foresee a shortened life expectancy, and this knowledge is accompanied by a sense of despair and fear/hyper-aggression. The author describes a kind of "perpetual conflict" in the lives of gang families at every level. Internalization of multiple marginality combines with self-preservation, as well as self-destruction, in some of these accounts. Vigil finds that there is community, parental, and intra-psychic denial at times concerning these aspects of negative behaviors in gangs and in some of the families. He comments that such a phenomenology of denial "surely is not a productive strategy" either for the families themselves, community activists, researchers, or policymakers.

Gangs are "institutions of last resort" for offering protection, resources, and a sense of power to youth and their parents. Vigil remarks that collective efficacy used to play a greater role in local community vigilance, and in the past there were some controls on gangs, but that this form of social capital has greatly declined. Gangs that in the past functioned at least in part to protect a community now are contributors to the much harsher current world of guns, drugs, and cash—the "cold despair" of today, as Vigil describes it.

Vigil identifies poverty as a key thread tying his story together. Persistent violence or the threat of violence (identified by residents as the most disliked aspect of their lives) is another central factor for children. Additionally, the author mentions that about a third of the families in his study were on AFDC in the 1990s; welfare policy changes have drastically reduced that number in recent years. What have these policy changes done to patterns of work and resources for families? And what about current policing practices—are they making a positive difference?

After inventorying the long history of community and intervention efforts, Vigil asks if we can develop better prevention and intervention strategies that fit poverty-stricken populations with gangs. There is tension in the community between wanting and needing outside intervention from police and others, and feeling anger at outside forces combined with a desire for community-based solutions. The long list of policy changes and recommendations that conclude the book, if enacted, would amount to a transformation of the world of the projects and gangs today, and I suspect that Vigil would be the first to admit that such a transformation is unlikely. We need much stronger research designs and evidence on what kinds of policies and programs truly have impacts on families, and that can be both sustained and scaled up in the real-world circumstances Vigil describes. *The Projects* offers those interested in undertaking effective interventions a full account of the contexts for which such interventions will have to be designed and implemented in order to succeed. It also suggests some outcomes that matter to families and children, which interventions might usefully address: fear reduction, the establishment of family routines, engagement in community programs, and an increase in positive connections outside the community.

Finally, it is very much worth appreciating that Vigil grew up in these barrio neighborhoods, sold papers on the streets there, and knows in a personal way whereof he speaks. Vigil does not offer easy, romanticized depictions of gang and community life, nor simple solutions, and he is clear that things are getting much worse, from the nearly fifty-year perspective he brings. He is one of those who not only did not have a gang life, but who has had a remarkable and successful research and teaching career, including, I am happy to say, his years at UCLA studying for his PhD and subsequently as a faculty member and colleague of mine. Throughout his career, Vigil has continued to bring new evidence and insight to our understanding of Chicano history, culture, gangs, and family and community life.

Thomas S. Weisner

PREFACE

In 1991, having just completed an on-site evaluation of a Los Angeles Housing Authority drug intervention program run by the Housing Authority in Pico Gardens, I approached Father Gregory Boyle to ask whether he would help me if I initiated a long-term study in that same housing development. Father Boyle agreed to do so, and soon after, I was able to write a proposal for a three-year study examining the connection between family life and gang membership. With funding from the U.S. Department of Health and Human Services (90-CL-1105), the study was begun in 1992.

I had already completed a book on barrio (neighborhood) gangs in Southern California (Vigil 1988) and was developing plans for a comparative work on gangs throughout the city of Los Angeles (Vigil 2002b). Earlier, I had assisted in studies conducted by my mentor, Joan W. Moore (distinguished professor emerita at the University of Wisconsin, Milwaukee) and her team of community researchers at the Chicano Pinto Research Project (Moore 1978, 1991; Moore and Long, 1981). This team primarily comprised ex-cons and ex–heroin addicts from the barrios of Los Angeles, mostly in East L.A. The team compiled longitudinal data on two barrio gangs dating from the 1940s, El Hoyo Maravilla and White Fence, carefully detailing family life going back several decades. One product of that work was an article I co-authored with Moore that summarizes some of the findings on the relationship between families and gangs (Moore and Vigil 1987).

For several reasons it was convenient to focus on this neighborhood, with which I had been familiar since childhood. Pico Gardens is a section of a public housing complex that anyone traveling north on Highway 101 passes; you can see it if you look to your left and down as the highway turns west, just before the Union Station and the Hollywood freeway. You can almost touch the skyscrapers that cover the horizon. Bringing to mind a Mexican saying ("so close to the United States but so far from God"), the projects are so close to the power center of downtown but so far from the resources needed to stem gang activity. From my earlier research, I was familiar with the gangs in and around Pico Gardens, two of which have storied histories like those studied by the Chicano Pinto Research Project. During the course of researching local drug use and drug trafficking for the intervention program evaluation, I renewed my acquaintance with Pico Gardens.

The focus of the long-term study would be family life and its connections with gang membership. While looking at the structure and organization and daily rhythms and routines of household heads and the members of the household, we might find differences among families that could tell us something about gangs. In the meantime, as with any good community study in the best tradition of anthropological fieldwork, we also might discover other things about the lives of the people who make up the projects. But, as I have said, the interrelationship between family dynamics and gang membership was our primary focus.

Research on this facet of the gang phenomenon goes back to the early gang researchers (Thrasher 1927; Ashbury 1927; Glueck and Glueck 1950) and has continued to be a focus of modern investigators. Some scholars have put the onus of responsibility almost entirely on the family, with little emphasis on other, larger forces in the equation. It was this position that I hoped to challenge and correct.

When Greg Boyle stepped in, little did I know that he would open so many doors for me. Almost instant trust was accorded me, something that urban anthropologists can struggle for months or years of fieldwork to achieve (sometimes without success), and our rapport was immediate. Particularly significant in the initial phase was when Greg took me to a household where I met a couple, Bebee and Pam McDuffie, who were deeply involved with the resident gang, Cuatro Flats. From then on it was a mostly smooth fieldwork experience. Bebee told me several years later that, when Greg crossed the threshold with me into Bebee's home, it was a clear sign that I was to be trusted implicitly, without reservation. Previous visitors brought by Greg to the threshold—political representatives and media folks out for a story—had been left right there, in the doorway, until Bebee and Pam made a decision about whether they should be allowed in. In other words, they had to earn the trust of the family before entering the inner sanctum of the home (and hearts) of those who were to become my community brokers and gatekeepers. As most fieldworkers know, once you've made a strong contact, then many other associations—perhaps not as strong but still welcomed and helpful—blossom into a larger network. Eventually, I had several key informants helping with the investigation, including gang members. It also helped that I was present there for a long time without any authorities showing up to arrest someone; this allowed me to be viewed as safe, and as someone to be trusted.

Even with this immediate foundation, and with the research team with which I surrounded myself for a primarily ethnographic study, we undertook a careful scientific approach to our research by randomly and selectively surveying community respondents and then quantitatively analyzing basic demographic information; all of this work is detailed in Chapter Two. We are fairly confident that this quantitative data—along with the more voluminous qualitative information stemming from intensive interviewing and extended observation over three years, bolstered by periodic visits by the author in subsequent years and up to the present—are sufficiently accurate, representative, and generalizable beyond this poor neighborhood.

Who made this work possible? A lot of people at different levels and with contrasting insights. First are the caretakers that serve the neighborhood and, more importantly, the residents who agreed to participate in the investigation. Especially significant is the research team and the method of involving community researchers that was learned from Joan Moore. Robert Garcia had been a key leader of the Chicano Pinto Research Project and, as an experienced community researcher, helped with the training. John M. Long, a professor of anthropology at East Los Angeles College who had grown up in East Los Angeles, supervised the community researchers day to day. Steve Yun, my undergraduate student from the University of Wisconsin–Madison who eventually became a medical doctor, collected and organized the different types of data we were gathering. Bebce and Norma Tovar were the community researchers who conducted the day-to-day interviews and observations, and met with the team weekly to debrief us on the field-work schedule and process. Pam McDuffie, familiar with many of the youth problems in the area, was invaluable as a key observer and as a contact with parent organizations.

Tom Weisner, professor of anthropology at UCLA, guided the staff in family studies and also graciously wrote the foreword to the book. Steve Lopez, a professor of psychology at UCLA, aided us in working out strategies for assessing family characteristics. David Diaz, a professor of Chicano Studies at CSU Northridge, gathered and compiled the initial data for the history of Cuatro flats. Charles Roseman, then a USC undergraduate and now a professor of anthropology at the University of Illinois–Urbana Champaign, drafted the framework utilized in Chapter Eight to help unravel the reasons why youths affiliate with or avoid gangs. Beth Caldwell, a UCLA undergraduate then and now a lawyer, researched and drafted a chapter on cholas, the females affiliated with the Cuatro Flats gangs—now Chapter Seven. Gisella Hanley, my co-author on another work and an adept graduate student, combed through the family histories with care and sensitivity to set the groundwork for Chapters Nine and Ten. Eric Taylor, a white student interested in and dedicated to slave revolt studies who received a B.A. in African American studies under my supervision at USC, and who was later my graduate student at UCLA, helped on different research projects of mine, including this one. Finally, Glenda Kelmes from UC Irvine ably assisted throughout the manuscript preparation and especially provided close scrutiny to the introduction, Chapter One, and the conclusion, Chapter Twelve.

Many other students assisted at various times and phases of the project, beginning with students at USC and continuing with those at UCLA and UC Irvine. At USC, Karin Stellwagon was superb as the visual anthropologist who caught many research episodes and scenes with both the still and video camera. Johann Diel and Nadine Diaz stand out as undergraduates who helped in many ways. There are too many students to mention at UCLA, but the names that stand out are: Carlos Ramos, Dean Toji—now a professor of geography at Long Beach State—Bong Vergara, Alfonso Gonzales, Ariade Della Dea, Ana Marie Lasso, Sophia Chang, Gemini Nolan, Ross Advincula, and probably others that I've slighted because there were so many of them. At UC Irvine, there are also too many, but the students that must be given recognition are graduate students Jesse Cheng and Tomson Nguyen, who both were always available to edit, research, and revise different parts of the manuscript; Richelle Swan, now a professor of criminal justice at CSU San Marcos, for editing throughout; and Dimitri Bogazianos, now a professor of criminal justice at Sacramento State, who drafted the first version of Bebee's biography, Chapter Six. The undergraduates who assisted were: Jennifer Kwon, Michelle Monreal, Erica Villa, Randi Odom, Rachel Tarras, Jill Anderson, and especially Hung Ho for composing Figures 5.1 and 5.2.

Many thanks to Scott Decker and Dana Peterson for their helpful comments and suggestions on the manuscript. And for assistance from the University of Texas Press, special thanks to editors Theresa May, Allison Faust, Lynne Chapman, and Rosemary Wetherold, as well as to the many others involved in the production process.

As always, I am grateful for the patient support of my wife, Polly, and my children, especially Joan Vigil-Rakhshani, who were there for me when I needed them. I take all responsibility for any factual errors and particular shards and peculiar "voices" of interpretation. I feel elated that this portrait of poor people will join the social science literature that aims to elucidate and provide insight into a major social problem.

CHAPTER ONE

INTRODUCTION

The strains and stresses of poverty in a public housing complex adversely affect family life, and those families that experience the greatest stress often lose control of their children to gangs. Losing children to gangs occurs in a social ecological arrangement, where there is already a generalized breakdown of major social control institutions. In this situation, street socialization of youths by one another and by slightly older youths becomes common. When street socialization takes over, a street gang with strong roots becomes a fixture. In the community this book focuses on, Cuatro Flats is this gang. Many youths in the Pico Gardens housing development in East Los Angeles have joined Cuatro Flats, but others have avoided doing so.

Why are some families vulnerable to having their children join gangs, and conversely, how have some families succeeded in having their children avoid gangs? How and why are there variances among poor families in a public housing project? If we know the answer to these questions, can we develop better prevention and intervention strategies that fit poverty-stricken populations?

I first learned of gangs as a young boy in this same Pico Gardens housing project. Pico Gardens became known to me when I was a thirteen-year-old selling newspapers on the street corner back in the early 1950s. Some of the other boys I worked with were from what we called "the projects."

My official introduction to the neighborhood came during a visit with one of its boy denizens. I remember the visit very well because it was that day that he related to me, in a low, awestruck voice, the adventures of "Geronimo," one of the infamous tough guys from the neighborhood. Geronimo, of African American and Latino parentage, was the leader of the Apaches, a gang from the projects.

According to the story, Geronimo was so tough and fearless that even the distant Los Angeles County forest fire authorities knew of him. According to the Paul Bunyan–esque tale, when there was a major forest fire, the forest ranger would pick up Geronimo and parachute him directly into the fire zone to combat the threatening blaze. Of such incredulous substance are myths born. Yet this myth captured at least some of the essence of Geronimo, as he eventually grew up to become Don Jordan, boxing's welterweight champion of the world.

The friend who told me the story was white—and probably "Okie." The projects in those days were populated by whites like my friend's family, along with African Americans and Mexicans. Over the decades there were many more tough guys and gangs in these same projects. By the time I returned to Pico Gardens again in the 1960s, twenty years after my first visit, that section of the projects was dominated by only one street gang—Cuatro Flats.

It was friendship that once again facilitated my 1960s visit to the projects. My associates, the Rodriguez brothers, were active members of the Chicano movement. Founders of a community center, they sought to steer youths in the right direction and away from drugs and gangs. "Casa de Carnalismo" (House of Brotherhood) was the center's name, and it was located on Fourth Street. The center achieved some success, yet struggled to stay afloat. Like many similar urban programs born of the War on Poverty, the center faced decreased funding over time. Its value was discounted, along with the population it was designed to help. In the end, Casa de Carnalismo was dismantled.

I reconnected again with Pico Gardens in the early 1990s, when I was asked to evaluate a drug intervention program. As I reacquainted myself with the area, I soon became aware of a government research grant that focused on family dynamics and street gangs. I wrote a proposal, funded by the Department of Health and Human Services (90-CL-1105), and soon was able to launch an in-depth community study of Pico Gardens, designed to expand understanding of family life in general. The focus of the investigation was to identify and explore the key forces that distinguish gang families from non-gang families.

Urban Poverty Research

Numerous ethnographic and survey investigations of low-income communities have addressed the many social, cultural, and emotional problems experienced by the impoverished (Anderson 1990; Hannerz 1969; Liebow

1967; Rainwater 1970; Suttles 1968). Utilizing a community study strategy, this book delves deep into the domestic and social habits and travails of family members, both adults and children, to show where and why larger forces and neighborhood effects have generated a gang and entrenched gang members.

Demographic characteristics of the population point to serious disadvantages that separate the projects from the surrounding area, the latter already a low-income enclave. What has transpired in this context of impoverishment is a gang with a long history and with deep cultural roots that persist into the present gang clique. The most marginalized males and females are the actors in this street drama, and it is clear that societal forces and family stresses are behind these developments.

As we unravel the differences between families, sifting through the structural and personal reasons, we can begin to understand why particular families have children in gangs and others do not; both family and individual histories shed light on and document these contrasts. Efforts to address and alleviate the worst effects of poverty, of which gangs are a part, are vitally important in the evolution of this community. Policy recommendations and practices must take heed of all information available if positive change is to occur.

This book adds to the tradition of poverty research and elaborates on the association of family dynamics and gang membership. Providing rich, in-depth interviews and observations, the present work examines the wide variation in income and social capital that exists among ostensibly poor residents of a mostly Mexican American background. Documentation on how families, from 1991 through 1995, connected and interacted with social and agency institutions in Greater East Los Angeles, helps chart the routines and rhythms of the lives of public housing development residents. Family life histories are presented to augment and provide texture to quantitative information. The latter are largely drawn from a random survey of project residents, followed by cross-reference with census data for the neighborhood precinct and with city, county, and state indices.

This investigation has confirmed what has long been suspected: Families of gang participants are poorer, have more children, and have less social capital than those of non-gang families. Furthermore, the gang family household heads in intensive interviews voiced a greater need for counseling, parenting training, and family therapy. From these candid discussions and interactions with parents and children, a series of policy recommendations have been generated to address other such low-income public housing developments and neighborhoods.

La Familia Reconsidered: Situating Analytical Frames

Despite my own early cultural and political ties to this area, an additional reason for selecting Pico Gardens as the research site for the study and book is that it lies in the heart of the Los Angeles barrios that have been adversely affected by the major socioeconomic developments of the past several decades (Moore and Vigil 1993). What has happened to the community has deeply affected families, children, and other caretaker institutions. Social control institutions (i.e., family, school, church, and police) in Pico Gardens are strained because of larger social and cultural forces. These include, among others, chronic unemployment and the pervasive lack of requisite economic or technical skills, as well as barriers based on race, language, and cultural practices, not to speak of the more than eight street gangs in the immediate vicinity. Moreover, youngsters in the projects are more likely to be socialized on the street. In previous work in two nearby barrios, it was found that substantially similar structural and historical forces existed (Chicano Pinto Research Project 1979; Moore 1978; Moore and Long 1981). At least three generations of gang members were identified in those two barrios, some coming from the same family; however, this trend was less true in Pico Gardens. Most of the members of these long-standing gangs were children from marginalized families who "grew up in the streets" (Moore and Vigil 1987). However, there is significant variation from one family to another within each barrio, as there is across barrios. Children from some families are much less affected by street socialization and are more likely to follow conventional lifestyles, avoiding the local gang. Residents of these two nearby barrios are subject to many of the same historical strains as those experienced by Pico Gardens residents, although the latter differed in many important ways. Toward this end, it was the main objective of this research to discover what additional factors make some families more vulnerable to gang membership. Further, the aim of the research was to determine why gang resistance was evidenced in similarly situated non-gang-involved families.

Two conceptual frameworks have guided this investigation of gang families, and the interplay between the macro and micro levels. The first entailed a macro-level examination of how certain factors, which have been referred to as "multiple marginality" (Franzese et al. 2006; Vigil 1988a), additively and cumulatively have shaped the functioning of some families, and the youth within them, to become more "*cholo*ized" (marginalized) and thus more at risk to street socialization vehicles such as gangs. The second level of analysis applied in this research dealt with the micro-level functioning of social control in the lives of the youth. It is the mechanism of the family and

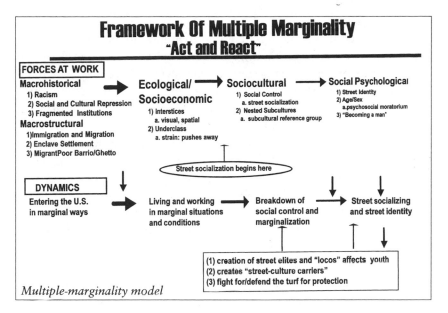

FIGURE 1.1.

associated institutions such as school and church that requires our attention (Loeber and Stouthamer-Loeber 1986; McLanahan and Sandefur 1994).

In previous work (1988a, 2002b), I have utilized the multiple-marginality macrostructural and macrohistorical framework to broaden and deepen the picture of which factors need to be considered, such as ecological, socioeconomic, sociocultural, and sociopsychological, in unraveling the breakdown of social control (fig. 1.1). This is especially the case in light of the maladaptation to cities that low-income, ethnic minority groups experience. All these factors intersect regularly with one another. To understand any of them, it is necessary to understand all of them in dissecting the gang phenomenon.

For example, Pico Gardens is bounded in such a way to make it a visually distinct and spatially separate enclave. Outside the mainstream of the city's economic life, a low-income, mostly immigrant group is subjected to low wages and unemployment, with a preponderance of families on welfare. Both private (family) and public (schools and police) institutions are attenuated and disconnected, making the residents' sociocultural experience disjointed and mixed. Finally, self-identification based on ecological, economic, and sociocultural patchiness and irregularities makes for fragmented and fragile sociopsychological moorings. Thus, gangs and gang members are found in marginal places, outside the mainstream of economic life, undergo social and cultural difficulties, and reflect a troubled identification trajectory.

The weight of all such factors leads individuals in each subsequent generation to repeat some type of gang adaptation, thus causing several siblings or relatives from two or more generations to follow older relatives into the gang. Living in the grips of poverty, or in a socioeconomic state bordering on poverty, gives residents of Pico Gardens considerably fewer avenues to improve their situation than those in other socioeconomic groups. Thus, it is common for youth who remain in the public housing development to model the path taken by older family members who have chosen to join gangs. Moore (1991) found that barrio family life was considerably affected by economic opportunities—which are, in turn, shaped by larger forces—and that when a neighborhood (again, such as a public housing development) experiences "persistent and concentrated poverty," the reverberations in other social and cultural realms are profound and must be understood.

Toward this end, a social control explanation is contextualized within a larger, macro framework (i.e., multiple marginality) that shows, in a second level of analysis, how major forces work to undermine or thwart family routines and functions and other control institutions that shape behavior (fig. 1.2). In short, a social control explanation is embedded in a macro framework (Barnard 2000, 17).

Barrio Life and Families

In a previous study (Moore and Vigil 1987), it was noted that four family types exist in most Mexican American barrios: (1) the "underclass," (2) the conventional/controlled, (3) the unconventional/controlled, and (4) the conventional/uncontrolled.

In the first type, the underclass, or what I have called the *cholo* family, it was found that family members have taken an unconventional turn and become as influential, if not more so, than gang peers in shaping barrio youngsters. ("Cholo" evolved from the Spanish word *solo* [alone] and meant cultural or racial marginality; today it is a label for the street youth.) Ineffectual in controlling its family members, the underclass also is involved in the gang/criminal subculture. The polar opposite to this type of family is the second variant, the conventional/controlled, which closely approximates what is found in stable working-class family units. Usually two parents, but sometimes a single parent, provide exemplary models for discipline and duty to their children and routinely and effectively maintain control over their household. The third type, the unconventional/controlled, are families that have adult members who may be involved in the gang and some deviant activities, such as drug sales, but maintain a conventional facade and conceal their deviance from the family. These individuals are still able to provide leadership to the children. Finally, the fourth type of family, conventional/

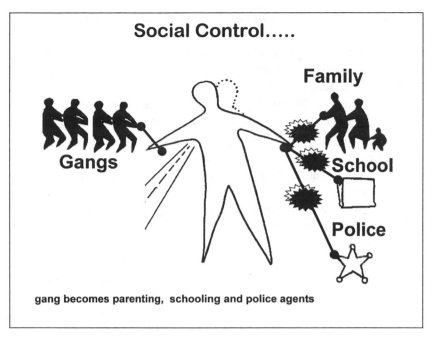

Social Control.....

Gangs

Family

School

Police

gang becomes parenting, schooling and police agents

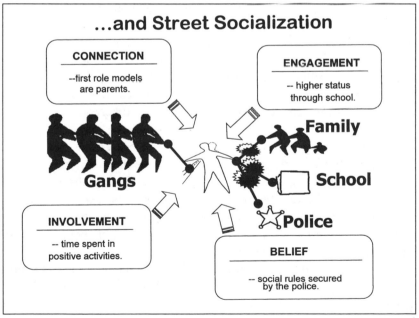

...and Street Socialization

CONNECTION

--first role models
are parents.

ENGAGEMENT

-- higher status
through school.

Gangs

Family

School

Police

INVOLVEMENT

-- time spent in
positive activities.

BELIEF

-- social rules secured
by the police.

FIGURE 1.2.

uncontrolled, simply comes up short, and there are many different variants in this category.

To reiterate, the breakdown of social control unfolds in the throes of these larger forces, and an examination of the breakdown must take this into account. Essentially, based on what I have witnessed and researched, I have concluded that the street gang is an outcome of marginalization, that is, the relegation of certain persons or groups to the fringes of society, where social and economic conditions result in powerlessness. This process occurs on multiple levels as a product of pressures and forces in play over a long period of time. Some of the gang members I have known have come from such stressed and unstable circumstances that one wonders how they have survived. The phrase "multiple marginality" reflects these complexities and their persistence over time. Other researchers have noted that multilevel and interactional analysis more accurately reflects deviant and delinquent behavior (Bronfenbrenner 1979; Elliott et al. 1989; Thornberry 1987).

Therefore, an examination of family structure and its relationship to delinquency was undertaken with an emphasis on the ways in which families facilitate or hinder gang involvement. Questions related to the ability of skilled parenting to serve as a buffer for youth who are otherwise feeling pushed and/or pulled into gang life were highlighted; in a subsequent chapter, a dynamic model of agent, push, pull, and interrupter explanations accounts for the variation among gang members. This topic is particularly relevant in light of both the popular and academic attention on the rise of single-parent families, along with the effects that such a family structure has on youth—effects that are particularly pronounced in urban areas characterized by economic stress (Smith et al. 1997; Thornberry et al. 1999; W. J. Wilson 1987).

By studying life in Pico Gardens, we can better understand how human agency interacts with structural factors to produce the reality that families living in public housing developments must contend with daily. In fact, this study examines the variety of ways the heads of households in both non-gang and gang families differ in their backgrounds and the choices that they make. Such backgrounds and choices tell us a great deal about the family situations and conditions that generate gang members.

Factors leading to both the broad category of delinquency and the more narrowly defined parameters of gang activity have long occupied scholars. Though the literature is vast, a number of consistent themes have emerged. Key to these discoveries are the social structural underpinnings of such behaviors (Loeber and Farrington 2001). In addition to family life and schooling patterns being altered under these situations and conditions, there has been a noticeable surge of violent gang activity in Pico Gardens during the last two decades. These developments can best be understood as an outcome of macro forces revamping micro ones; street socialization taking over conventional paths for social integration—in the voids left by schools, families, and religious or secular institutions—and thus turning out gang members.

The Economy and Housing

Many scholars in recent years have discussed the move to a global economy and the manner by which urban communities have found themselves without adequate opportunities for advancement, a process that was well under way earlier in public housing developments like Pico Gardens. This has certainly worsened the survival prospects for places like Pico, as manufacturing industries leave the inner cities of the United States and go abroad in the search for cheap labor (e.g., Hagedorn 1988, 2002; W. J. Wilson 1987, 1991, 1996); and Los Angeles is no exception to these macro changes (Moore and Vigil 1993; Vigil 1988a; Vigil and Yun 2001). This is particularly true for public housing communities, areas that suffer the indignities of urban poverty on an even more pronounced scale (Anderson and Massey 2001; Massey and Denton 1993; Massey and Kanaiaupuni 1993; McNulty and Holloway 2000; Vale 2000). Recent studies of public housing communities (e.g., Popkin et al. 2000; Venkatesh 2000) indicate that the multilevel disadvantages experienced by public housing residents are seemingly intractable and highly resistant to ameliorative efforts. As a result, residents are often left vulnerable to the forces of multiple marginality, restricted from economic routes to success, socially distanced from mainstream institutions, culturally disparaged, and personally disenfranchised (Vigil 1988a, 2002a; Vigil and Yun 2001).

In sum, the central and associated reasons for the rise of street gangs worldwide are poverty (i.e., where you work and live, or your social status and social space/place) and the repercussions and ramifications associated with it (Hazlehurst and Hazlehurst 1998). The nature of place and neighborhood effects is of primary importance when one considers the patterns of behavior present in Pico Gardens and other public housing communities (Vigil 2002a). One study of neighborhood effects on how residents develop, in both impoverished and economically stable areas, has shed light on this subject (Rubinowitz and Rosenbaum 2000). The authors demonstrate that in quasi experiments where families have been randomly moved from public housing to either urban or suburban environments, the latter environment proves to be much more beneficial to the development of the children, despite the discrimination that often accompanies the experience. In short,

Old house, the oldest home in the projects

lack of exposure to chronic neighborhood violence and stress is among the factors that allowed these new suburban dwellers to achieve substantially more in the educational arena than their urban counterparts. Similarly, some Pico residents have taken advantage of Section 8 public housing opportunities, moving to suburban areas to help their children escape street gang influences. Sometimes their exit was hastened by the One Strike rule instituted during President Bill Clinton's administration, which specified that any household resident involved in crime or drugs caused the whole family to be evicted.

Thus, deleterious neighborhood conditions have affected public housing developments nationwide and ultimately influence the vulnerability of individual communities to crime and delinquency. For example, Venkatesh's ethnographic and ethnohistorical study (2000) of the Robert Taylor Homes of Chicago describes the gradual transformation of that community over four decades as social programs were cut and globalization began to affect the region. With federal funding priorities shifting, gang activity morphed into a violent caricature of its original form. Gang activity that had once served as nothing more serious than mere nuisance took on a different look with the increasing availability of automatic weapons and involvement in the lucrative drug trade. As will be noted, it appears that a similar transformation has affected Pico Gardens.

Over time, the social controls that kept the Chicago community in check were weakened. Respondents lamented the breakdown of "mamas' mafias," informal networks of women heads of households who agreed to watch over the happenings in their buildings and keep the children in line. Such informal social controls eventually lost their positive influence as economically instrumental drug commerce became increasingly violent and the building maintenance became steadily neglected. Local involvement in community decision making also became diluted. As will be noted, Pico Gardens had similar community-based efforts to combat crime and gangs and build support networks, but those efforts met with uneven success. For example, an intervention effort by a Catholic church's Comite por Paz (Committee for Peace), a grassroots-based informal group of mostly mothers from the projects, often butted heads with a Neighborhood Watch program initiated by the police department.

Nevertheless, Venkatesh argues that the experiences he documents do not amount to a simple case of the "enemy within" perspective on crime in public housing. This perspective suggests that outside policing or social control mechanisms are necessarily futile because the "enemies" that community members are fighting are the members themselves. (As the comic strip character Pogo once stated: "We have met the enemy and he is us.") Instead, Venkatesh states that the experiences of Robert Taylor residents are more a testament to the complexity of the problem; gang members are reviled at times because of their often destructive activities, while they are simultaneously depended upon for financial opportunities and protection that are not sufficiently provided by outside agencies. Their role as the "enemy" is thus problematized, and the potential for an easy remedy to the situation is rendered highly unlikely.

Pico Gardens, of course, is a different public development with distinct problems of its own. However, our study supports the conclusion that Pico Gardens has experienced a deteriorating relationship with the police, a transition from a virtual crime-free zone to a war zone replete with shifts from violent police encounters, almost mini-riots, to a complete absence of a police presence and routine patrol. The Los Angeles Police Department (rightfully) fears the youth in the community, as numerous incidents attest to the dangerous situations that police officers face daily. Some memorable examples include the torching of a police car; the shooting of a motorcycle officer at the freeway off-ramp adjacent to the projects; and the brutal shattering of an officer's jaw when a youth threw a rock at him in the midst of one of the mini-riots spoken of above.

Popkin and her colleagues (2000) report other types of problems in their multimethod study of public housing in Chicago and show how gangs some-times are viewed more positively. They document that a number of crime reduction techniques employed in various segments of the larger public housing community were unsuccessful, partially due to the complex rela-tionships of residents with those active in gang activities. Since gang mem-bers do embody a number of different social roles, often including that of relative and friend, non-gang residents are reluctant to participate in com-munity crime prevention programs, due to loyalty as well as fear of retalia-tion. For example, as noted previously, consider in Pico Gardens the con-trast and conflict between Comite por Paz and Neighborhood Watch, the former a grassroots-based effort and the latter initiated by the police and often regarded as a "snitch" network. This factor interacts with others, such as irresponsibility on the part of housing officials and poor building design, to produce a highly challenging environment; more on these community issues will follow in later chapters.

Generally, the process by which neighborhood factors affect the quality of life in a given geographical area has been viewed through a number of dif-ferent conceptual lenses. The concept of "social capital" has attracted atten-tion in recent academic discussions of the topic. Social capital is commonly conceived of as the social ties between individuals, either kin or friends, that facilitate life chances (see Putnam 1993). These ties appear to function at the individual level, yet they are very much a product of the environ-ment. Recent studies have shown that the relationship between social capi-tal and neighborhood effects sometimes presents an interesting paradox: although close social ties among neighbors sometimes increase informal social controls and prevent crime and violence, under some circumstances they also sometimes hinder the development of social control. As discussed by Popkin et al. (2000), this may occur when non-gang-involved individu-als become unwittingly complicit in acts of violence transpiring in their neighborhood, by refusing to report them to the authorities due to personal loyalties. Conversely, in some suburban neighborhoods, there is a marked lack of social connections bridging ostensibly privacy-oriented residents, yet dutiful neighbors often informally patrol the neighborhood and report suspicious events to law enforcement authorities (Morenoff et al. 2001).

In order to elucidate the distinction between helpful and less helpful functions of social capital, Robert Sampson utilizes the concept of "collec-tive efficacy" (Sampson 2002; Sampson et al. 1997, 1999). Collective efficacy refers to a characteristic of communities whose members share a modicum of trust and expect others around them to proactively behave in ways that protect the community from harm, including violence and crime. Morenoff et al. (2001) found that low collective efficacy predicts increased homicide rates across neighborhoods. Kinship and friendship networks are related to violence primarily through their impact on collective efficacy. A few veteran Pico Gardens gang members (*veteranos*) often lament the breakdown in such "efficacy" traditions and accuse contemporary gang members of turning their backs on these roots.

Clearly, the structural and environmental setting of public housing contributes to the commission of crime and gang activity and strongly affects families and child-rearing practices (Dubrow and Garbarino 1989; McNulty and Holloway 2000; Weatherburn and Lind 2001). The disadvantages experienced in public housing complexes chiefly operate through a reduction in neighborhood efficacy and a reduction in social control as conceptualized by Hirschi (1969), that is, through a lack of social bonding to conventional others and conventional institutions. A lack of involvement in conventional institutions has been commonly noted in communities characterized by gang activity (Moore 1989; Short 2001). This observation holds true for the many families in Pico Gardens who have become involved in gang life.

Attention on the Family

Among the social control institutions that have received the most attention by scholars is the family. The connection between poverty, the family, and delinquency is an oft-examined topic in the scholarly literature; Farrington (2002) provides a summary of such family factors. Although some are wary of the implications that such studies hold for contemporary families (e.g., Hil and McMahon 2001), the majority of scholars of delinquency, dating back to the Gluecks (1950), have cited the family as one of the primary factors related to delinquency (McCord et al. 2001; Shelden et al. 1997).

Family-structural variables such as large family size, family disruption (divorce, abuse), and single-parent households (usually female-headed) have all been found to increase the likelihood of juvenile delinquency (Geisman and Wood 1986). In addition, family-functioning variables are important; Loeber and Stouthamer-Loeber (1986) found that four salient family functioning factors were (1) parental neglect, (2) conflict, (3) deviant behaviors and attitudes, and (4) family disruption. These factors closely approximate the family typology developed by Moore and Vigil (1987) noted above, although often labeled in different terms, and are generally agreed to be important in the discussion about delinquency and families (see Farrington 2002; Hirschi 1995). We will see later how these explanations are evidenced in the family life histories.

Gorman-Smith et al. (1998) examined the manner in which these four salient factors were related to patterns of delinquency in an inner-city community. They found tremendous variation in how different factors were uniquely related to the different types of behaviors by juveniles. What this indicated to the researchers is that blanket statements about family factors and delinquency may be inappropriate. They found that youth who were "nonoffenders" generally came from homes that were not characterized by multiple problems. Similarly, what I have referred to as multiple marginality is more than a laundry list of factors and more rightly suggests sequential linkages that additively and cumulatively shape delinquent behavior. According to Gorman-Smith and her colleagues, chronic juvenile offenders tended to be associated with families characterized by neglect, disruption, and conflict. In contrast, although youth who began getting into trouble at a later age were associated with disruption or conflict in the family, they seemed to have families without multiple problems. Their later involvement thus indicated that peer influences were more central to their experience.

Sampson and Laub (1994) reanalyzed the well-known study of the Gluecks and found four factors to be highly associated with official delinquent status among the five hundred juveniles studied: (1) parental rejection, (2) parental discipline, (3) mother's supervision, and (4) emotional attachment of the child. They found parental deviance, family disruption, and socioeconomic status to be less important. Significantly, family size and residential overcrowding were additionally found to contribute to the likelihood of delinquency. As in the present Pico Gardens study, it was found that gang-involved families were significantly more likely to have more people per household than non-gang families (Sampson and Laub 1994).

Overcrowding of residences is generally reflective of overall neighborhood disadvantage (Park and Burgess 1924; Sampson and Groves 1989; Shaw and McKay 1942; Vigil 1988a), and the question of how parenting processes can mediate the effects of the environment looms large. One highly influential factor in the development of delinquent behaviors is involvement in a delinquent or deviant peer group; but protective family factors can often mediate peer influences (Anderson 1999; Brody et al. 2001; Walker-Barnes and Mason 2001). Parental affection and nurturing have been shown to be negatively related to delinquent peer involvement, whereas harsh discipline and inconsistent parenting have been positively linked to deviant peer associations (Johnson and Pandina 1991); the more disadvantaged the community, the more noticeable the protective influences of effective, or authoritative, parenting (Brody et al. 2001). Additionally, Haapasalo and Pokela's study (1999) found that harsh or punitive, authoritarian discipline by

Hanging out in the courtyard

parents can backfire, predicting later delinquency. The manner by which parental factors influence behavior may not hold true across all racial and ethnic groups, however; there are indications that African American youth are more responsive to stricter parental discipline than are other groups of youth, primarily due to culture and socialization (Walker-Barnes and Mason 2001). In the case of the overwhelmingly Latino population in Pico Gardens, authoritarian parenting is actually counterproductive and can be harmful, as will be discussed in subsequent chapters. Not surprisingly, researchers have concluded the need for "precision parenting" in poor, urban neighborhoods (Gonzalez et al. 1996; Mason et al. 1996). These studies found that in urban neighborhoods the relation between parental involvement and monitoring is such that both too little (permissive parenting) or too much (authoritarian parenting) could result in problem behavior for children.

Yet, authoritative parenting clearly serves as a buffer that can lessen the influence of a violent environment or neighborhood on vulnerable youth (Tiet et al. 1998). Although effective parenting strategies tend to be hampered by structural adversity (Brody et al. 2003; Conger et al. 1994; Elder and Conger 2000; Gorman-Smith et al. 1999; Patterson et al. 1992; Weatherburn and Lind 2001), many resilient individuals nevertheless display substantial parenting skills in such circumstances. The effects of this buffer are further bolstered when the youth in a community have other healthy relationships with hardworking adults who are not involved with gangs or other criminal activities, such as drug sales enterprises. These relationships strengthen youth's social capital and often result in avenues to legitimate job opportunities that are not as readily available to youth without those connections (Coleman 1988; Short 2001; Sullivan 1989). Nevertheless, these positive and conventional relationships are harder and harder to come by in the most marginalized communities, as documented by Anderson (1990, 1999), Popkin et al. (2000), Venkatesh (2000), and W. J. Wilson (1996). Under these circumstances it is even more crucial that effective parenting be used as a protective influence against gang involvement, given all the obstacles that must be confronted.

In a synthesis of extant research on parenting and delinquency, Wright and Cullen (2001) partially replicate Sampson et al.'s concept of collective efficacy with their notion of parental efficacy, a term that refers to "parents who control and support their children." This notion is reflected in our own underscoring of how certain non-gang families used their time constructively, sought places for positive diversions and supervision, and built and cultivated social networks that exploited time and place to help build character in their children. In this vein, Wright and Cullen found that parental support is influential in and of itself—the affectionate parent who spends quality time with his or her children can oftentimes successfully prevent them from getting into trouble on the basis of the emotional bonds they have forged; even something as simple as sitting down to an evening dinner with the family reflects this orderly regularity. To reiterate, the non-gang families in this study demonstrate that parental efficacy can actually offset neighborhood inefficacy and assist parents in keeping their children out of harm's way. Indeed, the variation in household eating habits ranges from everyone eating together at an arranged time to a pot of food on the stove for members to partake in an irregular fashion to no food and no schedule, the latter being the most common practice among gang households.

Single Parents

The debate over single parenting and its relationship to decreased parental efficacy is a vigorous and ongoing one. There are many explanations proffered to account for the observation that single parents (often females) are less effective in preventing their children from getting into trouble. One explanation is that when there is only one parent to handle breadwinner and breadmaker roles and duties, there simply is not enough time or energy to do a good job of parenting (Matsueda and Heimer 1987; McLanahan and Sande-

Cuatro Flats and a *vato* (guy)

fur 1994). The other is that the single mother is uniquely less capable of supervising and disciplining her children—especially her male children. As will be noted later, and as Rebellion (2002) discovered at the individual level, it is not single parenting in and of itself that accounts for the "broken home" and delinquency relationship. Rather, the conflict and tension that surround the "broken home" arrangement is what counts. Indeed, Rebellion's statistical analysis of three panels of the National Youth Survey indicates that any type of marital disruption is related to delinquency on the part of affected children. Clearly, familial disruption of any type can be problematic in its repercussions, as this study will further demonstrate. However, Amato and Keith (1991), using a sample of divorced families, discovered that oftentimes the disruption inherent by unhappy couplings can have a greater negative impact than the disruption sustained in the separation or divorce. Although family disruption tends to be associated with gang involvement, it can also be said that family disruption does not necessarily always equate to future parental inefficacy; the non-gang family case studies presented in Chapter Eight are a testament to this.

Organization of the Book

Toward the end of offering workable public policies responsive to the concrete realities of public housing residents in general, and specifically to the families still struggling in Pico Gardens, the following chapters are organized to build upon one another. Gang families and the conceptual and theoretical constructs formulated to understand them are summarized in Chapter One. Like any other social phenomena, families and gangs do not arise in vacuums, as they occupy and are embedded within specific historical, economic, social, and cultural realities.

Chapter Two describes the physical and social location of the study in relation to the larger metropolitan area of which the community is a part. Census and other statistical indicators are used to sketch a portrait of the community and the residents therein. Here too, an explanation of the rationale and subsequent methodologies employed in the study is provided. Ethnographic survey techniques provide rich, contextually specific data facilitated by culturally trained community field-workers on-site over the duration of the study. The resulting samples are described, and key data features are teased out in an effort to clarify key concepts underlying much of the ensuing work.

In Chapter Three, a brief historical analysis of Pico Gardens and its residents is coupled with an elaboration on the origins and rise of the Cuatro Flats barrio gang. This chapter addresses the social, political, and economic transformations that define the complex, dynamic, and sometimes symbiotic-like relationship between the community's residents and the gang. Building on this historical analysis, Chapter Four describes the subculture that channels and directs the gang, especially looking at motivations and behaviors. Chapter Five takes an in-depth look at the contemporary street cohort that dominated the streets during the study, recreating some of the incidents and stories that provide the gist for this book. Particularly important here are details on the Pico Gardens cohort that rules today. Chapter Six elaborates on a single gang member and his family life, providing a micro-level perspective that details his growth and the continuity of his development as a gang member. Gender in the world of cholas is dissected in Chapter Seven to determine how the sisters, girlfriends, and other street females fare in the Pico Gardens neighborhood.

Chapter Eight introduces a causal framework for gang- and non-gang-involved families using an oversimplified bipolar gradient model. The different classes of effects acting on this model (i.e., pushes and pulls) are applied to the aggregate case history data in order to identify broad analytical themes endemic to gang involvement, resistance, or, even possibly, desistance. Chapters Nine and Ten are then devoted to presenting an in-depth meso-level narrative analysis of non-gang-involved families and gang-affiliated families, respectively. Utilizing the themes culled from the conceptual model proposed in Chapter Eight, case history narratives are disentangled in order to distinguish the peculiarities of individuals' lived experience as they navigate public housing's precarious terrain, ultimately concluding with family members' involvement in or avoidance of gang participation. An important feature of the detailed nature of this ethnographic data set is evidenced by the surface similarities of both types of families in terms of the structural challenges raised by daily existence, subsistence, personal improvement, and social reproduction, even though the non-gang families are somewhat better off. Patterns begin to emerge through examination of the coping strategies of successful evaders and the multiple, interacting vulnerabilities of those who fail to resist the lure of gang life.

Chapter Eleven examines the history and role of prevention and intervention strategies that mark the Pico Gardens community, citing specific programs and activities that have been in place to generally assist the residents and especially the youth. Finally, Chapter Twelve summarizes the salient themes evoked from the study. The prominence of family structure and interaction with regard to pushing or pulling residents into gang activity is a key theme in this chapter. This is so even though families, as social units, are themselves engaged in ubiquitous, dynamic power structures whose effects filter down to the micro level of personal involvement. Based on the findings and descriptions of this study, a reconsideration of the family as a mechanism of social control is in order. The remainder of this last chapter offers grounded evidence to generate public policy recommendations based on the substantive and cultural reality of the Pico Gardens community.

Conclusion

In sum, this broader community study is contextualized within macro developments to underscore the many issues that must be considered in the breakdowns leading to gangs. In the voids and gaps left in the wake of these social failures, the gang subculture has deepened its roots to continue to redirect the lives of too many youth in Pico Gardens. Of the various explanations for the association of family life and gang delinquency, the one that stands out is poverty and its ripple effects and repercussions on family stability and continuity.

CHAPTER TWO

RATIONALE AND METHODS

There are many rationales for selecting the Pico Gardens development as a research site. First, the complex contains a large concentration of low-income residents, many of whom have experienced persistent poverty over the span of generations. Second, a high percentage of families there rely on AFDC (Aid to Families with Dependent Children); many of these households are headed by a single parent. Third, the development features a local established gang, with at least seven other gangs inhabiting surrounding areas. The definitions for gangs are many, but the working one for this book is this: gangs are groups of male adolescents and youths who have grown up together as children, usually as cohorts in a low-income neighborhood of a city, and bonded together by a street subculture ethos that maintains an anti-social stance which embraces embracing unconventional values and norms. Finally, the local gang boasts a long history and a self-generating structure in the form of numerous age-graded cliques—a component that makes it possible to examine intergenerational change and continuity through retrospective interviews.

Finally, the fact that crime, drug trafficking and use, and violent gang conflicts are rampant in the area enables an examination of relations and daily interaction with law enforcement, which this study has found to be often antagonistic and hostile (Websdale 2001). For example, and as will be noted, numerous incidents occur involving the Los Angeles Police Department on a weekly or daily basis for all residents, such as officers stopping youths or adults on the streets if they look suspicious, irrespective of whether they are gang members or not; police car patrols checking license plates of all residents after a mini-riot or confrontation to instill fear; and a police observational presence at outdoor family gatherings to show authority even if the event is well organized and everyone is behaving properly. For gang members and their families the incidents are more extreme and frequent and include constant police monitoring; real and imagined beatings of gang members for no reason; officers stopping and questioning gang members in order to fill in field identification cards even if no crime was committed, so that the cards can later be used as evidence in courts to show gang affiliation; and overaggressive physical manhandling of gang suspects during investigations. During an interview for this study, for example, one female adult resident said, "Police always take our boys to the empty buildings to beat them up before taking them to jail." This observation was common earlier and based on fact then, but it is incorrect today, as police have eliminated this practice, according to a local caretaker.

The demographic characteristics of the population point to serious disadvantages that separate the projects from the surrounding area, the latter itself being a low-income enclave. Indeed, Pico Gardens attracted attention for this study in part because it lies in the heart of the East Los Angeles barrios that have been adversely affected by the major socioeconomic developments of the past several decades (Moore and Vigil 1993). Because it is a project of rented apartments, it may be that Pico Gardens' residents have fared worse under the impact of these transformations than have most area residents who reside in single-family, stand-alone houses. Furthermore, local public schools and health services have become increasingly overburdened in recent decades because of the continuing state and local government budget "squeeze," compounding the stresses on residents. In these conditions, participation in secondary and marginal labor markets, including illegal markets, has grown greatly (Moore 1989).

The pervasive and overwhelming reality of most Pico Gardens residents is the often heartbreaking poverty experienced in the face of metropolitan Los Angeles' opulence and opportunity. Just out of reach but always in sight, living in the background of wealth's possibilities brings into sharp focus the structural and functional contrast of public housing neighborhoods; if only they were farther apart and thus out of mind. A non-gang-member mother once told me, "I always feel like I'm alone and locked in even when I'm outside." Yet for all the physical and symbolic isolation imposed on these barrios, their residents raise families, are economically engaged in some capacity, and are otherwise interested in the same conditions of stability, personal growth, and self-improvements as their affluent counterparts. Moreover, there is the tacit acknowledgment that the service-oriented labor provided by public housing's immigrant residents is integral to maintaining the status quo.

Pico Gardens and another public housing development lie just east of and

Raspata (snow cone) vendor

across the Los Angeles River from downtown Los Angeles, on the northwestern edge of the Boyle Heights neighborhood. The skyscraper skyline to the west dominates the western horizon. With two other adjoining housing projects—Pico-Aliso extension and Aliso Village—it covers 57.5 acres of "townhouse-configured units." The three projects together have a total "official" population of 4,762 as well as an "unofficial" population that the government estimates to be quite substantial (Housing Authority 1990, 3–4). Latinos compose 85 percent of the residents and include "an unknown, but undoubtedly significant, number of individuals and families with non-legal immigration status" (Housing Authority 1990, 3–4). In the Pico Gardens development, the average reported annual income per household is $10,932 (see Condon 1989 and Jencks and Mayer 1988, for discussions concerning the relationship between recorded levels of official criminality in public housing projects and extreme poverty, respectively). The principal source of income for more than one-third of Pico Gardens households is AFDC payments. Although many households derive their incomes principally from employment, most jobholders work in the low-pay, low-status service and light manufacturing jobs that have largely supplanted the unionized, high-paying jobs once available to East Los Angeles residents (Moore and Vigil 1993).

While residents have more open space and grassy lawns than people living in the apartments and residential hotels of downtown Los Angeles, the facilities in Pico Gardens are visibly less well maintained than most of the freestanding homes and small apartment buildings in the residential areas of Boyle Heights. Moreover, Pico Gardens and the adjacent housing developments are isolated from downtown and the rest of East Los Angeles by physical barriers, including decaying industrial buildings and warehouses, the riverbed, railroad tracks, and freeways. In effect, the area is cordoned off and demarcated by practically all the boundary markers common to low-income neighborhoods.

As one of the oldest public housing developments in Los Angeles (dating from 1942), Pico Gardens also suffers from a deteriorating infrastructure. Electrical shorts, leaks in the plumbing and roofs, and insect and vermin infestation are recurring problems. The courtyards and parking lots provide open space, but the paved areas are potholed and cracked, and most of the large trees and shrubbery have been removed to eliminate hiding places. (This strategy was developed in the wake of a major police-resident clash in 1978, an incident made famous during the O. J. Simpson trial because police officer Mark Fuhrman had chased and beaten a suspected drug suspect then.) All of these characteristics have made Pico Gardens a somewhat barren, desolate place to live and raise a family. Recreation and social facilities are somewhat better than the residential buildings and their spartan exterior, but they are still limited and show similar signs of neglect. Most residents complain at one time or another about the condition of their neighborhood. A mother of one of the gang members lamented, "There were no things for my kid to do when he was young. He always just went outside to disappear someplace with his friends. All of them used to go places."

Such place and other pressures have contributed to an increasing inability to maintain effective social control in the streets and within many families (Moore and Vigil 1987). The per capita arrest rates for drug-related offenses and crimes of violence among residents of these projects were much higher than the national average—40 percent and 50 percent, respectively. For example, the national average for drug arrests and violent crime, respectively, was 0.43 percent and 0.73 percent for 1990 and 0.56 percent and 0.68 percent (FBI 1996; Housing Authority 1990; see also Dunworth 1994 for comparable reports). While, of course, those arrested are not exclusively gang members (many non-gang street dealers inhabit these housing developments), these circumstances have unsurprisingly given rise to a substantial degree of gang activity (see Venkatesh 1996). Of the eight known street gangs active in the Pico Gardens housing project and the two other projects contiguous with it, two gangs—Primera (First Street) Flats and Cuatro (Fourth Street) Flats—

Vatos hanging on clotheslines

have been in existence for over forty years (Housing Authority 1990). Gangs are an entrenched, multigenerational social institution not only offering an avenue for illegal markets and deviant associations but also, in a very tangible way, providing cohesion in the vacuum left by ineffective or unavailable conventional social institutions.

The Cuatro Flats gang predominates in Pico Gardens. There are still veteranos (members of the earliest cliques) who either live in this housing project or regularly visit family members currently living there. Importantly, many gang members are not only first-generation participants in gang activities but also first-generation, or "1.5 generation," immigrants (newcomers who arrived in the United States between the ages of four and seven years; see Vigil 1997 for a discussion of the 1.5 generation). At one time, families that were closely connected to Mexican culture generally succeeded in preventing their children from joining gangs (Vigil 1988a). This is much less true, however, as more and more first-generation Mexican and Latino children either join established gangs or spontaneously create new ones alongside previously existing gangs (Romo and Falbo 1996; Suarez-Orozco and Suarez-Orozco 1995; Vigil 1993). With eroding conventional opportunities for many of these youths, a middle-class lifestyle is out of the question, and instead marginalization ensures gang membership. For these reasons, the carriers of the gang subculture are continually replenished in Pico Gardens.

Researching Marginality

In order to better understand the variation in families associated with gang activity and drug problems, this investigation employed a combination of survey, interview, and observation techniques (Copeland 1991). A quantitative/qualitative mix of approaches and information was used for this study and involved the following four research steps:

1. *Baseline sample.* A random sample of 30 of the 239 units in Pico Gardens was drawn for a two-hour, questionnaire-guided interview with adult household principals. Four of the selected 30 households had at least one gang member. All of the interviews covered basic demographic, family, household, and other personal data. The instrument, constructed on the basis of field testing, focused on the social control issues of connections, engagement, involvement, and beliefs (Vigil 2002b). Research assistant trainees conducted the interviews. The latter were recruited from the community in the earlier intervention study in 1991, based on their willingness to gather data and maintain a cultural competence and sensitivity to respondents' concerns. A former male gang member and a female whose brother was a gang member were chosen to act as community researchers,

Bebee interviewing *vatos*

cultural brokers, and key informants—a tall order that greatly facilitated the research. Along with data from housing project management, the census, and other sources, this survey information became the baseline data source for all families in the research site.

2. *Intensified observation of housing project families.* Simultaneously, informal observation of overall family life was conducted by the two community researchers throughout the entire community (that is, not merely within the 30 selected households). All families exhibiting some sort of "ganging pattern" were designated for further study. A ganging pattern would include early street socialization and bonding among young children; close associations with similarly street-socialized friends in public school; and identification with the older street role models, learning and acting out the habits and customs of the street gang.

3. *Gang-based selection of second sample; intensified observations of gang families.* The community researchers determined that of all the remaining households (209 of 239) in Pico Gardens outside the original sample, 24 had members belonging to local gangs. Principals from these families were interviewed with the same survey instrument mentioned above. Taking together all families with at least one gang member (the 4 gang families from the first random sample plus the 24 families from the second gang sample), we pooled all information on Pico Gardens families with at least one active young gang member. Therefore, the final count for the gang-involved families in our study was 28, and for non-gang, 26.

4. *Focus on gang and non-gang families.* After initial analysis of this body of information, along with contact outreach and interviews with local leaders and service providers (church, probation, school, etc.), we undertook a more in-depth examination of the two types of families: gang families that showed an intergenerational ganging pattern (two or more siblings or two or more generations in the gang or, rarely, members of different gangs), and non-gang families.

This four-step framework was incorporated into a three-year longitudinal study that took place from 1991 to 1994. Much of the research on cultural transmission and enculturation of family members has benefited from extended examinations of selected families. Within the context of a public housing barrio, this study initially cast a wide net from which to select "ganging" families. Once identified, these families were observed and engaged for most of the three-year period. We gathered and recorded information in different settings, adapting to the constantly shifting personal and family dynamics that inevitably played out with the passage of time. Our database has accumulated detailed records of incidents, moods, attitudes, accomplishments, and failures for each family.

In addition to observations and individual and family histories, we sought important collateral information that would provide a more textured analysis of the socioeconomic conditions and interpersonal dynamics of the neighborhood; in effect, a way to triangulate qualitative and quantitative information (Lofland and Lofland 2005; Moore and Pinderhughes 1993; Weisner 1997; W. J. Wilson 1987). In sum, hard demographic data are joined with longitudinal observations and intensive interviews to provide the actors with the motivations and feelings that reflect a gang community and gang life. These data included the following:

1. During the first year of the research project, we compiled an ethnohistorical record of the Cuatro Flats (Fourth Street Flats) gang—a history that spans five decades. This information was based on interviews with older members and former members. We also recorded a less complete history of that gang's chief rivals. This historical record is discussed in depth in the following chapter.

2. During the second year, we sought the help of a person who worked with the local gangs to write a year-long chronicle of all public incidents involving violence, especially gang activities. This informant, a person who has lived in Pico Gardens for decades, is frequently sought out by residents (including gang members) for assistance and advice in dealing with service agencies and authorities. It goes without saying that the help of such a connected informant added invaluably to the quality of the evidence.

3. During the third year, we nonrandomly interviewed senior gang members chosen by our community researchers who represented the Pico Gardens clique. These interviews, primarily focused on household conditions and family structures, were based on an abbreviated form of the same questionnaire used in the surveys of resident households. The purpose for selecting these respondents was to show major trends and tendencies of gang affiliation and participation (e.g., drug use, parties) if not all gang patterns (e.g., gang conflicts, drug trafficking). Such respondents gave us a feel for broader community conditions in which the Pico Gardens housing project is situated.

4. We gathered extensive photographs and videotape footage in both public and private family settings within the housing development. Most of the photographs were taken by Vigil. A graduate film student at the University of Southern California trained the community researchers to use a videotape camera so they could videotape events themselves.

5. Finally, throughout the research period, Vigil in particular regularly interacted with local police, school officials, and public and private social service providers serving the area. One prominent community figure with whom Vigil communicated regularly was Father Gregory J. Boyle, formerly the local parish priest and currently the director of a renowned job development program designed to address the employment needs of local gang youths.

A study of this nature and scope would not have been possible without the cooperation of many parties—academic professionals, informants, observers, students, and community researchers (not necessarily mutually exclusive categories). The collaborative research strategy was similar to that used in earlier efforts of co–principal investigator Joan W. Moore and her coworkers at the Chicano Pinto Research Project (CPRP 1979; Moore and Long 1981). As previously mentioned, community research trainees who were longtime residents of the research site conducted most of the formal interviewing and served as principal sources of data based on their long experience in the community and personal knowledge of most of the residents; they conducted what is referred to as "street ethnography" (Weppner 1977).

Methodological Deviations from the Plan

Despite the successes of the project, the rigor of our methodological discussion would be compromised if the numerous problems that affected the course of the research were ignored. Foremost among the problems were the repeated outbursts of gang-related violence and other crime in the neighborhood. Several shooting deaths occurred in Pico Gardens and the Boyle Heights area during the final year of the study. Police-community relations remained troubled throughout the study period but were especially acute in the weeks following the shooting of a motorcycle officer just outside Pico Gardens in May 1994. During one 1993 episode, large numbers of police swarmed into Pico Gardens, beating and arresting several young men. One of our community research trainees was arrested during this incident while attempting to help a neighbor explain to the police that he lived in a nearby apartment. The trainee's wrist was injured during his arrest. The proximity of violence, not only in the lives of study participants but also for those collecting the data, surely colored responses and observations made during this exceptionally volatile period.

Other sources of tension in the housing development potentially affected the residents' confidence in the researchers' efforts. For example, just before the study got under way, the Los Angeles Housing Authority announced its intention to renovate Pico Gardens by demolishing and replacing most of the buildings there. Community meetings to discuss these plans were held thereafter, raising residents' apprehensions about who would have to move out of the development, for how long, and with what compensation and assistance. Similarly, in the fall of 1994, there was a proposition on California's ballot that would severely limit immigrants' access to public health, education, and welfare services, another source of concern that raised suspicions among immigrant residents regarding the role of the research team.

These tensions may have affected residents' responses during our study as well as their trust in our motivations for undertaking the project. Even with courteous prodding by the community researchers, two or three times adult household heads refused to talk to us, as did certain gang members who remained suspicious throughout the investigation. Community researchers were trained in this context to maintain a measured pressure of encouraging residents to cooperate. Weekly meetings, debriefings, follow-ups, and academic and community exchanges ensured that the investigation was kept on track.

In any event, most respondents in the formal interviews—which involved not only questionnaires but also tape-recorded sessions, subject to interviewees' approval—denied any involvement on their own part or that of any family members with gang activities, an attitude perhaps inspired by the One Strike rule of eviction if crime and drug charges were brought against any household member. During the field testing of the questionnaire, one trainee interviewed her mother, who denied that she or others in the family had ever imbibed in alcoholic beverages. Almost all respondents, in fact, actually denied that their household members drank any type of alcohol. In many of these instances, our interviewers had firsthand knowledge suggesting otherwise, and the data were corrected to reflect the actual facts. Thus the importance of having research assistants grounded in the research site proved to be an important check on the reliability of information gathered from the respondents, who were quite open and candid on most other demographic and household matters.

Despite these snags, however, the ultimate value of this study lies in its distinguishing features. Taking a broad analytical approach to the processes of enculturation (learning one's culture, and in this case the Mexican culture) and acculturation (learning the American culture) that families underwent, this book has combined interviews, life and family histories, and observational techniques in tracing the acquisition and retention of cultural patterns. We devoted attention to relations between youths and their adult siblings, as well as other adult figures. Given the longitudinal nature of the study, many family members were able to present their stories as a continuous narrative unfolding through the course of time. From the fragments of this complex mosaic, the investigators pieced together nuanced family stories that offered an understanding of gang families. This approach allowed us to achieve a level of texture and depth uncommon in comparative studies of gang and non-gang households.

The remainder of this chapter situates the Pico Gardens community within the larger social, economic, and cultural context of Los Angeles County. It also provides a geographical, physical, demographic, and social context for the community, employing official indicators in order to make greater sense of the use of the respondents' own narratives in later chapters. A descriptive and empirical analysis of the data collected from the sample is also included here.

Scenes of a Community Both In and Out of the Margins

The residents of Pico Gardens came to live in the housing development for a variety of reasons, whereas most remain there primarily because of economic factors. Several household heads in our sample were raised in Pico Gardens or an adjacent project. Most, however, lived elsewhere before moving into the projects. They relocated in Pico Gardens to take advantage of cheaper rents, larger apartments, the allowance of a large number of children, or a combination of these reasons. As a result of the benefits of living in the barrio, the households in Pico Gardens are much more stable than might be expected in such a poor environment. There are some exceptions to this rule, however, because particular individuals within households may come and go (such as "shadow" spouses, discussed later). Well over half of the families in Pico Gardens have resided in the same place for more than five years (see table 2.1 for a comparison of characteristics of residents of Pico Gardens, nearby communities, and Los Angeles County at large). This number is similar to that of their immediate neighbors (downtown and the rest of Boyle Heights), as well as the county's population in general. The average household size in Pico Gardens is considerably larger, however, than those in nearby neighborhoods (which are themselves larger than the county average).

The families in the barrio contain many more children than those in the surrounding communities, a characteristic that significantly lowers the average age of Pico Garden residents. The level of economic distress in Pico Gardens is evident. More than half of the households receive government

TABLE 2.1. *Selected Characteristics of Households in the Pico Gardens Sample and Other Areas*

	Pico Gardens	Boyle Heights and Downtown	East L.A.	Los Angeles County	U.S.
Mean number of persons per household	5.2	3.4	4.2	2.9	2.6
Mean age (years)	22.2	30.4	28.6	32.7	35.3
Percentage of population under age 18	57	28	34	26	26
Households receiving public assistance (%)	57	18	12	7	3
Households without a car (%)	27	42	20	11	10
Households in same residence for 5 years or more (%)	57	54	43	55	46

SOURCE: U.S. Census Bureau 2000 (for all areas except Pico Gardens).

AFDC payments and/or food stamps, eight times more often than residents of L.A. County overall, and more than a quarter of Pico Gardens households have no car (two and a half times the county-wide figure)—even though the nearest supermarket is two miles away. Downtown residents are even less likely to have a car, however, due to the larger number of elderly poor and, to a lesser degree, the lack of available parking for people living in residential hotels. It must be reiterated that housing residents are even worse off in an already-poor section of East Los Angeles, Boyle Heights, where 43.9 percent of all households have an income less than $15,000, 45.6 percent of all families with related children under the age of five live below the poverty level, and 13 percent of adults are unemployed (U.S. Census Bureau 2000).

The employment careers of Pico Gardens residents are marked by fits and starts, and less than a third of the households in our survey included people who were employed in a salaried or wage-paying job. (Several household heads and/or their spouses earned some money by making and peddling goods in the informal "underground economy.") Not surprisingly, the residents frequently express the need for jobs and skill training programs. Pico Gardens is surrounded by buildings that at one time housed thriving industrial plants and warehouses. Most of these buildings, however, were abandoned in the 1970s and 1980s and are now empty and decaying. The

Drying the clothes; sitting on the stoop

obvious distress of the immediate physical space is symbolic of these residents' invisibility and marginality. Across the river, service jobs are available to Pico Gardens residents in downtown hotels, restaurants, office buildings, and the booming garment district. Residents seeking work in these
places, however, compete with recent immigrants who are willing to accept
minimum wage or, all too often, even less. Most of the adult residents (even
those who immigrated long ago) feel that the entry-level jobs they might
have been willing to take years ago no longer provide them with enough income to sustain their families. Thus the lure of the informal job market has
become more attractive as the formal job market offers them less and less.
Moreover, they now know what constitutes a good job in America: merit
salary increases, career ladder opportunities, benefits, decent working conditions, and job security. Having learned this the hard way—by losing jobs,
being fired without cause, being lodged in below-minimum-wage jobs, and

working in unsafe and insecure working conditions, for example—they now realize that personal growth and improvements go hand in hand.

Compounding matters for the residents who want to work are the biases that potential employers have against people from the projects. Directly across the street from the housing development is a chicken-processing factory where *no one* from Pico Gardens works. Knowing the importance of job opportunities for the residents, a local city councilman and an activist priest who works to secure jobs for the residents met with the owners of this facility when it first opened. The discussion gave rise to mutual assurances that the city would expedite business permits and the employer would hire some of the housing development residents. The first half of the bargain was met, but as of early 2000, no residents had been hired by the factory. Similarly, a block away from the research site, a small brewery has employed hundreds of workers for various jobs in processing, warehousing, and truck driving, but, again, none of them are from Pico Gardens.

Most Pico Gardens residents say they would like to work, but they know that their earnings would barely cover what their households are getting now from AFDC, food stamps, and Medi-Cal coverage (California's version of Medicaid). This tension is often relieved by innovation in the informal economy by motivated residents. Some people in Pico Gardens have risen to be entrepreneurs within the context of a low-status reality (for example, one woman makes and sells nachos every Friday). Crossing boundaries between formal and informal economies appears much more normative when we remember that the average annual income reported in Pico Gardens—at $10,932—is far below the poverty level for families. The end result of this dismal economic situation in Pico Gardens is a large potential workforce that is unable to find decent-paying jobs. This group of people finds themselves trapped by a welfare system that allows them to make only a minimal amount of money before they lose their benefits. The economic conditions for residents who live in Pico Gardens are depressing. Adding to the lack of economic opportunity available to residents is that the community has been stigmatized by public officials and the media as a haven for welfare recipients, criminals, and drug users.

Tendencies and Trends of Sample Families

Our research identified some important differences among families in Pico Gardens. Many families have had greater success at resisting the worst elements in their environment. Frank Furstenberg's research (1993) supports our findings. As he observed, "Poor people, even those living in entrenched poverty, are not all alike. Indeed, differences among the underclass may be as conspicuous and consequential as any commonalities" (231). Furthermore, although Pico Gardens is renowned as a center of gang activity, only four of the thirty households in the random survey reported having an active gang member in their family. A majority of the gang families did, however, state that they had more than one family member who was gang affiliated. Usually, gang affiliation involved two or more siblings, and as many as eight in one family. A few of the gang members had parents who had been active gang members in their youth. One household head had a daughter and a grandson who lived with her and were gang members. Three households in the combined sample were headed by active gang members (their children were too young, however, to be involved with the gang). Even within this low-socioeconomic, mostly minority population, some households were markedly worse off than others, and their children were more at risk to fall prey to local problems, including gang involvement.

One of the most visible differences between the randomly selected households and households in the gang sample is the number of people in the households. Gang families have significantly larger households, with a mean of 5.43 members, whereas the mean in non-gang households is 5.00 ($t = 1.86, p < .05$). When only households with children are included, a visible, albeit marginal difference between the samples remains (mean 5.79 vs. mean 5.23, $t = 1.58$, $p < .10$). The difference is apparent even though there is also a larger proportion of households headed by a single, female parent in the gang sample. When we compare household size for only the single female–headed households with children, the average size of such households is also larger for the gang families (mean 5.69 vs. mean 4.27, $t = 2.93$, $p < .005$). Both larger families (and the consequent crowding that ensues) and single female–parent households have been commonly cited in the literature as being associated with youth gang membership (Franzese et al. 2006; Klein 1995; Vigil 1988a). Even though such associations are common knowledge, it was somewhat unexpected to find confirmation within the residential population at the research site.

Comparison of the responses of random-sample household heads with those of the gang-sample household heads shows additional differences that, although not significant by themselves, cumulatively suggest that the gang families face greater socioeconomic obstacles. For example, less than a third of the household heads in Pico Gardens have completed high school, but only half that many gang-sample household heads have done so. Similarly, seven of ten households in the general population do not have any member earning a regular wage or salary (this excludes income from "hustling," i.e., participating in the informal economy), but 8 of 10 gang-sample households fit into that category. Gang-sample households are marginally more likely to receive public assistance. On the quintessential Californian indicator of general well-being, we find a significant difference between the two types of households: about three-quarters of the randomly surveyed households have an automobile, but two-thirds of the gang-sample households do not (chi-square = 8.06, $p < 0.005$).

In addition to economic and overall quality-of-life differences that are described in depth in the remaining chapters, the families shared some commonalities. Most notably, the large family sizes of both gang and non-gang respondents meant that parenting for couples as well as single mothers left many children at risk for street socialization and gang recruitment (Vigil 1988a). For some families, this may indicate large generation and cultural gaps resulting from the relatively advanced age of parents still raising children, the sheer number of children parents must be responsible for, or the prevalence of single, female heads of households in this sample.

These brief examples suggest that family structure and function, especially as reflected in survey-collected quantitative data, provide a starting point for understanding the dynamics of family life and its relationship with either encouraging or deterring gang membership of the children in the family. Many of the single, female household heads occasionally had adult male companions who stayed in the household. One mother, who had young teenage children whom she said she could no longer control and who were involved with a gang, had a series of boyfriends staying with her for short periods of time during the research project. The woman reported, and the community researchers' observations confirmed, that the boyfriends took little or no interest in her children and contributed little to the household budget while they were there. Thus, if anything, the effect of these "shadow" spouses (so called because they are not listed on the Housing Authority roster of residents) on familial and child involvement was minimal. In another household, however, the mother's husband was a heavy drinker and was often away from home. The mother tried to ensure that when he was home, he would interact publicly with the children—playing with them or accompanying them to school or on shopping trips. The mother's motive for this was so that the children "will know they have a father, and so will the neighbors" (i.e., the children will not be stigmatized by local gossips as perhaps being "illegitimate").

Family structure is an important indicator and determining factor in whether or not youths become involved in gang activities. Parental practices and family relations, however, within any type of household can be

an even greater indicator. Also, the social capital inherent in the relationships, friendships, and overall competence of the parents can make a difference. When household heads were asked, for example, to whom they would
go for help with a problem, one third of the gang-sample respondents said
they had no one outside the household to turn to, but only a fifth of the
random-sample household heads had the same response. More than half of
the random-sample household heads said they could turn to family members residing nearby, while only a third of the gang-sample respondents
said they could rely on relatives for help. Similarly, only about one-eighth
of the random-sample household heads reported that no one outside their
households came to them for help, while over a third of the gang-sample
respondents did. Gang-sample household heads reported being less aware of
and taking less advantage of services offered by nearby service agencies, and
they also demonstrated less involvement in community groups such as the
Residents Advisory Council and the PTA. Less concretely, but importantly,
many of the gang-sample household heads did not have memories of their
own parents to help guide them in supervising their children. Several single
mothers in this group talked about childhoods that were full of misery, conflict, and, very often, abuse. Mothers in the random sample, however, often
recalled memories of effective parental child rearing as well as frequent con-
tributions of numerous other adults in extended kinship networks during
their childhood years.

Parental competence is central to one's ability to seek out and cultivate social capital in an environment. David Hamburg (1992) argues that
parental competency and access to social networks are essential to positive
child and youth development. He states that "the family that is embedded
in a strong network of social support is buffered against stressful experiences" (308). Furstenberg (1993) has also found there to be benefits associated
with higher degrees of parental competency. He suggests that parents with
stronger social support networks have an increased ability to regulate "their
children's behavior outside the home and in dealing with the formal and
informal institutions in which their children participated" (236). One exemplary mother in Pico Gardens follows the stereotypical tradition of being
an overworked and underappreciated suburban housewife; balancing four
or five tasks a day while working part-time. She regularly made snacks and
items for use in ceremonial affairs, which she sold to residents on a daily
basis. She picked up her children from school, took them to their music
lessons, taught dancing and singing classes twice a week (which, of course,
her children attended), and kept a sharp eye on her children during after-
school play groups and homework time at night. Despite doing all of these

activities, she remained active in the local church, which included not only religious observances, but also Comite por Paz and other community-based groups.

In general, then, the parents in the random sample of households differ from those in the gang sample. These differences appear to have contributed to their children's noninvolvement with gangs. This is not to suggest, however, that these non-gang families were without troubles. As was noted above, for example, the father in one of the non-gang households had a drinking problem that exacerbated the financial difficulties of the family. In another non-gang family discussed above, the teenage daughter of a single mother was briefly involved in a romantic relationship with an older boy who was a gang member. Other children in households that had no gang involvement still often became involved in delinquent behavior. This behavior included underage drinking and/or drug use, truancy, theft, and fighting. One youth who was raised in a non-gang family was serving a sentence for manslaughter at the time of the study. Although many of these young people still engage in some delinquent behavior, there are noticeable (but not significant) differences in the extent to which such troubles occur within the gang families and the non-gang families (more often in gang families).

Throughout the time we conducted our research project, gang violence was a major part of life in Pico Gardens. Not surprisingly, residents reported that gang-related activities (especially violence) were the most frequently disliked aspect of life in the housing development. Household heads in the gang sample were somewhat less likely than random-sample household heads to say this, although a majority of both groups did. Several youths known by members of the research team were injured by this violence. Two members of gang-sample households were killed.

Despite the dangers it poses, the gang life continues to fill voids left by conventional institutions; pushed out into the streets leaves such youth with few choices except what the streets have to offer. Several of the children in grammar school with whom the researchers met when this study first got under way had started to hang around with gang members by the end of the project. The pattern they exhibited was consistent with the usual pre-initiation behavior (Vigil 1996). One cohort of nearly a score of teenagers, who had attempted to develop an esthetically oriented graffiti club like those found in West L.A. and San Fernando Valley communities, were instead "jumped in" (initiated into) the local gang en masse, in large part because of pressure from gang members.

The data we collected on public agencies and school authorities and from criminal justice system officials are important in comprehending the family dynamics behind gang membership and behavior. As is discussed later, it appears that poor home socialization leads inexorably to street socialization. This means not only that children are prone to getting caught up in delinquent behavior, but also that they are socialized by their peers on the street. This is one of the most important areas we examine; echoing similar, earlier discoveries made by other researchers (Cartwright et al. 1975; A. Cohen 1955; Klein 1971; Thrasher 1927). The absence of parental and home-based influences, combined with limited schooling and teacher interactions, means that there are few positive institutions for youngsters, and thus they find socialization agents elsewhere. In an environment like Pico Gardens, the children who live there will encounter gang members. The gang alternates threats with offers of protection to youngsters.

Additionally, gang members show obvious emotional support for one another. The gang is a multiple-age peer group that has readily available values and norms of its own. All of these factors mean that the gang is the institution of last resort, filling in where other caretakers have failed. The overall effect is to make parenting and the development of successful families more difficult for the residents of Pico Gardens.

Our research addresses how stable families and parents armed with appropriate resources can (on average) make a significant difference in the likelihood that children will not become active in gangs. When these factors are absent, the costs are high to public safety, community cohesion, and personal well-being. It is in the public interest, then, to find ways to promote family stability and the acquisition of appropriate resources for parents.

In Chapters Nine and Ten, the dynamics of family life, with full descriptions of the nuances of our sample, are examined in order to make distinctions between those families that offer a protection against dysfunctional aspects of street socialization and those that succumb to the lure of gang life. However, before that, it is important to understand the historical roots of gang life in this community, as well as its great symbolic and cultural significance. With this in mind, the next chapter is presented as a descriptive, historical analysis of an important socializing institution in the neighborhood, also known as the Cuatro Flats gang.

A HISTORY OF THE CUATRO FLATS BARRIO GANG

An important part of the investigation into gang and non-gang families in the Pico-Aliso family housing community in East Los Angeles is understanding the history of the dominant gang in the area—Cuatro Flats. It is a long and deep history that began in the 1930s and has continued to the present. This chapter presents the background to the gang and shows how it began, grew, and slowly transformed itself into a street entity with so many of the self-destructive elements common to gangs in Los Angeles today. Family life in the project community also deteriorated during this span as what began as mostly working poor, two-parent households gradually evolved to include many more poor, single-parent households. The measured devolution of the Cuatro Flats gang and its original intentions to serve as a community protector parallel the descent of Pico Gardens itself into its present state of disrepair and despair.

Both gang and community began as strong, reasonably connected entities serving to hold together the people of Pico Gardens, a concentration of low-income citizens who congregated in one place to receive public assistance in weathering the tail end of the Great Depression. At the beginning of World War II, the New Deal provided public housing aimed to help people who helped themselves, and Pico Gardens residents were the working poor. However, both the people and, shortly thereafter, the gang were affected by the poverty and isolation that arose in Pico Gardens and other communities. It was a shaky but still-tolerable foundation. In the ensuing decades, however, a slow but steady disintegration transpired.

Pico-Aliso (two contiguous housing developments, Pico Gardens and Aliso Village) is the largest grouping of public housing projects west of the

Mississippi River and is home to as many as eight thousand residents. More than half of these individuals are under the age of eighteen, and some 60 percent of households have no source of earned income. In the aftermath of funding cuts in social services and poverty program contractions in the 1970s, persistent and concentrated poverty and unemployment gained a viselike grip on the community. Self-respect among individuals and the neighborhood began to decline in the 1980s and continued until the end of the century; it was during this time that crack cocaine appeared, and drug trafficking acccelerated among the street youth. The Cuatro Flats gang similarly abandoned its erstwhile image as protector and transformed itself into a much more individualistic, fragmented, and destructive force. The history of this significant change is outlined in this chapter to provide an accurate portrayal of the emergence and growth of a street gang and the ways in which young people in the community respond.

Early History of Cuatro Flats: 1930–1950

In the 1920s and 1930s, the area from which the Cuatro Flats gang arose was known as Russian Flats, for its first group of ethnic settlers. This area originally covered a large portion of Boyle Heights, bounded on the east by Lorena Street, on the west by the Los Angeles River, on the south by Olympic Boulevard, and on the north by Mission Road. Sometime in the mid-1930s, the Cuatro Flats gang emerged here, beginning as a group of youth claiming Fourth Street as its domain. Like the rest of East Los Angeles residents, the group had as its activities mostly just hanging around together and partying.

Early in the 1940s, the area became known as Tortilla Flats, and later in the decade the *placa* (graffiti logo) "Cuatro Flats" came into extensive use. In these early days, the gang resembled many of the other youth clubs forming in the city around this time. Whether among Latinos, African Americans, or other ethnic-based groups, young people were mobilizing within their communities to maintain the integrity of their cultural heritage on the one hand, while fighting the steadily encroaching consequences of racism and discrimination on the other. Indeed, as Mexican American families began to concentrate in the Pico-Aliso area in the late 1940s, largely due to their inability to move up the economic ladder as quickly as their Anglo counterparts in the boom years following World War II, gang membership provided a sense of personal pride in the face of social and economic powerlessness. Cuatro Flats was no exception and began as a Latino-oriented sports and social club. The local church and community center, Bronson House, offered

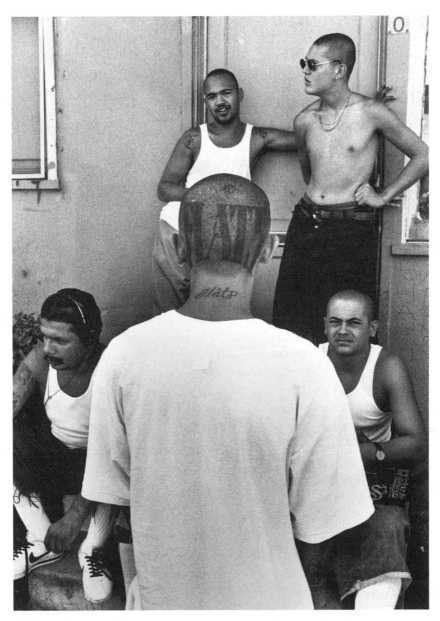

"Flats" tattoo; *vatos* relaxing

many outlets similar to those at the All Nations Club on Soto Street. Members sponsored dances and other social events and participated in boxing clubs. The Catholic church had a program, Catholic Youth Organization (CYO), that organized citywide boxing matches between different neighborhoods. In fact, a number of Cuatro Flats members later fought professionally during this era. Hollenbeck Park was one of the focal points of the gang's sphere of influence at this time. The park was a place where members could freely congregate and socialize.

The modern notions of gang activity, including homicides, drug sales, and assorted misdemeanors or felonies, were by far the exception among Cuatro Flats members at this time. Community cohesiveness was still strong, and ties of race, class, and neighborhood tended to dominate lesser differences. Of course, this is not to say that Cuatro Flats and its members were immune to negative influences. Relatively small-scale drug use, focusing on marijuana and heroin, was certainly making a mark on the community by the early 1950s, and gang fights were a common occurrence, more rumbles than shootings. However, community conflict in this era differed markedly from the violent skirmishes we tend to see today. Indeed, a pattern of "set battles" in which the protagonists mutually arranged a time and place for gang fights was the norm. Members of Cuatro Flats and other gangs in the area would clash with such weapons as fists, sticks, bats, chains, bumper jacks, and knives, but accidental maiming rather than intentional murder was usually the outcome in most instances (see Canada 1995 for how gang aggressions deteriorated into serious violent and life-threatening activities). Robert Garcia, or "Viejo," was one of the members of the first clique in the White Fence gang in the late 1940s. According to Garcia, his gang was the first one to start using guns, because it was surrounded by many other enemy barrios and was always outmanned (see Chicano Pinto Research Project 1979, Moore 1978, and Moore and Long 1981). White Fence and Primera Flats were two large Eastside gangs that coexisted with Cuatro Flats during this time, but while set battles occasionally erupted, no major gang wars occurred between them.

1950s and 1960s

Although gang violence gradually escalated during the 1950s and 1960s, the nature of this violence remained self-contained, following the original custom of set battles. Internal fights within Cuatro Flats occasionally occurred, and ordinarily were one-on-one or two-on-two affairs, in which the fellow gang members ensured that the protagonists faced each other without drawing their personal feud into a larger conflict. Similarly, inter-gang rivalries, while a common aspect of gang life, continued a pattern that rarely led to major injuries. Guns were almost never used, and knives were not the main weapon of choice. Veteranos (veterans, or what later became known as OGs, for "original gangsters") from Eastside gangs were raised in the tradition of settling conflicts from the shoulders up. Fisticuffs or boxing, rather than shooting, was thus the conventional method of settling disputes. The key figure in these disputes was the gang's toughest leader, who was considered to be the *más chingón* member (baddest dude) of the gang and the person who best understood the gang's place in the larger context of the barrio.

In addition to these relatively small-scale battles, frustrations and rivalries were also acted out in other ways. Aggression could be released, for example, during the football games between different gangs that began to be organized in the 1960s. The CYO played a major role in outfitting barrio youth in uniforms for each sport, especially football and boxing, and scheduled regular boxing events. After the 1943 Zoot Suit Riots, the Catholic church had been able to generate a lot of resources from more upscale Los Angeles residents to support such youth activities. I was one of the recipients of this largesse, and I vividly remember boxing at a Santa Monica church recreation hall in 1949 where Tom Harmon, the popular former Michigan University and L.A. Rams football player, auctioned off his All-American sweater to raise monies for the CYO.

Clearly, the modern notion of the ultraviolent street gang, or superpredator, as some observers maintain (Bennett et al. 1996, 26), did not prevail at this time. Gangs like Cuatro Flats remained on the fringes of respectable society. Street youth then were more like the Dead End Kids, with mischief, not malice, dominating. While perhaps feared and hated by some in the community, they did not spend their efforts in intimidation, random violence, and crime. Surely they were in the first stages of a process that ultimately transformed them into something entirely different. In the 1950s and 1960s, however, this metamorphosis was not yet complete. I have described this historical change in other venues for Mexican gangs in Los Angeles (Vigil 1988a; Vigil and Long 1990), as the street youth groups evolved from *palomillas* (youth cohorts) to boy gangs (Bogardus 1926), then to gangs (Bogardus 1943), and finally to a gang subculture deeply rooted in the urban landscape. Exceptions to these steady developments were short spurts of social programs to temporarily slow gang growth and activities (mainly the late 1940s, early 1950s, and late 1960s). In short, gangs became so deeply rooted because of enduring social isolation and neglect of marginalized populations.

Much like mainstream society at that time, Cuatro Flats was on the cusp of the social and cultural revolutions that would occur in the 1960s and 1970s. (Detailed information regarding the War on Poverty is presented in Chapter Eleven, because it deserves more than a passing mention, as it played a significant role in tempering and redirecting gang routines.) Still, informal organizations like Cuatro Flats gave young Mexican American kids in the Pico Gardens area a sense of family, of self-respect, and of responsibility. By fighting other gangs in minor scuffles, members were waging small neighborhood battles aimed at representing the community to outsiders and trying to maintain its structure and health from within, not at protecting some coveted drug turf or other entirely selfish or negative motives. At least that is what gang members recall of the times back then when comparing themselves to the contemporary gang member.

1970s and 1980s

The 1970s brought about major transformations in the very nature of gang culture for members of Cuatro Flats and the residents of Pico Gardens, in much the same way that African American gangs in L.A. changed at the time. Cuatro Flats was now becoming a rooted gang subculture and could claim some generational continuity, with sons following in the street footsteps of their fathers. The early part of the decade saw the increased use and sale of PCP, and substantial amounts of drug money flowed into the gang. As a result, gang members began to purchase guns in larger quantities and to use them to protect their newfound wealth. The presence of such an unprecedented number of guns, especially inexpensive Saturday night specials, in the community also led to a substantial evolution in the nature of community conflict. Whereas disputes had formerly been settled with fists, fistfights might ignite an encounter in the 1970s, but firearms were the inevitable retaliatory response. Guns made gang members of all ages equally deadly and filled them with an inflated sense of confidence, indestructibility, and cockiness. As a result, the influence of veteranos (OGs) as mentors to younger gang members began to wane severely. As one older gang member confessed to me, little dudes who could not fight their way out of a paper bag now became *matones* (killers or bad dudes).

Cuatro and Primera Flats remained the major gangs in the area at the time. A few African American gangs also began to crop up in the territory, beginning with the formation of the Brims in Aliso Village, a gang that was gone by 1984. As the Brims faded, they were replaced by the East Coast Crips, an African American gang based in South Central Los Angeles. Over a two- to three-year period in the 1980s, the Cuatro Flats gang periodically clashed with the East Coast Crips. In the mid-1970s, Cuatro Flats had also warred with the Juarez Maravilla gang. In spite of this escalating violence, however, Cuatro Flats continued to be known throughout the 1970s as the group to party with on the Eastside. People from other barrios frequently came to the Flats to party. Cuatro Flats had good relations with a number of major gangs, such as Florencia, Varrio Nueva Estrada (VNE), Maravilla, White Fence, and others. Cuatro Flats apparently provided a nonthreatening atmosphere in which members of different gangs could coexist in relative peace.

Groups on the periphery of formal gang membership also coexisted with Cuatro Flats at this time, beginning in the 1980s. These included the Clarence Street Stoners (CSS) and the Mob Crew (TMC, sometimes derisively referred to as "the Mexican Crips"), which actually were intertwined. These groups were not considered gangs during their initial formation but were instead "stoner" groups who focused on rock music, dance clubs, and drug use. They tended to avoid direct gang involvement and existed essentially as alternative groups for young adults to join without having to pledge formal allegiance to Cuatro or Primera Flats; some observers claim that the groups actually struck out on a new path as a form of repudiation of gangs and all that they represent. The football games that had begun to be organized between gangs in the 1960s during the War on Poverty continued in this decade, however, suggesting once again that Cuatro Flats and the other gangs in the area had not yet fully completed their fateful transformation into modern street gangs.

The 1980s ushered in a difficult and disruptive era for Cuatro Flats. The fabric of the gang changed dramatically. There were gaps in the leadership, and the younger members did not seek tutelage from OGs. Younger members established their own rules, began to disrespect the neighborhood, and failed to actively recruit new members. Additionally, the veterano leadership within Cuatro Flats had become relatively inactive. Older members were in jail, some had died, others had become drug addicts, and some had left the gang altogether. Thus, a critical period of evolution within the gang materialized, with an absence of more or less positive street role models to school younger members and new recruits. And this absence of example and mentoring occurred at precisely the moment when the gang was undergoing substantial transformations caused by the new flood of guns and drugs that would determine its future character. Bad role models, guns, and drugs made a volatile combination.

Interestingly, the use of the term "veterano" itself began to undergo a transformation that paralleled the changes taking place at the time. Indeed, the designation veterano had been very restricted, given only to those privileged members who had earned the ultimate level of respect by having actively participated in and experienced pivotal moments in the history of the gang. However, as younger gang members began to think that they deserved respect simply because they were now armed and dangerous, the terms veterano and OG began to lose much of their meaning. Members began to call themselves and their homies OGs after just a couple of years of gang life. Younger gang members no longer needed to prove their loyalty to the gang before earning the coveted title, and even those outside the barrio were sometimes called OGs. Though fairly minor in and of itself, this change in the usage and meaning of the term "original gangster" mirrored the breakdown in order that both the community and the gang were dealing with at the time.

Cuatro Flats had become severely splintered and was losing its raison d'être within the community by the 1980s. Indeed, by mid-decade, four groups had formed within the barrio: TMC, CSS, the Pico Stoners (which soon changed its name to the PGs, or Pico Gardens), and the Ghetto Boys. One faction of the gang did not even live in Pico Gardens but instead consisted of a gang of "weekend warriors" who would come into the barrio at the end of the week to sell drugs, socialize, and gangbang and leave when the weekend was over—an example of how Pico Gardens had become a "free crime zone." Alternative groups, whose members shied away from direct gang involvement, also continued to develop within Cuatro Flats territory. Their members formed as social and drug-based party crews. All of these groups were able to develop because the barrio had become weak and failed to exhibit the leadership required to keep the neighborhood in order. By mid-decade, party crews within Cuatro Flats' sphere of influence had developed throughout the Eastside, including the Boyle Heights Stoners, the Evergreen Stoners, the Tiny Boys, and the MCF (Michigan Criminal Force). Most of the members of these groups originally met at either Hollenbeck Junior High or Roosevelt High School.

The sale and purchase of PCP and crack cocaine, along with heroin use, also heavily influenced the actions of Cuatro Flats. Gang members began fighting with other young adults within the barrio, further alienating potential recruits in the process. Cuatro Flats' influence diminished, and its internal structure had become irreversibly fragmented. Throughout the Eastside and the rest of Los Angeles, the era of the "drive-by shooting" took hold in earnest in the 1980s. There were more gangs and less turf to fight over. The increase in larger numbers of Mexican/Latino immigrants and the marginalization process that chews up so many of its young were generating more and more gangs and gang members. Thus, continual conflict increasingly characterized gang experience. With the availability of Uzis and other auto-

Throwing signs, C-Four-Flats

matic weapons, as well as the money to purchase expensive cars, younger gang members perceived themselves as being similar to the glamorized gangsters of the 1920s and escalated their acts of violence to new levels. Both TMC and Cuatro Flats were heavily involved in crack cocaine and the more advanced criminal life, just two of the eight gangs on this path in the immediate vicinity.

Rather than formal gang wars, most of this conflict was based on personal disagreements, vendettas, or mindless paybacks that led to cycles of violent retaliations. The objective of drive-bys is to get in, shoot, and get out. The main method was to obtain a "G-ride," or stolen car, for the job and then dump it afterward. By the late 1980s, gang members increasingly relied on "baseheads," or PCP addicts, as drivers. High on drugs, these individuals would rarely remember what they had participated in the next day. Innocent victims—referred to by gang members as "mushrooms" because they pop up unexpectedly—were regularly caught in the cross fire of drive-by shootings, bringing the amount of death and mayhem inflicted on the community by gang members to new levels.

1990s to the Present

The problems that had been so prominently exposed in the 1980s only intensified in the following decade. Younger gang members continued to resist receiving advice from OGs about the codes of the street that had helped in some ways to control behavior within the barrio. Loyalty to community, respect of one's neighborhood, and generally using the lessons of the past to determine conduct in the present all became of secondary importance to the new generation of gang members. For example, respect for older adults and children always kept them out of the line of fire, whereas today the bullets whizzing around are marked "For Whom It May Concern." Not only was the old code being left behind, but fewer and fewer new gang members were familiar with the habits of the past, and thus they were unable to maintain even a modicum of responsibility. Formerly holding a very unspoken position, informal gang elders of the past were responsible for keeping other gang members in check. They influenced the ebb and flow of the gang's activities and relations with the immediate community, and they were required at times to develop a more or less clear approach toward gang wars and drug sales. Without such guidance, there is no real direction for the gang, and younger members run wild. When police targeted the barrio, for instance, it was sometimes the actions of the gang elders that put younger members in check by forcing them to tone down their aggressive behavior for the short term. If the gang was to maintain its reputation, all members had to recognize this type of street code that modulated the gang's activities.

To reiterate, however, it is the voids in other conventional realms that push youth into the new set of beliefs and habits of a gang. Most new recruits by the 1990s were joining for the money, the prestige, and the street party lifestyle, especially on weekends when young females from all over—cholas as well as wannabe cholas—descend on the neighborhood to find a "bad boy" to party with. (This is a very interesting area that requires some significant research. Why do girls like "bad boys"? It is well known among the street people that girls like guys who look and act tough, whether the boys are gang members or not. This predilection drives police officers crazy, as they wonder why nice-looking girls, perfectly decent otherwise, would want to go with a gangbanger.) New members, while desiring the aura of respect that comes with being a gang leader, rarely want to take on the responsibilities and difficulties that come with being a true leader. The breakdown in leadership and order caused by this new mentality has led to further splintering of the gangs within the Pico-Aliso area. Consequently, the level of conflict between the different gangs has continued to intensify. As a case in point, there is an active shooting war that started in 1991 between the Cuatro Flats, TMC, and CSL (Clarence Street Locos) gangs. This inter-gang rivalry has only intensified as more and more gangs establish themselves in the Pico-Aliso community. As of 2007, at least eight established youth gangs are operating in the area, and there are several dozen other on-again, off-again quasi-organized gangs. The Hollenbeck police say the number of gangs located in Pico-Aliso is unequaled anywhere.

The newer and larger TMC and the long-standing L.A. 13 Dukes are still very active in the area, along with smaller gangs such as the CSL, Rascals, and Al Capone gangs, as well as the last surviving remnants of the East Coast Crips, the sole African American gang in the neighborhood. These gangs vary in size from a couple of dozen members to nearly a hundred. Although there has been only one official girl gang in the area (the Hang Out Girls, who were affiliated with the East L.A. Dukes), young women usually become attached to gangs in an auxiliary capacity. Because of the limited room in Pico-Aliso, the territory that each gang claims is extremely small—no more than a couple of blocks for each gang. The Pico-Aliso gangs are involved in a continual process of claiming and reclaiming turf and of asserting and losing gang identity based on territory, violent behavior, drug commerce, and style. It is a battle waged largely by young people, not simply to control drug trafficking territory but to find a locus of personal control over their environment and their identity, to identify with what is perceived to be a sense of honor, and to feel a belonging in a world that has largely rejected them. It must be underscored, however, that it is a process driven more by a flight from negatives such as poverty and family and school problems than a pursuit of the shootings, drugs, and so on associated with gangs.

Efforts to mediate between rival gangs have enjoyed a certain level of success, with a high point reached in the 1960s, when there were more well-funded social programs and interventions (see Chapter Eleven). At the institutional level, a mediator from Community Youth Gang Services or Comite por Paz will attempt to negotiate a truce. Alternatively, a neutral third party with a strong reputation and a high degree of credibility within the community can serve as a mediator at the local level. These individuals communicate with designated liaisons of the rival gangs. This individual may know opposing gang members from school, jail, family relations, or juvenile hall. The representative must be a person whom both gangs look up to. The situation itself is what dictates how best to orchestrate peace. A mediator understands that every situation is different.

In developing the crisis intervention framework, the mediator negotiates with one or two representatives of each gang. This negotiation is always done in person. Discussions then focus on how to achieve a cease-fire. The idea of a cease-fire is circulated throughout the community either prior to or just after the first meeting. Two meetings are normally sufficient for an agreement to be reached. This temporary treaty occasionally includes the signing of a written document that is enforced by the word and reputation of the respective gang leaders. Their role is to inform their members about the truce and convince them that their gang's respect, honor, and pride are at stake in the matter.

After a truce has been called, the mediator will attempt to maintain a semblance of a dialogue between the gangs. This dialogue is designed to address ongoing problems, keep members who have been in jail in line and informed about the truce, and minimize the extent of conflicts between individual gang members. The objective is to prevent any potential hostilities from escalating. Clearly, effective gang leadership is an important part of minimizing the hostilities between rival gangs, for only through this leadership will the intentions and suggestions of the mediator be carried out.

Sadly, the lack of leadership in today's street gangs often dooms meaningful mediation to failure. Furthermore, growing poverty has continued to contribute to the perversion of gang life. With many parents either unemployed or strung out on drugs, increasingly younger children are forced to fend for themselves. As a result, the average age of drug sellers is getting younger and younger, with many youth peddling drugs simply to eat and provide basic sustenance for their family. As gangs continue to transform themselves into ever more sophisticated drug distribution organizations, their attractiveness to such youngsters remains understandably high. In spite of leadership problems and the presence of numerous rival gangs in the Pico-Aliso area, older gangs like Cuatro Flats continue to find ways to flourish. This is accomplished by abandoning many of the traditional elements of the gang and adopting new styles and codes of conduct in order to remain visible and contemporary.

When this fieldwork ended in 1996, the Mexican Mafia (EME) was just beginning to establish its "green-light" directive, ostensibly to intervene in gang conflicts by making gang members return to the old practice of facing an enemy by walking up to shoot him rather than wimping out and racing past him in a drive-by. In fact, fisticuffs were preferred rather than wanton drive-bys. If anyone in a gang disobeyed this order, a "green light" was issued on him, meaning that he should be shot and killed by anyone. However, this street directive did not work, because it turned out that what the EME really wanted was to extort monies gained by individuals or collectives of gang members that were into drug trafficking.

Conclusion

In little more than a half century, gangs such as Cuatro Flats have been transformed into bastardized versions of their former selves. Whereas youth

Youngsters and a *veterano*

were originally pushed into the gang to fill voids in their lives by adopting a meaningful identity, the nudge now is increasingly motivated by the lack of adequate formal economic prospects and the irresistible lure of quick, easy money provided by illegal drug markets. Respect of community and self have descended downward and become negligible in relation to the cold despair of today. Thus, no matter how understandable the motivation for engaging in the criminal underworld, the collateral costs to their own neighborhoods and families are lost on these tough, young gang members. In this negative, destructive scenario, communities are decaying from the inside out. While larger forces of racism and poverty provide the impetus for such transformations, it is the gang members themselves who unleash the greatest damage on the community.

Indeed, a few short decades ago, Latino and African American gangs in Los Angeles formed as street youth groups. Gangs formed to protect the community rather than to prey on it. Outsiders were intimidated, trouble-makers were reprimanded, and neighborhoods, though still impoverished, angry, and marginalized, were nevertheless respected and protected. In this climate of a semblance of respect and sense of community, gangs as we know them today were prevented from forming.

A number of forces brought an end to that situation. With the passing of civil rights legislation beginning in the 1950s and 1960s, for instance, the working poor in the community who had the drive, money, or determination began to get opportunities to leave their impoverished neighborhoods behind and forge better lives for themselves and their families in the Los Angeles suburbs. The War on Poverty and, later, CETA (Comprehensive Employment and Training Act) helped such families and individuals. The youth who remained behind in neighborhoods such as Pico Gardens in the wake of this out-migration were left to themselves. Problems and issues formerly sorted out on a community basis and with public assistance now began to be neglected and ignored. Thus, more impulsive and individualistic behavior took center stage.

However, this was only part of the problem. Indeed, while a certain loss of community stability was bound to occur in such a situation, that would not have inevitably resulted in the kind of self-destructive behavior that gangs practice today. Although gangs did take on an increasingly criminal nature as the communities that spawned them grew poorer and more unstable, the history of Cuatro Flats into the 1970s shows that gang activity remained far from the purely destructive force that it has become in recent times. In some sense, the gang actually continued to provide members with important social outlets, albeit with many more negative and destructive ones overall. In short, while the transformations brought about by the flight of stable, working-poor and working-class individuals from their former communities in the civil rights era and the end of the War on Poverty certainly did negatively affect neighborhoods such as Pico Gardens, they cannot be seen as the key factor that led to the violent permutation of gang life in Los Angeles.

Instead, the true turning point came with the increasing prevalence of guns and drugs in the community. Guns leveled the playing field and allowed the last remnants of the former order and regulations governing street gangs to disappear. A thirteen-year-old kid packed just as much power as a veterano who had been through the struggle from the beginning. Honor, rules, and respect seemed outdated, and guns inflated the egos of young-sters—desperate for an identity not based purely on images created by a wealthy, Anglo society—who mistakenly thought that weapons were the answer to their structural helplessness. An "every man for himself" atmosphere prevailed, distorting the original ideal of the gang, which came to be considered little more than a long lost irrelevant remnant. The new gang subculture had norms and values of its own. Drugs only exacerbated the situation, for their large-scale introduction made the profits to be reaped by the now armed street youth even greater. More and more groups with less and less in common now preyed on the community, and the level of conflict increased exponentially.

It is important to view the history of Pico Gardens and the Cuatro Flats barrio gang as a microcosm of many of the key features occurring simultaneously in American society (Hayden 2004). Gang members' behavior in the informal drug market mirrors that of large corporations in the 1980s and 1990s that deregulated, splintered, and conducted business ruthlessly to increase profits. Consumers incurred much of the collateral damage associated with self-indulgent corporate behavior. At the same time that American society was becoming more concerned with "law and order" and less concerned with social welfare, those most vulnerable to marginality also morphed into something less lawful and more disconnected from society.

The history of the Cuatro Flats gang of Pico Gardens is an excellent example of precisely this type of transformation. It is clear that the gang's original intentions, and ultimately its reason for existence, have become clouded if not lost altogether by the dramatic changes that have gripped the community in recent decades. Understanding this radical shift in the motivations, character, and membership of Cuatro Flats will go a long way toward appreciating the complexities faced by gang and non-gang families, which are described in the following chapters.

CHAPTER FOUR

THE GANG SUBCULTURE

Change and Continuity

He used to sneak out of the neighborhood and successfully avoid where gang members hung out. Going to high school was enough of a challenge, but trying to keep away from the guys who hung out all over the projects was an even tougher job. But he did it; he grew up in the projects, poor, with a struggling mother and seven other siblings, and he found a way out. He became a cop, an LAPD officer!

This is what the projects are all about, even though the screening he went through to become a police officer was extraordinary in anyone's book. Being from the projects isn't easy even for the people who go straight. People are poor and fighting to get out, and some of them make it. They get out and up and away from the poor areas of town, East Los Angeles in this case. A lot of them don't make it like this guy did, becoming a part of the establishment, a cop. The gang members knew him but never were able to connect with him in any way; his younger brother almost got sucked in, but he, the cop, and his mother and other siblings stepped in to pull him away. A former gang member who "matured out" (left the gang and its world) very early before getting into any serious trouble said it best: "When you grow up on the streets and there are no adults around in your life, then it is hard to get away from the guys who run the streets. I got out when I worked two jobs so I never had time to be around the neighborhood."

There are many more from the projects who just acquire a good working-class job, as a postman, a UPS (United Parcel Service) truck driver, a security guard at Montebello Town Center, or a receptionist at a local government office, for example. The comparatively few who don't make it wind up following what the streets offer, a life of destruction and meandering, losing themselves in violence and an aimless preoccupation, with nowhere to go. The gang members of Cuatro Flats fall into the last group. Interestingly, they have also captured a little bit of an illicit dream of the lower class by securing a street occupation that makes their lives a little bit better. Far from being middle class as gang members, the drug trafficking gives them opportunities to show off every now and then.

There is something else about the projects that needs to be told, an ethos and sentiment that are conveyed in different ways by a lot of residents, young and old. Everyone in the projects is connected because the people are so close together, many residents say. You are into everybody's business because you see and hear what is going on all the time. Further, in the projects there is a sense of safety that is hard to explain, except that you know the other residents cover your back even if they don't belong to the gang. Because all of you are poor in comparison with everyone outside of the projects, that feeling creates a bond of "us against them." As an older, female former gang member stated, "We knew we had nothing, and other outsiders had more. There was tightness there. We were like in a mansion with different wings that made us one, like in the same house."

Sometimes when you hear the beating one of your friends is receiving from his father, you can't help but show *cora* (empathy, or heart; from the Spanish word *corazón*) the next day when you see him, one of the young gang members told me. The same is true if one of the female residents is being beaten up by a boyfriend from the outside. Everyone feels the obligation to come out and intervene, for they are all members of the "family." In contrast, outsiders have a hard-and-fast position on the projects. Meeting people from outside the projects is always the same: "You're from the projects?" with a look that indicates you are rough and tough. After a while you try to live up to that image. This is the social glue that exists in an area that is poor and blatantly stigmatized, and it lays the foundation for what comes later: the gang. In fact, gang members think they act as a shield for the barrio. They make sure outsiders behave properly when they enter the project space. If they don't, and if something appears to be unusual on the face of it, then they act accordingly to step up.

Following up on the history of Cuatro Flats that was presented in Chapter Three, this chapter and the next one elaborate on the gang dynamics that drive and direct the lives of the contemporary gang, and Chapter Six provides insights into the gender scheme of the cholas who are friends and supporters of the males. First to be examined is the development of a subcultural pattern that has lasted for more than fifty years. Every few years a new cohort picks up the mantle of the barrio to defend it from intruders and to preserve and continue its street traditions. What do members of these cohorts do to uphold the tradition? Are there any changes that each cohort undergoes? How are gang members recruited and infused with the code of the streets? What is the gang structure and organization? When and how do they learn the street subculture and become street warriors? Ethnographic vignettes of the daily rhythms and routines will augment what they do, who they do it with, where they do it, and why they do it, all important features of understanding any gang.

Part of the Flats region just east of the Los Angeles River, Cuatro Flats came into existence soon after the Pico Gardens housing development was built in 1942 and over the decades has undergone evolutionary but also abrupt changes in its gang style and customs. The Flats as a distinct locale was recognized as early as the late nineteenth century in an area that was avoided mainly because it became dangerously inundated during the rainy season. It was uninhabitable, and only the poor and undesirable elements of the population would live there (Vigil 1988a). In fact, the area was flat because occasional heavy rains would swell the river and the spillage would level out the land until it reached the bluffs of Boyle Heights.

Close by the city's center, less than a mile away from what is now known as the Union Station, some of the Mexican settlements around the area, including the Flats, were referred to as "cholo court" in the 1920s because of the rundown shacks that were hastily and meagerly constructed by immigrants. So it was true then, and it is true today, that it is an undesirable place where the most destitute and impoverished live, a place that is home to one of the classic gangs of East Los Angeles.

As noted, Mexicans were usually the primary residents of the area. In the early twentieth century, however, the Flats area, along with Boyle Heights, became the Ellis Island of Los Angeles when Russian Jews, some blacks, Christian Molokans, Japanese, and other ethnic groups, including Mexicans of course in large numbers, arrived there to make their way through the maze that would make them American. Through the first half of the twentieth century this part of East Los Angeles was a thriving ethnic mix. Various commercial establishments, entertainment and social spots, religious and cultural activities, and political events centered there. The sounds, smells, and sights reflected a diversity that has not been matched in East Los Angeles since.

The early youth street groups in the 1920s included the above ethnic mix, and studies of their street group activities are well documented (Bogardus 1926; Kitano 1989; Waters 1999; Young 1929). Except for that period of time, the place has before and ever since been primarily Mexican, and so have

The author and Bebee in abandoned, industrial section of housing neighborhood

the gangs. Today there are many more gangs in the area because Mexican (and other Latino) immigration has continued unabated to the present, and thus the process of multiple marginalization mentioned earlier continues to churn out youth from the most stressed immigrant families.

"Multiple marginality" refers to being outside the mainstream of the dominant middle-class population of Los Angeles, literally across the river from downtown and on the other side of greater Los Angeles, with limited access to wealth and power. To reiterate, differences between the Pico Gardens world and the upscale Los Angeles one are stark and deep-rooted. There are ecological contrasts (visual and spatial distinctions); economic strains (underclass and secondary labor market); social dysfunctions (family stress and school failure); cultural discontinuities (hybrid mixture, syncretic cholo); and psychological ordeals (adolescent status crisis and group identity). As a result, youth in such communities spend most of their time being street socialized and learning the values and norms of the street in order to survive and maintain their lives as street people.

The Pico Gardens gang has generally relied on a territorial imperative, such as defense of the barrio and protecting one's street friends, as a raison d'être. Gang conflicts stem from this belief, and gang banging is considered a necessary activity that, in the participants' minds, protects the neighborhood. Banging may mean actually participating in gang conflicts or simply tacitly supporting it from afar. Over the years this conflict-based explanation has undergone some modifications with different immigrant populations, especially with the introduction of drug trafficking and related criminal activities, in which even youth outside the territory have begun to take part. The sociocultural mechanisms that maintain this continuity are many, but more important is that there has always been a cohort to carry on the gang goals. One of these mechanisms is an initiation ritual to induct a person into the gang (Vigil 1996). If you have lived in the barrio most of your life and grown up with the children your age, experienced attenuated parental and schooling influences, and undergone street socialization with them, then you are inclined to be informally "walked" into the gang. Some of the youth with such a background have mentioned that when they do have an initiation, it usually is a pro forma affair—a couple of punches by close friends and they are in.

Even though the initiation event, formal or informal, takes place during the junior high, adolescent-passage phase of a person's life, it is quite common to have many street socialization and school-related experiences that precede it. Many stories abound from a number of gang members on how street socialization would include long hours away from home exploring the downtown area of Los Angeles, just a short walk across the river on the Fourth Street Bridge. Department stores, the garment district, a dozen or more movie houses, and many shoppers and business folks made for a lively and entertaining magnet. It was common for these errant, hooky-playing youth to scrape up the price of a movie ticket, and one would attend and sit near the fire exit door and at the appropriate time open the door to let the others in. As a Catholic myself, I knew this was tantamount to a venial sin, as no one was hurt, and it was simply an inconvenience for the theater usher; and less money for the theater owners. Shoplifting, petty theft, and panhandling, among other mischievous ploys, as well as encountering street boys like themselves from rival neighborhoods for minor skirmishes, helped educate them in the ways of the street and prepare them for a life in the gang; earning their "bones," so to speak, mafia-style.

Similarly, many pre-gang bonding incidents occur in the schools, both in and outside classrooms (Vigil 1999, 2004). Most of the gang members have had learning difficulties since starting Second Street Elementary School, even though in recent years many have benefited from preschool learning programs like Head Start. Because of this shaky start, one of the first things that a teacher attempts in order to reverse the decades of educational neglect and isolation is to start subject-matter study groups to help them catch up in reading or math, for example. This means putting all the poor learners, with a myriad of contrasting educational handicaps, in the same learning group.

It is no coincidence that it is often the same children who have weak home and family socialization routines who are being put into these learning groups, the ones wandering around downtown L.A. and undergoing street bonding. Ergo, the schools additionally cement what happens on the streets, thus speeding up the induction into the gang. Moreover, almost all of the gang members are early nominees for being kicked and pushed out of school by the first year of high school, a statistic that is politically charged in a carefully couched phrase by school authorities as a process of "dropping out."

Simultaneously, another issue emerges: the psychosocial moratorium (Vigil 1988b). Erikson (1968) has referred to this human developmental passage as that time when there is a transition from childhood to adulthood (adolescence) and a person, for a number of reasons, experiences ambiguity and confusion over his or her identity. During early adolescence these street-reared youth have serious trouble with their self-image, strains that largely stem from family life and early childhood experiences. As has been noted, once an unfavorable self-image is set, a person is compelled more than attracted to join a gang. There is more of a need for group affiliation and activities in this phase of life. To assuage the confusion over self-identity, the group provides uniformity of opinions, uniform rules, and a "uniformed" appearance. In the absence of stability in the barrio, family life, and school, the gang provides a haven and outlet for unsupervised and unguided youth. Cuatro Flats, like most other classic barrios, is representative of this multidimensional process.

In summary, junior high school, coupled with adolescent passage and street socialization, is the social arena where the major shift in gang connections, engagements, involvements, and beliefs occurs (Vigil 2002b). Peers in this environment take command and have an inordinate influence over others, and more so for youth who are susceptible to the wiles and whims of the gang. The presence of other gangs, the formal and informal initiation rituals, the acquisition of cholo signs and symbols, the ratcheting up of aggression and conflict to more serious levels—all hasten affiliation with a gang and signal a type of surrender of the self to the group (i.e., *mi barrio*).

Preceding this passage into the gang is the process known as street socialization, whereby youth raised in the streets more earnestly learn the ways of the street. Being molded into an effective participant of the gang occurs away from traditional institutions such as the family. Most of the members of each *klika* (clique or gang cohort) have had this type of upbringing; otherwise they would have great difficulty fitting into the gang. Those few individuals who have had a limited or short street socialization often have to stretch beyond their capacities to measure up. To be subject to street socialization is to be bereft of conventional supervision and guidance, as a person must now contend with a multiple-aged peer group that dominates the streets. In addition to being introduced to new social networks and new models for behavior, values, and attitudes, youth also receive, in return, security and protection from being fair game for anyone. In all instances, if a person is street socialized, he or she must come to terms with the gang that controls the neighborhood.

Sometime earlier—but certainly by junior high school, when peers take on a new importance—the youth in Pico Gardens begin to be more earnestly connected to the local gang and for a number of reasons are tempted to join it. For one thing, arrival at junior high school exposes a person to youth from other barrios. In this case, it would be Hollenbeck Junior High, where at least a dozen gangs are present. White Fence and the King Kobras are historical enemies of Cuatro, and even before school starts, most of the project youth are prepared to have their guard up. If a student is not yet officially affiliated with his or her barrio gang, this time and place help secure that affiliation. At Hollenbeck, adjusting to the new demands of teachers and schedules is accompanied by coping with the various groupings and cliques that have carved out their social niches there. Each one of the groupings has a mini-territory on the school grounds, and Cuatro's is near the restrooms by the gym area. Interestingly, gang and non-gang children hang out in their respective areas, for sometimes the non-gang youth gain residual protection from the presence of their own barrio's gang members.

Youth from different barrios may have occasionally come into contact with each other and experienced a brouhaha when they were younger, but most certainly it happens in junior high school. Most of these contacts consist of giving challenging looks (mad-dogging) and deliberately crowding another's space, but occasionally a more serious affair materializes. In one case, two rival gang members who had the same class decided to arrange a fight after school, with each bringing their group with them.

At the predetermined place, an alley near the school, the two groups squared off (some were officially gang members, and others were not). One of the guys who made this arrangement decided that the biggest, tallest members from each side should "duke it out." Each group pushed its designated fighter forward as a type of group-selected volunteer, and the two unwitting designees, who had nothing to do with arranging the meeting, met in the middle. After a few punches were thrown, one fighter effectively landed a telling blow that stopped his opponent from fighting, and the celebration was on. The winning group jumped and shouted with joy, as the losers slipped away in shame and defeat. This event was reported to me by the winner of that arranged conflict, who by then was a seasoned gang member in his early twenties, with many serious gang conflicts under his belt. He playfully acknowledged that younger gang members had fights too, but those affairs were mostly *chavalo* (kid) stuff.

Aside from a "psychospatial identity" with their territory, or turf, gang members are taught, by direct instruction and modeling in the ways of the gang, the thinking and behavior that are expected of them. Often unnoticed by gang observers and authorities are the values ("ought-to's") and norms (blueprints for action) that guide gang members, even though these standards have been changed in recent years. The following examples give some indication of how this works for an older gang like Cuatro Flats: protection is valued, so watching other gang members' backs is expected; gang loyalty is important, and claiming a turf demonstrates it; respect is crucial, and deference to older gang members is shown; and emotional support is given as if gang members are family members.

If Cuatro Flats members who are still going to high school encounter a challenge like "Where are you from?" from rival gang members (such as TMC and White Fence) while walking home from school, they regularly relay this information back to fellow gang members, who will register it for future considerations. The latter could be stored for a similar retaliation of "hitting up" (verbally accosting) someone from White Fence, sometimes just anyone from that neighborhood. Of course, if the encounter involves either the brandishing of a weapon or its use, then the "payback" would be ratcheted up.

Similarly, demonstrating loyalty to the gang can occur in the same situation just described. Younger gang members sometimes are challenged with "Where are you from?" by veteranos of their own gang to test them. Those who aspire to be loyal to their barrio gang will answer the question affirmatively and take their chances, even if it means trouble. A couple of the younger gang members who were interviewed mentioned that they were scared but had to maintain a hardened, tough front when tested in this manner. It is also relatively common for the police to pick up a gang member and then drop him off in a rival gang's territory, dramatically announcing on the car's loudspeaker that —— from —— (name of gang) is in the vicinity as they drive away.

Finally, though gangs claim to be egalitarian, there is a special place in members' hearts for the veteranos. These veterans have been through all the gang wars and withstood the prison experience many times over. Therefore, they are accorded great respect, even if they no longer are active "bangers" or "slangers" (i.e., participate in shootings or drug dealing). Bebee, the community researcher for this study, was much older than the current clique, but the gang members looked up to him with the greatest deference and respect. In their eyes, even though they were the active bangers and slangers, he had forever earned a status.

Keeping your word (*palabra*) and showing heart (cora) are common values too. These practices aid in the reciprocal relationships that pervade gang members' interactions over time. Perhaps second to the protection and security afforded by gang members, a requisite practice for street survival, are the affection and friendship that radiate from the gang. The gang replaces what has not been received or experienced at home or school or in any other arena that would normally fulfill this basic human need.

Both in group discussions that I initiated with gang members or when I spoke to one of them alone, the idea of gang-as-family was never far from their utterances. "I think of the homeboys as my family," said one sixteen-year-old. The more popular, formal words or phrases to underscore this belief, such as *camarada* (comrade) or "homeboy," were used on a regular basis. Actions almost always followed these words. As an example, sharing resources such as food, drugs, alcohol, or even money was a core value. As one gang member proudly stated, "I throw a big party when I made a lot of money." Anyone who showed a self-centeredness or selfishness would be "thrown a *leva*" (sanctioned)—a gesture indicated by clenching the right hand in a fist straight up over the head, with the index finger pointing to the sky, simulating a pistol.

According to gang members who have been imprisoned, this sharing, egalitarian behavior is what distinguishes Chicanos from other ethnic groups. In fact, although outside the scope of this study, prisons served as another arena for gaining stature and respect and reaching a higher level of gang commitment, involvement, and perceived toughness. Doing time in a youth detention facility (a "camp") or the CYA (California Youth Authority) works more as a reification of gang membership than as rehabilitation. A pundit once remarked that the concept of rehabilitation does not work for gang members, considering how messed up their past lives were, and that returning them to that life would be a disaster. Thus, a more appropriate strategy is "habilitation"—setting them on a completely new, sounder foundation.

In any event, another value that shapes behavior, also played out in

Hanging and "toking up"

prison, is to show that you are or can act like a "man" in order to make it in the street gang world. Enculturation to street values and customs proceeds apace with these young males' social interactions and networks. Fear is omnipresent in street life, especially if one is unprotected, and must be managed; one gang member, Triste, was always afraid and wanted out of the gang. He began to use his birth name to signal this inclination, but before he could make his exit, he was shot and killed in a drive-by by a rival gang member.

To aid in managing this fear, there is a "manly" mind-set, or *locura*, a role and role performance especially instrumental in the context of street reality. Locura is a state of mind in which various quasi-controlled actions denoting a type of craziness or wildness occur, giving the appearance of a lack of impulse control. A person who is a *loco* demonstrates this state of mind by alternately displaying a destructive fearlessness, toughness, daring, and other unpredictable forms of behavior. Getting loco on drugs and alcohol or excelling in gang banging are manifestations of this. Such traits are more or less considered gang ideals. Showing that one is tough and can take it, in this context, involves many behavioral levels: posturing with a sullen, mean look; laughing at a drive-by near miss (gallows humor); showing no mercy to a rival gang member who is considered deserving of death; plotting a drive-by in which innocent victims are present; and many other sorts of physical and emotional outbursts around fellow gang members that reflect a locura mind-set.

Two other examples of this mind-set will suffice. Thumper, twenty-seven years old, once carelessly walked to the corner liquor store in broad daylight to purchase more beer to feed the buzz he had started earlier in the morning. The store was located on the street that is the boundary between Cuatro and its arch gang enemy, the Mob Crew (TMC). This was a period when the two gangs were locked in a vicious, months-long gun battle. When someone from TMC saw Thumper, drunk and flaunting a fearless front, he either shot Thumper on the spot or informed someone else who came and shot him. Hit in the stomach area but surviving the attack, all Thumper complained about was that his tattoos in that area of his body were forever ruined. He seldom was seen shirtless after that, dropping the gang-member habit of appearing in public naked in the upper body to show off one's tattoos.

The other incident demonstrates a mind-set of playing with death and coming out alive. Tiny Wino, age twenty-six, was walking down a street one day in a neutral neighborhood when he was spotted by a rival gang member who was driving by. The rival pulled out his gun and fired from a distance of about fifteen yards, hitting Tiny Wino in the shoulder and causing serious injury. Many months later, when Tiny Wino had recuperated, he ran into the shooter in a social context, at a party when there was a casual gang truce in the neighborhood. Coolly and with plenty of bravura, he complimented the shooter on his skill with the handgun, saying, "Te aventarse" (from the Spanish *aventar*, "to blow away," meaning "You displayed great skill").

Acts of violence can be both public and private. Violence occurs against others in the form of rampant gang fighting and slayings, and against oneself through the careless use and abuse of drugs and other chemical substances. In effect, it represents the destructive, debilitating habits that separate the gangs from most other adolescent peer networks. For Pico Gardens gang members, there are public and private destructive acts, meaning that the locura mind-set can take external and internal paths. To assist in this locura orientation, the gang has evolved a cohort tradition. Other barrios have similar hierarchies, defined by age and status, and Cuatro Flats has sometimes had three or four cliques simultaneously, particularly if some members are unable or refuse to mature out. Roughly, for Cuatro Flats, there are the twelve- to fifteen-year-olds in junior high who are just getting into the gang, the fourteen- to eighteen-year-olds who are in high school or have dropped out and are somewhat proven in the gang, and the eighteen- and twenty-year-olds who are seasoned (the majority of the current clique and the subject of the next chapter). These age ranges are not fixed, and successive cliques may overlap.

Each clique has selected its own name to go with the barrio name, and in the gang graffiti the moniker, clique name, and barrio name are sprayed on walls, fences, and other vertical surfaces. Thus, Snapper would graffiti his gang identity in this manner:

Snapper

P.G.

Cuatro Flats

Age grading is both an informal and formal mechanism to aid the barrio gang in its duties of defending its turf. When there is a locura binge, as there once was between Cuatro and TMC, then the cliques can collapse and older, somewhat inactive members are called into action to form a single extended, multiclique gang (a multiple-aged peer group) to carry out sorties and/or remain at the ready. The planned drive-by sorties are interspersed with opportunistic moments, such as the shooting of Thumper, that keep the conflict going. Such a coiled readiness guarantees that the nearby barrios, whether rivals or allies, maintain a deference and respect for Cuatro Flats.

The name of the clique running the streets as of this writing and when this study was initiated is Pico Gardens, or P.G. after the name of the projects. The current group is still recruiting and active. Years ago, cliques that were active for such a long time were unusual, but the gang's involvement in drug trafficking has changed that. There have been fourteen active cliques (age-graded cohorts) going back to the 1940s (with some loosely organized and short-lived groups included). For a classic barrio gang like Cuatro Flats, situated in a government project, this is about the typical number. Joan Moore (1978, 1991) provided the framework for clique formation and history in her studies of two similarly classic barrios, El Hoyo Maravilla and White Fence. Each of the Pico Gardens cliques has its own name and is listed in table 4.1 with the years that it was active.

Each clique, or klika, represents a cohort, usually starting with thirteen- or fourteen-year-old members and usually lasting until they are twenty or twenty-one years old. Occasionally, as in the case of the Pico Gardens klika, it continues well past its heyday because new members desire to become a part of a still-popular, active clique. Cliques are common organizational attributes of Chicano gangs, as Moore (1978) underscored with this statement:

TABLE 4.1. *Cuatro Flats Cliques*

Clique Name	Years in Existence
Apaches	1945–1955
Continentals	1962–1965
Sinners	1965–1970
Enanos	1968–1975
Peacemakers	1968–1975
Penguins	1969–1976
Chicos	1970–1977
Termites	1970–1975
Dukes	1973–1979
Night Owls	1974–1980
Pico Stoners	1983–1986
Countdowns	1987–1990
Chicos (new clique)	1989–1993
Pico Gardens (P.G.)	1989–present

"Chicano gangs are age graded, with a new klika, or cohort, forming every two years or so. Regardless of the degree of discipline and cohesiveness of any klika, their origin lies in the interbarrio conflicts between teenage boys in school or sports" (35).

The recorded data of the Pico Gardens project gangs shows that the Apaches (the one Geronimo, or Don Jordan, belonged to) were the first clique, beginning in 1945 when different barrio gangs were emerging in the area (see Duran 1992 for information on Tortilla Flats). By the mid-1950s this cohort had wound down, with no new cohort taking its place. In large part, the success of social intervention programs had slowed the generation of new gang members. Both DAP (Deputy Auxiliary Police, run by the LAPD) and the CYO (Catholic Youth Organization) had initiated sports, social outings, and recreation programs and activities to occupy the time and redirect the energies of barrio youth. The county's probation department also innovatively guided probationers in new ways with its outreach program of street caseworkers. Another effort, supported by these groups and others, was to start car or social clubs to replace the gang and create new names for these more pro-social entities; I was a member of such a car/social club named the Diablos, a CYO effort to replace the local Thirty-second Street gang. Unfortunately, many of these groups morphed into gangs when the staff and resources for the clubs dwindled and then ended. In sum, this slowdown in gang formation resulted in no new clique names until the early 1960s, when an entirely new phenomenon appeared.

Fashion changes throughout the United States regularly affect the population, especially youth. In this case an Ivy League look was dominant for a while, but by 1962 a "Continental" look came into vogue and for a while replaced the traditional street gang appearance of long, greasy ducktail haircuts and the garb of khakis, white T-shirts, long-sleeved plaid Pendleton shirts, and dark leather dress shoes. The Continental dress was much slicker, with tightly fitted dress slacks, fashionable shoes and shirts of various designs and hues, and a slightly shorter but slickly combed-back hair (think of the early Beatles with shorter hair).

This was the new Continental look and the street style in many barrios. By that time black music had evolved from rhythm and blues (cholo-preferred music) to Motown, the music of the Continentals. In Cuatro Flats, as in other barrio street gangs, this became a generic style that prevailed for a short time. It was a generation that had partially lost touch with the cholo influence and look, in part because of intervention and prevention successes. Additionally, the Vietnam War took more Mexican kids off the streets to be sent to Southeast Asia. Street role models were in short supply then, and the void cultivated experimentation with new "fronts" (Vigil 1988b).

The Continental era was short-lived, however, and by the mid-1960s a new klika arose named the Sinners, reviving the old cholo garb and style. This cohort experienced and reacted to the War on Poverty and the Chicano civil rights movement. Gang conflicts were toned down during this time, and the street youth released their frustrations and aggressions on school officials (e.g., a major high school walkout in 1968) and police departments (see Chapter Eleven for elaboration of these events, and see Franz Fanon's *The Wretched of the Earth* for an explanation of how oppressed groups often resist their oppressors and experience a catharsis).

Following the Sinners, who had mostly disbanded by 1970, was the Enanos (Midgets) klika, who began in 1968 and lasted until 1975. The latter were gang members turned activists. From this point on, a mix of klikas appears, all spawned by a quasi-hippie cohort known as the Peacemakers, which gelled in 1968 at the peak of the counterculture, civil rights era. This klika affected a more scraggly cholo style, with natural, longer hair and baggier khakis, and ironically were considerably more deviant than other klikas. They stole from and preyed on their own families and neighbors. (The man mentioned in the O. J. Simpson case as having been beaten up by Mark Fuhrman in 1978 was once a member of the Peacemakers.) From the Peacemakers came the Penguins (1969–1976), the Chicos (1970–1977), and the Termites (1970–1975), all coexisting throughout the early 1970s. For the reminder of the 1970s two other cliques coexisted, the Dukes (1973–1979)

Playing dice in between other diversions

and the Night Owls (1974–1980), the latter a mix of Chicanos and blacks. (Although the project gangs are mostly Chicano, there have always been a number of blacks in Cuatro Flats and sometimes a large number. The single all-black contemporary gang is the Eastside Crips, and much earlier there was the Ghetto Boys.)

As the 1980s began, a few remnants of some of the earlier cliques still remained, with most members having matured out and the rest either in prisons or victims to homicides. Around 1983 or 1984, another phenomenon similar to the Continental phase transpired. A resurrected youth style, with clear hippie overtones, emerged and was known as the Pico Stoners. It began as a party crew but eventually splintered into different klikas. The Stoner style consisted of wearing longer hair, riding Sting-Ray bikes, playing video games, and mostly smoking marijuana, ingesting methedrine, and dropping acid (LSD).

"Stoners" was a generic name for what was happening in different East Los Angeles barrios, and the Stoners phenomenon perhaps stemmed from the void in cholo role models, who were by then filling California prisons. Immigration from Mexico had also slowed, and this lull allowed the second generation to show off its knowledge of the United States. With this immigration gap and the lower number of cholos, a subcultural street void was occupied by the Stoner innovation. This front included a preference in communicating in the English language, clearly leaving Spanish behind and, more importantly, refusing to speak the cholo language—*calo* (Spanish slang) or Spanglish (a mix of English and Spanish). This shift was prevalent in how some Stoners changed the barrio names; for example, El Hoyo became the Hole, and Jardin became the Garden. Police experts even maintained that the Stoners practiced satanic rituals, such as sacrificing dogs in local cemeteries.

Soon, like the Continental phase, the barrio youth returned to its roots: *choloismo* and the ubiquitous khakis. Spinning off from the Stoners, which probably ended around 1986, were several klikas. The Countdowns surfaced first, about 1987, and were followed by the Chicos (another, newer Chicos cohort) and the current klika, Pico Gardens, which both arose in 1989. The latter has lasted longer than any other klika. As was discussed in Chapter Three, the evolution of these subcultures has resulted in a very dangerous and lethal gang style. Drugs, drug trafficking, and the ready availability of powerful guns have contributed to displays of violence that dwarf early gang conflicts, which were more like the rumbles portrayed in the film *West Side Story* than full-blown urban street wars. As previously noted, because drug trafficking has become a source of steady, and usually sizable, income and power, that might account for the Pico Gardens klika's having lasted so long. Most of the earlier klika members matured out to follow conventional pursuits: jobs and a family life. Though these paths are still pursued, it seems that today's gang members simultaneously keep their hand on this extra source of money as they mature out piecemeal.

An additional pressure encountered by the contemporary gang is the intrusive presence of the prison gang, the Mexican Mafia, EME. In the early 1990s, after the release of the film *American Me*, EME took to the streets, "taxing" (extorting) different barrio gangs a percentage of their drug sales; its ostensible purpose was to stop wanton gang shootings, a practice that interfered with drug trafficking. If a barrio didn't pay up, then it was given the "green light," meaning that barrio members in prison would be threatened or killed. Cuatro Flats, as part of the Flats confederation of barrios (i.e., Cuatro, Primera, Eastside Primera, Westside Primera, Compton, Verdugo, Paco, and Tortilla), was able to unite somewhat to resist this Mafia intrusion but not as successfully as the Maravilla confederation (El Hoyo, Kern, Arizona, Ford, Juarez, Lopez, and Rock).

In conclusion, it is clear that marginalization is behind the creation and persistence of the Cuatro Flats street gang. Defending their territory from other similarly marginalized youth is a way to show that they control something in their lives, when in fact they control nothing. The roles and goals that are set for them come from unconventional sources and certainly are not entirely of their own choosing. The attitudes and behavior they adopt are fashioned by previous generations of similarly out-of-control street populations. What accounts for this persistence? Pico Gardens has always been a low-income port of entry, and today immigration is a prominent element in the dynamics that perpetuate gang life; in fact, the current clique has a large number of foreign-born gang members (see Chapter Five). After all, choloization and street socialization go hand and hand, in that the maladaptation of segments of the children of immigrants is what leads to the breakdown of social control. Street socialization takes over thereafter, and the newly minted street subculture then guides the identity of the street youth, the gangs.

Chicano barrios are more geographically bounded than other gang neighborhoods, and this insulation and isolation are perhaps the geosocial explanation for why social problems fester there. The presence of plenty of unattached boys makes belonging to a gang inevitable when nothing else is available and there is no way to be transported someplace else. Why else would the gang make such a fuss over the barrio, giving it names at all levels—place, cohort, and individual—and then claiming it with pride to the death? Adding other signs and symbols makes it like a mini-nation, a place to call home and defend from would-be threats and attackers, when it is blatantly clear that the family and school life have fallen short. At first, gangs resulted because street realities imposed pressures and strains on youth, but now, with the passage of time and the steadying of a gang subculture, the gang has become a street fixture, and newcomers must contend with it whether or not they are street socialized. In the next chapter, an indepth look at the present clique, Pico Gardens, shows what this reality is all about.

CHAPTER FIVE

THE PICO GARDENS CLIQUE

One of the fascinating aspects of the gang member's persona is how he works at and consciously maintains a sullen, hard look and demeanor to show the world; for some, it is real. When you attempt to interact with gang members for the first time, you get this stony front; forget about questioning them right away. The advantage of long-term fieldwork, however, is that people eventually let their guard down, relax, and behave more like their true selves. Then you see normal young faces, a little scarred and tattered in some cases because of the traumatic lives they've had, smiling, grimacing, frowning, or evincing whatever emotion that befits them once they feel comfortable around you. There is one story that tells it all.

Bad Boy was one of the first gang members I met when I started the investigation. He was the younger brother of a woman who helped me throughout the time I was there, and she introduced him to me at her home. When you get to know someone at the home of his sister, a relaxed, informal setting, he usually acts like her brother, smiles, and acts graciously. Several months later I was at a wedding of one of the adults in the area—at the International Institute on Boyle Avenue, in fact, where I was shooting the affair (several times I was commandeered to photograph events like this, a functionary habit common to anthropologists who are trying to "win friends and influence people"). I ran into Bad Boy and his girlfriend, who was draped on his arm. He was all "choloed out," in freshly pressed, starched khakis and a nice white tank top to show his tattoos, and standing straight but laid-back at the same time, a common cool, cholo look. I wanted to take their picture, so I said, "What's happening, ——?" (I used his birth name, which his sister had used when she introduced me to him.) He was in the cholo mode, so he looked at me hard, uncaring, and answered testily: "Who are you?" The look lasted only a few seconds, as his girlfriend, part embarrassed and part incredulous, quickly nudged him with these words: "He called you ——, didn't he?" (She meant that I knew his private name.) No sooner had she uttered those words than he slipped smoothly into the guy I had been introduced to: smiling and gracious, as before. I reminded him where and when we had met and who introduced us. This experience, for me, was a harbinger of things to come, a type of smoke and mirrors of the street that one must learn.

Charting a Gang Subculture

This chapter provides similar ethnographic vignettes to highlight other personal and social habits of the Pico Gardens clique. Because of the barrio's location near downtown L.A., the clique draws from other ethnic groups, primarily Central Americans and Vietnamese, in making up a gang of mostly Mexican Americans. In addition, some of the basic information that reflects this group's situations and conditions is summarized here, such as the number of gang members at the time of the fieldwork, their nicknames, and some of the activities they were known for then and what has happened to them since the late 1990s, when this investigation was entirely completed.

Because of a number of factors, I was not able to meet and talk with each gang member in this clique. There were thirty-five individuals in this cohort, all males, and they ranged in age from sixteen to twenty-three years old; the females affiliated with these males and their beliefs and activities are covered in Chapter Seven. I saw some of the guys every day I was at the projects, which was about two or three times a week, and the greater majority I encountered only on occasion. The community researchers lived in the projects and interacted with these gang members on a daily basis, were privy to a lot of private intrigues, and reported these developments to me weekly. A couple of gang members questioned my presence there several times, and a few gave me ominous, pre–mad dog looks and refused to interact with me or allow that their photo be taken.

For example, I was taking a couple of friends on a photo shoot of the projects along with the community researchers. One guy I had never seen before was following us, broom in hand, and every time we stopped to talk or take photos, he would act like he was sweeping the sidewalk or parking lot. Well, when we eventually reached one of the porch steps of the community researcher, this guy loudly and with agitation shouted out to Bebee (and mostly us, the outsiders taking pictures) that he was a homeboy just like Bebee. He walked up to Bebee and shook his hand Chicano-style (three

The group psychology reigns!

moves: regular hand grip, shift to hand grip for arm wrestling, then back to regular hand grip), gestured proudly with his chest pushed out, and said, "We can take care of business." He then strutted away and left us transfixed, not knowing what to do or say.

Bebee interrupted our thoughts and explained that Tiger (who was a veterano from an earlier clique, probably the Countdowns) didn't like that we were using the projects as a zoo, a place to study people, even though Tiger never said those words. Bebee just knew that was what the whole show was all about. In fact, Bebee added that Tiger was a loco, and if the two of them ever got into it, they would have to go the distance, meaning one or the other would be killed. That was the first and last time I saw Tiger; and don't think I didn't keep my eye out for him the remainder of the fieldwork stay, as one must do with a loco who is volatile and unpredictable.

Even though I rarely, if ever, saw Tiger and some of the others in the study, that does not mean they were less involved than the rest; they did participate in many activities, conventional and unconventional, on a regular basis. It is just that they were not there every day and were busy doing other things, like working or engaging in other activities, informal or illicit.

Local dances and Friday night gatherings were held at the parking lots, hidden away from the main thoroughfares, and afforded interactions and socializing with many females from all neighborhoods—cholas, chola wanna-bes, and adventurers. Some of the latter "good girls" cruised the neighborhood looking for "bad boys." They enjoyed the challenge and excitement that a roughneck brings but also the knowledge that the inferred tough guy would likely "be down" for them, meaning he would protect them at any cost. This strange but interesting male-female relationship psychology is detailed in Chapter Seven.

This was a weekly affair for the clique; some members attended faithfully, and others showed up occasionally. There were even special "parties" called *momos*, when a motel or hotel room was rented and a few select associates were invited to "party." Drinking alcohol, smoking marijuana, cholo dancing (slow dancing), and, on occasion, running trains (guys lining up at a bedroom door and taking advantage of a drug- or alcohol-loaded chola) took place there. In all these socializing instances, a slight majority of the guys were all choloed out (dressed in their best gang garb)—wearing khakis (the Dickies brand is the preference) and bright white T-shirts or tank tops, sometimes going shirtless to show off their tattoos. More recently, as part of the DL belief (staying "down low," or under the radar, to avoid detection by others), some of the cholos dress more "square," the way regular youth their age dress. However, wearing large and baggy regular dress shirts and slacks gives them away, as the clothes hang distinctively on a posturing street dude. As several have observed about deeply experienced street people, there seems to be an aura about them that clothes and other "fronts" (image management) cannot hide.

These were the nights when a lot of guys appeared from earlier Pico Gardens cliques, even a few veteranos from the 1980s, to reconnect with their homeboys. Oftentimes, these contacts also meant making a drug connection with active drug dealers who were closer to the market and had ready access to whatever was desired. It was the time for such exchanges or for catching up on rival barrio news and incidents, pinpointing who is tagging the neighborhood (with graffiti), and other such intelligence gathering that reflected the daily gang cycle. This assemblage also showcased the sport of choice among cholos, handball, an activity acquired in prison and diffused to the barrio. There was one large wall on the side of one of the apartments, right next to the parking lot, and the game would run continuously until sunset. Different one-on-one players or double matches, allowing for dozens of players to get in on the action, made for strenuous physical exertion. As might be expected, some of the players had had plenty of time incarcerated away from the barrio to practice and perfect their game. These individuals showed mastery equal to or better than what one would find in a sports facility or country club handball court.

This social ritual would sometimes be a three-day weekend affair, especially Friday and Saturday nights, with quick forays to the liquor store to purchase refreshments, beer mostly but also soft drinks and occasionally cheap wine (white port mixed with a can of concentrated lemon juice, Thunderbird with an envelope of powdered grape Kool-Aid, and Ripple are still around, but ones like Strawberry Hill and Annie Green Springs are the current favorites) to accompany the "chronic" (the best, most expensive marijuana, at approximately $20 for a dove [one gram] or $500–$600 for an ounce, and from a kilo [2.2 pounds], $20,000 could be made) that was being passed around by any number of people. Spontaneous parties at someone's home occurred on some of these weekends, but rarely on weekdays. At these affairs, it usually was a small gathering of about eight to ten people, with drinks and chronic keeping them high while "oldies but goodies" music was played (slow 1950s rhythm-and-blues songs proclaiming love gained and lamenting love spurned and lost) and couples danced. Because of the excessive amount of drinking and smoking, it was not unusual for the party to end up in a brawl, even among friends who "got stupid," in the words of Bebee.

The cholo/a dance was stylized for both practical and romantic purposes: the dance allowed people who were high to simulate dancing, and the slow, close minor movements nurtured physical, amorous contact. Observers could say with some conviction that the couples were readying for coupling, as the tightly hugging, rocking side-to-side motion was more a subterfuge. In this cholo version, the girls, mostly cholas, were held very close to the guy with one of the girl's arms held behind her back, arguably a sign of surrender. Planted in one place on the floor, the couple would slowly rock back and forth with the music and mostly scrunch closer together throughout the night. If there was mutual agreement between the couple, the evening would end in the bedroom of that same home, even if it was just a friend who was hosting the party.

Hanging Out and Selling

During the day every week, awakening in the early afternoon from the previous night's partying, small groups of about four or five cholos would hang out in different spots in the projects; there were two or three groups like this, making it about ten to fifteen members every day. Gossiping about who's out of line, what the other barrios are doing, and who's slinging (selling drugs) occurs then. If they were smoking marijuana or drinking alcohol, maybe doing a little methedrine, the hangout was sure to be in the interior of the projects, behind a hidden isolated building or in an alleyway or driveway. In this way they would minimize being observed by the Neighborhood Watch adults, and, of course, the housing and regular police patrols. Interestingly, it was mostly the housing police they avoided, since the LAPD patrolled on an irregular basis. A few would "hot-box" the marijuana, smoking at someone's home with all the windows closed to keep the fumes in.

When they weren't hiding out, so to speak, in the interior of the projects, they brazenly walked over to the fringes of the development to sell their wares, with parking lots, sidewalks, or someone's front lawn becoming the place to score drugs. Rock cocaine was the drug of consumer choice, and these gang members kept a handful of plastic bags of the drug at the ready, along with a handgun in their waistband. Gang members who used rock were disrespected and thus learned to keep it DL. When a customer would appear, almost always in a vehicle of one sort or another, and slow down in either the street or the parking lot, this would be the cue to all that they were interested in purchasing a bag or more. Unlike the long line at a bank or similar establishment, where people wait their turn, the drug sellers would all respond to the sign and rush the vehicle. Whoever would arrive there first was the one who clinched the sale. To ensure that there were no shenanigans, the seller pulled out the handgun and pointed at the customer while handing over the bag. With the deal thus consummated, no one was ripped off. Drugs handed over, money paid, and gun put away. This was a common occurrence in the projects, and because police patrols were limited, even nonexistent from time to time, drug traffickers from outside the projects were drawn to the area to sell their wares. As noted earlier, the

Waiting for a customer

area often became a free crime zone. It was quite common to observe an adult male manning the local public telephone that hung on the side wall of the mom-and-pop store. When a vehicle would stop by the curb, he would go make a transaction and return to the telephone, which was left dangling until his return.

Sometimes incidents occurred when drug sales went awry. One time a drug buyer, actually a non-gang member from the community, attempted to rip off one of the young dealers and took the drugs, knocked the gun out of his hand, and stepped on the accelerator. Before he was a car length away, one of the other guys, who had rushed the car along with a couple of others, fired his pistol several times, hit the driver, and killed him. This turned out to be a very messy affair. Later, when the police investigation was initiated, the shooter was apprehended because the drug dealer, the wronged party in this instance, informed on him. The snitch, in this instance, had to leave the neighborhood, and from what I heard from the gang members, he is still running. The other gang members were incensed over this incident. The culprit not only "ratted" on a homeboy but also broke the street pact common to drug dealers.

As noted previously, violence is a way of life for gangs in general, and there are too many incidents to recount for a classic barrio like Pico Gardens in the space provided here. Drive-bys were the most common, even though the proximity of TMC and Cuatro made for many street-level shootings where the participants were on foot. Members of Cuatro killed Sad Boy from TMC that way. Sad Boy had ventured out of his home to visit a friend in another section of the apartment complex. Walking through their own neighborhood, Sad Boy and his friend stopped at a mom-and-pop liquor store. Somehow the guys from Cuatro got wind of this opportunity and were waiting for him right outside the store. When he exited, he was shot and killed. Sadly, as his name attests, he was at that time hoping to get out of the gang. He had grown weary of it; he was always in fear of his life and was fed up with others insisting that he measure up to the reputation of his klika, TMC. Father Boyle informed me just before his death, Sad Boy had written a note to the priest in which he confessed this desire to get out. The message ended with his signature, his birth name, to indicate that he no longer wanted to be Sad Boy.

Locura and Gang Banging

The intensity of locura reaches such a high level that some gang members opt to go out swinging, whatever the consequences. Loco, a veterano, had served so much time in prison that by the time he was thirty years old, he had vowed that the cops would never take him alive. He never stopped breaking the law, however, and once when the police came looking for him for a parole violation, he was in his house and on the run. Entering the house with a warrant, the police approached Loco, and before they could put the handcuffs on him, he bolted and dove headfirst through a glass window. With major lacerations all over, as would be expected, Loco was taken to the emergency ward of the nearby White Memorial Medical Center but bled to death before he arrived; some observers stated that he was allowed to bleed to death before the police whisked him to the hospital (see Fremon 2004). As the story goes, the police had taken Loco to the burned-out industrial factories across from the projects and allowed him to bleed some more before trying to save his life. This common belief has become so ingrained in the residents that it is an automatic response to any questions about the incident, irrespective of what the truth is. Father Boyle carefully pointed out that this was not what happened, although there was an earlier time in the neighborhood's history when such unfeeling, neglectful episodes transpired. Unfortunately, community and police relations to this day reflect this muddled state of affairs (Garrison 2006).

Nothing matches the Big Shoot-out, however, for locura, as the following story shows. There had been a lull in the street war between Cuatro and TMC for two or three weeks, and I guess everybody was getting itchy and wondering when the retaliations and paybacks would start again. They had been locked in a street war for several years, so long that by now most of the young gang members had forgotten how it started; the older members from the 1980s Countdowns and Chicos klikas remembered when the gangs were allies, even having close relatives on both sides. By the time of the Big Shoot-out, Father Boyle had buried close to 70 members from various Boyle Heights gangs who had succumbed to gang warfare over a seven-year period. (As of January 2007, the number had reached 155.)

The shoot-out started on Fourth Street, the boundary line between the two gangs. Two enemies viewed each other from opposite sides of the street. Then they reached into their jackets, pulled out handguns, and began firing at each other. It was about six-thirty at night, and the sun was beginning to go down on that late summer day in August 1993. A few adults were walking with their children on the sidewalks. Some young teenage boys were playing basketball, and younger, pre–junior high kids were running around the baseball field. When they heard the gunshots, they all scattered, the adults disappearing into the housing projects, and the children ducking and throwing themselves on the ground and crawling as fast as they could in any direction away from where the loud noises came. Seven or eight bullets whizzed by.

The sounds of the shots carried far, followed by the almost-as-fast word of mouth among residents and rival gang members on both sides of the street. The restless gang members jumped at the opportunity to get involved, for it was a hot, smoggy day, and hot tempers made them run for their weapons, if they didn't already have them on their person. Each side was able to quickly wield a sizable arsenal, with automatic rifles now the weapons of choice to join the handguns. Hiding behind buildings and cars, Cuatro mounted a fusillade of missiles in the direction of the playground. It was empty of people by now, as were the sidewalks, and vehicular traffic in both directions on Fourth Street had come to a standstill. Initially, traffic stopped, but before a long line of motorists formed, cars, vans, trucks, and buses began to turn onto the side streets to find another route to their destination.

This recounting of the event as it was reported to me by several observers (adults and children, gang and non-gang members, and authorities of various stripes and persuasions) may sound overdramatic, but it is how the story was imparted, with excitement, awe, and emotional tension. It started with the two rival individuals, and eventually there were eight to ten shooters all told in the fray, with TMS members scaling the two-story building in the playground area to gain a vantage point on the roof for a clear view of the Cuatro side of the street.

According to witnesses, the shoot-out lasted anywhere from fifteen to twenty minutes, and hundreds of shots were fired, most hitting the sides of buildings and cars but a few passing through windows and missing dwellers, who had pancaked themselves on the floor when they heard the first gunshots. Viewing the holes in the buildings and cars the next day, and talking to a number of residents, some of whom I knew and others whom I met for the first time, I was able to gauge the severity of the incident. Amazingly, no one was killed or even wounded, except for minor scrapes and abrasions from stucco, plaster, or cement explosions where bullets had hit. More amazingly, the LAPD had responded to the call almost within five minutes, three or four cars arriving a block or two away. However, because the firepower of the weapons and the rapidity of the firing were so extreme, they had to wait thirty minutes for the exchange to end before moving in to restore order.

This event is obviously a rare happenstance, not just for Pico Gardens or housing projects in general but for other gang neighborhoods throughout the nation. In the nineteenth century, in places like Chicago and certainly New York, pitched battles—with less firepower, of course—were common, with many more participants and a variety of the weapons of that time period. In the modern period, violent gang conflicts are usually forays (such as drive-bys) or encounters that involve three or four individuals and last for just a few fast moments. These are just some of the extreme examples that depict the patterns and daily routines and activities of the Pico Gardens clique.

Now let us take a look at some demographic information for a better understanding of the personal and social backgrounds of these individuals. In addition to hard survey data that reflect the lives and patterns of the household heads and their children, the clique-based analysis below helps contextualize the daily reality of the gang members themselves. Toward this end, a focus on the active members of the clique will help elaborate the more notorious activities of the gang, the crimes, and the violence that mark their lives. These unconventional and destructive acts may occupy only a small portion of their lives, but it is these dramatic gang events that have caught the public's attention. However, we must remember that gang members spend the majority of their time, as briefly summarized above, participating in mostly conventional behaviors. Even alcohol and drug consumption among gang members, although excessive, is representative of what has become a national pastime for a large portion of America's youth.

Survey of the Pico Gardens Clique: Trends and Tendencies

There are thirty-five members in the Pico Gardens clique, and a survey questionnaire was administered to a nonrandom sample of thirteen of them. It was found that the demographic baseline information gathered from these thirteen corroborated much of the ethnographic details and insights gathered during the intense 1991–1995 fieldwork period; the number thirteen is approximately one-third of the thirty-five members and is representative only insofar as these members were more regularly hanging out in the neighborhood. Interviews over a long period of time and participant observation of daily gang activities were the preponderance of evidence that showed a very strong street gang presence. Gang members from the community were asked a number of demographic questions as well as questions relating to their involvement in gangs and drugs and their perceptions of gangs, gang involvement, drugs, and drug involvement. The age range of those who participated in the survey was sixteen to twenty-three years, with the majority under the age of twenty-one.

Home life was extremely difficult for these individuals, as nine of the thirteen respondents reported living in a single-parent household. The reasons for this situation included mother or father deceased, parents divorced, or parents separated. Paralleling the initial survey findings of gang members coming from single-parent households in Chapter Two, the gang members had mostly negative reactions to such domestic arrangements. One of the individuals sampled stated,

> My father never was around, and when he showed up every now and then, he only wanted to deal with my mother. He gave me a quick hug and then got into it with my mother. They liked to argue, I think, because that is all they did. He said he was an electrician and an accountant, but he said he was so many things. But I never felt or thought he was my father.

Financial difficulties, as already noted, also contributed to a stressful home environment when there was only one breadwinner.

Immigrant parents entering the United States generally encountered a number of obstacles such as language barriers and racial discrimination, according to the respondents. Foreign-born parents were very common; 69 percent of fathers and 92 percent of mothers were first-generation. The gang members who took this survey were largely second-generation (about 70 percent). Acculturation to U.S. society was an extremely difficult process for many of the family members and children; household heads noted as much when they listed language classes as one of their goals for self-improvement.

For the parents who could find work, the jobs were of a menial nature: in housecleaning, the garment district, or nearby light industries. Sixty-one percent of the respondents reported that their households depended on federal assistance—in short, welfare. For example, one individual described his mother's job before they moved to the projects as that of an assembly-line worker in a fruit-processing factory. Another stated that his mother's job before coming to the United States was planting corn in Mexico. Such employment positions and experiences made for difficult times when the American economy required other skills and sources of knowledge; this, among other reasons, accounts for why immigrants fill positions in the service economy, such as dishwashers and janitors, and generally this is what the respondents' parents did. Parent educational level also contributes to the unskilled work that is usually sought and attained. Only one of the thirteen individuals reported having a father whose education went beyond the high school level. Not surprisingly, it was also reported that none of the mothers of the sample respondents had an academic background that included higher education.

Considering that 83 percent of the respondents reported having more than six people in their household, financial problems had become a pressing issue, due to aforementioned factors. As noted previously, crowded households are also one reason that youth seek public space (parking lots, alleyways, shady park areas) for privacy. In large part, big attenuated families and limited space and play areas account for the push out into the arena of street socialization.

One ripple effect stemming from inadequate support or resources, such as lack of parental readiness for supervision and/or lack of social capital, was the nagging problems these kids faced when they attended school. Although most of the individuals had a positive attitude toward education—77 percent reported "liking school most or some of the time"—their actual academic behavior and performance demonstrated otherwise. All of the individuals questioned reported that they had been sent to the office for problematic behaviors while in school. Of these incidents, 46 percent were for fighting.

Other noted problematic behaviors in school included excessive absences, low grades, and, worst of all, possession of weapons and/or drugs. As one individual stated, "I used to be a schoolboy back then. Then I got into a fight at Second Street Elementary, where a friend gave me a knife to use. I was going to stab him. Then the principal caught us and kicked us out of there because she said I started everything." This individual had attended five different elementary schools.

It was also discovered that 69 percent of the respondents had received an average grade of C or lower. Maintaining good grades is a task in any case, even for individuals with strong support networks and adequate resources. Basic reading materials were lacking in the respondents' homes, however, as were adult models for learning. Street associates were the only informal teachers or examples available to them. It should not be surprising that only one of the individuals surveyed went beyond high school to consider attending college, but he changed his mind at the last minute.

What is clearly obvious is that blocked access to social resources and networks had redirected these youth to a group network that fit their needs and levels of competencies—namely, the gang. They were proud to claim Cuatro Flats, probably the most dominant gang within the projects and the Boyle Heights community; in fact, many non-project youth joined this gang because of its reputation. Belonging to a gang for them, as well as other gang members, worked as a replacement for the family to provide care and affection. In addition, the voids in schooling influences that are required for life were also taken over by the gang. Two voids; two replacements by a surrogate family and educational experience.

Further reinforcing this almost coerced lifestyle was the influence of relatives that also belonged to gangs. Of those sampled, 46 percent said that they had a brother who belonged in a gang, while 54 percent reported having a cousin in a gang. It is especially important to note that peers were explicitly cited less often as models in my previous study than were male family members (Vigil 1988a). Male relatives who were (or had been) gang members provided an image to live up to, as well as encouragement (sometimes inadvertent) to join a gang (Vigil 1993). One individual illustrated the influence of family role models when he stated: "My uncle is in the Mexican Mafia, and he made a lot of money. My uncle was selling drugs. He gave a lot of money to his family. They had brand-new cars every month. . . . My first experience with the law was at fourteen years old. I sold heroin to an undercover police officer. I sold it to him for three hundred dollars." Pico Gardens generally, and this P.G. clique specifically, have old and continuing ties to prison gangs, and as Sureños (mostly urban, southern Californians, living south of the Tehachapi Mountains near Bakersfield), the members of those gangs are associated with the Mexican Mafia.

Street life had become an important part of these individuals' lives, especially considering that many of them had obtained street comrades that they considered "family." One member of the clique stated, "Having a lot of friends, a place to go, homegirls, and things I need are some of the reasons I liked the gang life. My devotion went deep enough to die for my homeboy, who I know would die for me." Furthermore, members joined at a very young age, some as young as seven years old. Thus, these individuals had grown up on the streets with their "homeboys" rather than their family. Though rare, one young gang member stated in an interview that he had been around seven years old when he was initiated into a gang: "I was jumped into Pico Gardens when I was around seven years old. After my initiation, I began to dress cholo and learn how to throw the gang sign. I participated in robberies using cap guns [fake guns] and learned the importance of defending my homeboys." More than 50 percent of the individuals in the survey had joined the gang before they turned fifteen years of age. More surprising yet was that all reported being solidly in the gang by seventeen years of age; this finding corresponds with evidence from other researchers (Moore 1978, 1991; Morales 1982; Vigil 1988a).

Individuals surveyed also expressed an upbeat perception of gangs and gang life, particularly since family and school had fallen short. There is a special closeness among youth who have undergone street socialization. When these individuals were asked whether they felt that being in a gang was important, 77 percent said it was. The reasons varied: one gang member felt that it was important because of the "family" he had acquired, another felt that it was simply a way "to survive." Whatever the reason, the gang had become a central part of their life. Incidences such as fights, drugs, and contact with law enforcement invariably become part of the gang experience. Gang violence, such as gangbanging incidents, become common and accepted as part of the gang member's culture. These trends were no exception among the respondents' experiences. During an interview, a member described an incident in which he was beaten up by three gang members: "There were three of them, and they started thumping me. I was on the ground, and one of them got me good in the arm. The next day we got them back. All the time when you're in a gang, you got to watch your back." Within the sample, 91 reported participating in gang fights, ranging from minor fistfight skirmishes to drive-by shootings.

The possession, use, and sale of drugs are also part of the contemporary gang experience. One individual noted, "I enjoy getting high. When I get fucked up, it's because I don't want to do shit. I only use cocaine, marijuana, PCP; none of my homeboys shoot up. We drink a lot of beer and stuff, Miller, Tecate . . ." Of those surveyed, 61 percent reported using drugs often, and 23 percent reported occasional drug use. The most commonly reported substance used was marijuana, followed by alcohol and cocaine. However, ingestion of acid (LSD) and crack was also noted. Supporting such a lifestyle requires money. Considering that these individuals were mostly unemployed, money was obtained through illicit and informal means. One prime method of making money on the streets is selling drugs. Of the individuals interviewed, 69 percent reported that they had sold drugs. One gang member stated, "The gang gets money by stealing cars, selling drugs, burglarizing homes. . . . We do anything to get money."

Inside P.G.: Then and Now

In addition to the above information, the community researchers and I compiled the names of all the gang members in the Pico Gardens clique. To reiterate, there were initially four gang members in the random household sample. When we then conducted our purposive sample, we identified all the other gang members in the remaining housing complex households, who numbered twenty-four. Thus, twenty-eight gang members lived in the projects. We then were able to identify seven others who were from outside the projects but lived nearby in the Boyle Heights neighborhood. All together, as noted, there were thirty-five members in this clique. Having identified all of them, we were able to interact with at least twenty on a daily or weekly basis. Since the community researchers conducted most of the interviews and observations, they also interacted occasionally with the other members. What follows is some general information on all of the clique members, especially the ones we were able to interact with regularly or who responded to the survey instrument mentioned above.

The nicknames of the clique members, their ages, and other basic data are provided in table 5.1. As noted at the beginning of the chapter, the gang is primarily Mexican American and Mexican, with some blacks, Vietnamese, and an El Salvadoran comprising a small minority. Concentric circles in figure 5.1 indicate the relative level of gang involvement for individual members at the time of the study; those within the inner circle were central to the gang as regular members, and others were more or less peripheral. Ten years after the intense fieldwork, few of the original members remained in the gang. Figure 5.2 shows where the gang members from the original survey were in 2005.

TABLE 5.1. *Pico Gardens Cohort*

	Member	Locale	Age	Birthplace	Level of Involvement	Latest Information
1	Hobo	Center	20	Mexico	Drug seller/gangbanger	Shot a cop/recently got out of jail
2	Joker	Peripheral	19	Mexico	Drug seller	Didn't do anything/wangster (wannabe gangster)
3	Bad Boy	Center	19	Mexico	Drug seller/gangbanger	On the run for many shootings
4	Lil Gordo	Center	17	U.S.	Drug seller/gangbanger	Active/brother was killed by Eighteenth Street gang
5	Whitey	Center	19	U.S.	Drug seller/gangbanger	Unknown
6	Tripper	Center	18	U.S.	Heaviest gangbanger	In and out of jail/on the run
7	Sad Boy	Peripheral	17	Mexico	Drug seller	Killed in drive-by shooting
8	Cowboy	Peripheral	18	Mexico	Drug seller	Didn't want to bang
9	Pato	Peripheral	18	Vietnam	Drug seller	Moved out/became a counselor
10	Turco	Center	20	U.S.	Drug seller/gangbanger	Unknown
11	Lil Lonely	Outside	18	U.S.	Gangbanger	Fugitive on the run
12	Chato	Outside	18	U.S.	Gangbanger	Doing 17 years to life for killing rival gang member
13	Grenudo	Peripheral	16	Mexico	Drug seller	Moved out
14	Bosco	Center	18	Mexico	Drug seller/gangbanger	Unknown
15	Panson	Outside	17	U.S.	Gangbanger	Family man
16	Teco	Outside	17	U.S.	Gangbanger	Lost contact/moved out
17	Snapper	Center	17	U.S.	Drug seller/gangbanger	Jail; shot by rival gang
18	Raccoon	Outside	19	Vietnam	Gangbanger	Moved out
19	Wizard	Outside	18	U.S.	Gangbanger	Locked up for a bit/now working
20	Puppet	Peripheral	20	U.S.	Drug seller	Currently working/doing well
21	Midnight	Center	17	U.S.	Drug seller/gangbanger	Unknown
22	Crow	Outside	17	U.S.	Gangbanger	Just out of jail/with wife and baby now

	Member	Locale	Age	Birthplace	Level of Involvement	Latest Information
23	Zooter	Peripheral	17	Mexico	Drug seller	Matured out of gang after first gunshot/ originally a tagger
24	Sneaky	Peripheral	19	Vietnam	Drug seller	Short-time banger/moved out of projects
25	Tripa	Peripheral	17	U.S.	Drug seller	Raised in gang but not all into it/nominal member
26	Goofy	Peripheral	17	Vietnam	Drug seller	Didn't want to bang
27	Timid	Outside	16	Vietnam	Gangbanger	Short burst of gang and slang/moved out
28	Silent	Peripheral	17	Mexico	Drug seller	Moved out of projects/never visited again
29	Rapper	Outside	17	U.S.	Gangbanger	Mildly active/moved out
30	Jaws	Peripheral	17	Mexico	Drug seller	Big-time drug dealer
31	Zorro	Center	17	El Salvador	Drug seller/gangbanger	On the run for attempted gang and slang
32	Trucha	Center	21	U.S.	Drug seller/gangbanger	Moved to Texas/MIA
33	Psycho	Peripheral	18	Mexico	Drug seller	Drowned in swimming pool
34	Shaky	Peripheral	17	Mexico	Drug seller	Moved out of projects/never visited again
35	Curious George	Peripheral	17	Mexico	Drug seller	Moved out of projects/never visited again

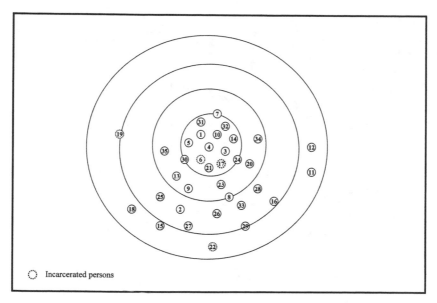

FIGURE 5.1. Gang entrance, 1995

A summary of groups of members follows, from the most active to the least active ones, with a commentary on what they were like then and what has happened to them since the study was completed. According to our analysis, almost all of them, with some variation depending on the time and place, were supportive of gang conflicts, joining in them when called upon, and participated in drug trafficking (i.e., they were bangers and slangers). This type of confidential information could be considered an "ethnographic rap sheet" for each individual, revealing the discoveries of social science, as opposed to the criminal rap sheet kept by law enforcement. Names and other identification markers have been changed for confidentiality and to maintain the anonymity of the research respondents.

Regular gang members were closest to the center of the circle, which means that they were perhaps the most active members. "Active" in this instance means that they were the most loco and were involved in the more dangerous and illicit activities on a regular basis. The eleven who fit this category are as follows (including their age and, for those born outside the United States, their birthplace): Hobo, 20 (Mexico); Bad Boy, 19 (Mexico); Lil Gordo, 17; Whitey, 19; Tripper, 18; Turco, 20; Bosco, 18 (Mexico); Snapper, 17; Midnight, 17; Zorro, 17 (El Salvador); and Trucha, 21. The most active members are located near the center in figure 5.1. Ten years later, only two of these eleven members remained in the center (fig. 5.2).

Of these eleven, four were born outside the United States, immigrating as members of the 1.5 generation when they were between the ages of four and seven. Moving into the projects as young children with little supervision from parents (either a single mother or both parents, who worked late hours), they were subjected to early street socialization and experienced limited schooling successes. Ten years later, two of these eleven were on the run from the law: Bad Boy, for many shootings, and Zorro, for joining with four others to kill a rival gang member but mistakenly killing a five-year-old girl instead. Both Bad Boy and Zorro were into banging and slanging in the 1990s. Three others—Hobo, Trucha, and Tripper—were also very active. In addition to committing many shootings, Hobo shot a cop, and Trucha was so heavy into drug trafficking that he decided to move his operation to Texas, where, according to his gang member friends, he disappeared. They suspect that either the police or other drug dealers killed him. Tripper, perhaps the top gangster of them all, was a heavy banger/slanger then and was in and out of jail. He once kidnapped a drug dealer, and in 2005 he remained outside the law with a number of warrants for his arrest; he was considered the most loco of the clique.

The other six were among the most involved in banging and slanging. Lil Gordo had a brother who was shot and killed by members of the Eigh-

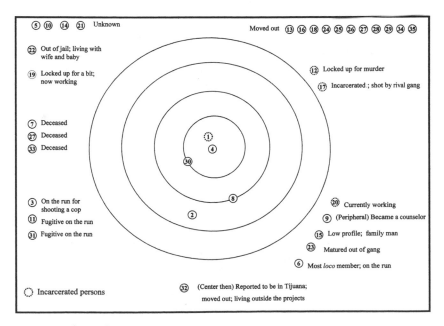

FIGURE 5.2. Gang exit, 2005

teenth Street gang; by 2005, Lil Gordo was in jail for attempted homicide. Snapper was periodically jailed and eventually shot by rival gang members. He survived the shooting and partially turned his life around. In 2005 he was working and helping to raise his son. He still kept his hand in the drug trade, though. The other four—Midnight, Bosco, Whitey, and Turco—disappeared from the neighborhood and perhaps are somewhere else doing the same thing or have met their ends.

Fifteen members belonged to the peripheral category of gang members. They were only mildly involved in using weapons and were less apt to encourage or join in gang homicides or anything remotely connected with them. The main crime that they regularly indulged in was drug sales. These members were Joker, 19 (Mexico); Sad Boy, 17 (Mexico); Cowboy, 18 (Mexico); Pato, 18 (Vietnam); Grenudo, 16 (Mexico); Puppet, 20; Zooter, 17 (Mexico); Sneaky, 19 (Vietnam); Tripa, 17; Goofy, 17 (Vietnam); Silent, 17 (Mexico); Jaws, 17 (Mexico); Psycho, 18 (Mexico); Shaky, 17 (Mexico); and Curious George, 17 (Mexico).

The most interesting factor in this category of fifteen is that thirteen of them were born in a foreign country (Mexico or Vietnam). As very young immigrants, these thirteen still approximated a second-generation group, some coming as 1.5 immigrants and others arriving closer to age ten. Generally, as young immigrants, they did not have the gang role models, street socialization, and other deeply rooted family strains in their backgrounds. In contrast, the regular gang members had such backgrounds to expedite their deeper gang involvement and participation. Moreover, six of the regular gang members were second-generation Mexicans, and one was third-generation, a characteristic that seems to support the stance of many researchers that gangs are generated most often in the second generation (Vigil 1988a; Vigil and Long 1990; Waters 1999).

One of the Mexican-born members (Zooter) actually was a K Clover tagger before a P.G. friend brought him in, but not for long; he matured out very fast. The first time he heard gunshots nearby, he decided to stay away from the neighborhood. Sneaky was a banger/slanger for a short time and then moved out of the projects. Joker was ostracized by other gang members because he never wanted to do anything wrong; he was mostly a "hanger." After about two or three months of hanging with the gang, he just drifted away. Moderate slangers like Cowboy and Goofy never wanted to gangbang. Cowboy stuck around but never moved beyond dealing, and Goofy moved out. Tripa was raised in a gang family, but his home socialization was not enough to make him a committed P.G. member. He was more of a nominal member who got in because of his family's street pedigree; the family later moved out of the barrio. Several of the peripheral members—Pato, Silent,

Grenudo, Shaky, and Curious George—were light drug dealers who eventually moved out of the projects, and to my knowledge, they have not returned even to visit old friends. The other individuals have met different endings. Psycho drowned in the recreation swimming pool at night, and Sad Boy was shot and killed in a drive-by. Jaws was an outsider who started off small-time and had become a big drug dealer. Finally, Pato became the survivor and outdid them all. After starting unconventionally, on the DL (and never being apprehended even though he did his banging/slanging stint), he got married, earned his B.A., and secured a job as a street counselor. The latter occupation, by the way, is a common one for former gang members who want to help the younger generation avoid the worse effects of gang life and mature out before it is too late.

For a variety of reasons, the remaining 9 P.G. members were outside the main circle, functioning as irregular gang members. They are listed here, along with their circumstances ten years later: Teco, 17, lost contact or moved out; Raccoon, 19 (Vietnam), moved out; Crow, 17, out of jail, with wife and baby now; Lil Lonely, 18, black member, fugitive from the law; Chato, 18, heavy banger/slanger, shot and killed someone from TMC, doing seventeen years to life in prison; Rapper, 17, mildly active, then moved out; Timid, 16 (Vietnam), short burst of banging/slanging, then moved out; Wizard, 18, short involvement, did time, then got out of gang and was doing well working; and Panson, 17, early maturation out of gang, became a family man.

The Pico Gardens clique is unique in that it has lasted for a very long time, since the early 1990s. According to local observers, the drug trafficking and continuous rivalry and warfare with a neighboring gang have kept it a viable gang. Its reputation and the respect gained thereof have made this clique attractive to younger recruits, who prefer to become P.G. members rather than start their own clique. What should interest us, however, is that there were only thirty-five members during the time of the field stay, with most eventually finding their way out of the gang; about 70 percent left the gang, a percentage similar to what has been reported in earlier studies (e.g., Short 1996). The mix of entrance and exit processes of this clique must also draw our attention as an example of the variations and complexities that exist in a gang.

Conclusion

The mix of quantitative and qualitative information in this chapter provides some baseline demographic details that are complemented by the interviews and participant observation of the fieldwork experience. Community researchers were vital to the insights that were gathered and as insiders were able to aid me in the analysis that followed. In its simplest form, multiple marginality was evidenced in the space that these gang members and their families occupied, in the status that shaped their lives, and in the socio-cultural rhythms and routines that took an unconventional and destructive route. Street socialization was summarized, the development of a street sub-culture that flowed from it was outlined, and finally the only identity that springs from these influences was underscored: a street identity.

The qualitative information and insights that were gathered tell us how and why someone becomes violent, what the significance of turf is to a gang member, when the gang becomes a surrogate nurturing and learning influence, and finally, what gang members do with most of their time. The dynamic gang processes make more sense if we know what it means to live in a crowded household and thus to seek privacy in public spaces. These dramas play out on the streets. A lack of resources of all sorts destabilizes youth and sends them in misguided directions, and no one knows where they will land. Anthropological theorizing and methods can add significantly to the gang literature, because field researchers specialize in nonspecialization, gathering data from all persons and all places in a holistic fashion. For example, an integrated framework showing actions and reactions among factors is what holism is all about, and the multiple marginality framework is merely another step in that direction. Taking this broader and deeper perspective is an essential anthropological enterprise. Especially important is talking to and watching people over a long period in different settings. Assessing the social ecology of a place while people display different moods and behaviors adds immeasurably to the motivations and proclivities of the actors. What are their actions and reactions to the social ecology of place, why is human aggression so predictable in this context, and when does this social identity prefigure personal identity? Though street gang members are a difficult population to investigate, as many researchers have discovered, it is important to integrate intensive, in-depth interviewing of gang members as part of large-scale surveys. Self-report surveys only go so far.

This chapter attempts to do just that. The contexts of time, place, and people are an important part of the equation. We have noticed the increase in drug trafficking in recent years, for example. Gang members today are more inured to the absolute brutality that high-powered weapons dictate. Newcomers, heretofore culturally insulated from joining gangs, now rapidly undergo acculturation to the isolated, segregated urban America they are introduced to, which is a street subculture. Because gangs have been a fixture in Pico Gardens for at least a couple of generations, many of the young-

Father Boyle with the males at a wedding party

sters learn gang culture at home, accelerating what they learn on the streets. To reiterate, the cohort network functions to maintain the size of the gang as older members "mature out" and younger gang members take over the banner of defending Cuatro Flats from intruders. Now, however, much of the gang lore is so fraught with myths and falsehoods that no one knows when or why the hostilities and antagonistic relationships started that have made barrios bitter enemies. The next chapters dig into the family lives of these gang members to chart what went wrong or right to set them on their paths, either into or away from the gang.

CHAPTER SIX

A GANG LIFE

Turning his stingy-brim hat around in his hands and contemplating its shape and the red feather in the headband, Bebee thought about his life in the projects. Born and reared in the projects, knowing no other life than public housing and support, he had been able to survive even though he had done almost ten years in prison for a killing. As a member of Cuatro Flats from the early 1970s, he had established a reputation as a reliable black Chicano, one who could be trusted to back someone up but not go off the deep end and start unnecessary trouble. Almost everything that could happen to a person to funnel and compel him into a gang had been a part of Bebee's life: poverty, displacement, single-parent household, no male role models, early street socialization, trouble in school, and friction with law enforcement. Yet he eventually matured out, his prison experiences aiding natural maturation, and returned to the barrio to become president of the Residents Advisory Council to help initiate and supervise various programs to aid the betterment of the residents.

Bebee was raised in a family of seven children—two brothers, four sisters, and himself. His mother was born and reared in Texarkana, Texas, that region of East Texas that is adjoined to western Louisiana and sent a large number of rural black migrants to Los Angeles in the early to mid-twentieth century. His mother had been with a common-law husband in Texas and had had the six older children with him, and then she moved to L.A., leaving her daughters with relatives in Texas and bringing only her two sons with her. In the late 1940s, she needed assistance, so she settled in public housing. She met another man and had Bebee and his twin brother, who died as an infant.

Bebee has no memory of anything before he went to school at the age of five years, except for stories his mother told him. One such story has him crossing the street to go visit relatives who lived in a different section of the projects, an event that shows either how adventurous he was or, as Bebee put it, how stupid he was; he used the word "stupid" a lot, to cover all the attitudes and behaviors that get gang youth into trouble. Until his stepfather came into his life around the time he was in junior high school, Bebee and his siblings were raised by just their mother. Memories of their first apartment are doubly tragic: both Bebee's twin bother and his grandmother died there. The family soon moved to another address nearby, however, and most of Bebee's memories during his elementary school years revolve around this second apartment. He also had fond memories of his then–"road dog" (close buddy he spent most of his time with), an Okie named Norman Green, who belonged to a family of twelve with an abusive, alcoholic father. Norman and Bebee were inseparable as they grew up together in elementary school, walking to school every morning, playing after classes ended, and, especially, rummaging the dumpsters behind every light industry factory by the river for sugar, cereal, bread, Hot Wheels, T-shirts, school supplies, jawbreaker candy, and any number of other products.

Bebee loved school, or at least the social part of it. He attended Second Street Elementary and had fond memories of kindergarten, especially of nap time, during which he liked to look up the girls' dresses and also the teacher's dress when possible. Unfortunately, Bebee was removed from kindergarten after being diagnosed with tuberculosis and was quarantined in a section of Olive View Hospital in the San Fernando Valley for an entire year. Bebee recounted a particularly traumatic event during this time, when an older child, about twelve years old, jealous of the gifts Bebee's mother would bring, tried to smother him with a pillow. After Bebee had endured such experiences, it was later determined that he had been misdiagnosed and did not have TB, so he was sent home. Nevertheless, he had to stay home and received home schooling for a few months after that; he hated having to look out the window and watch all the kids go to school while he just waited drearily for his home teacher to arrive. With this unsettling start and near-death incident as a child, Bebee never was able to catch up with his classmates, even though he was a bright child who became a capable adult.

Bebee recalled that during his elementary school years he was "the typical child"; he followed a routine set by his mother, who was religious and adhered to an ethic of discipline and respect despite the poverty and turmoil that surrounded the family. She only knew the rural culture she had come from and was unfamiliar with city life, much less places like the projects,

Members of a family on the porch during a hot summer day

where all the poor people were piled together along with their problems and proclivities. Poverty was reflected in the family in many ways. For example, Bebee was instructed to make sure that his friends were not around at dinnertime, as Bebee's recounting of his mother's words shows: "Don't you invite nobody around here near dinnertime. . . . Why do you have your friends coming over here when you know we're ready to sit down? You know we don't have enough food to feed everybody. . . . Now you got Billy out there, and we got to feed him . . . and he's gonna have some of your food. Now sit down at this table, and give Billy some of your food." And Bebee added, "He eats a lot. Billy eats a lot."

This home foundation, albeit unsophisticated and rural based, was set for Bebee at a young age. He even recalled that if he was outside playing with his friends and his mother called him by his full name—Breavron McDuffie—in a commanding tone, his friends would laugh and snicker. After he obediently answered his mother in the affirmative, he then turned to his friends and threatened to kick their asses. Early on, he tipped his hat to two voices, the home and the streets, but in time the latter overpowered the former.

Although his mother got involved with his school only when he was in trouble, she was strict about making him do his homework. A typical day after school consisted of changing from his school clothes to playclothes, washing his hands before snacking on fruit, and doing his homework. This was a disciplined routine, but since his mother had not had much formal education, she was unable to help with some of the more difficult subject matter. His teachers, from what Bebee could remember, were not particularly helpful or interested in the kids from the projects. The only stories he recalled were those that involved punishment, a not especially helpful assessment given that Bebee himself acknowledged that he was a class clown, more interested in gaining the attention of his friends—similarly "fuckups" all, in Bebee's opinion. If he should go to the office for some misdeed or another, he would see a friend there and think, "There's Johnny. Now, that's a guy I want to be like. I want to be with him." Looking up to such role models because they get attention is a common problem in low-income school districts where gangs are rampant.

Corporal punishment was very much the norm when Bebee was coming up. Being pushed around by teachers and other school authorities was de rigueur, for social order and decorum in the classrooms had to be maintained at all costs. Unfortunately, it didn't work. Bebee and his friends still messed up. However, they did walk cautiously around some of the teachers. One male teacher, a former marine, was known as being very tough, and students learned not to mess with him. According to a story Bebee told me, this teacher had once rammed a kid's head against the wall in the cloakroom and made a dent there. This dent became a type of cause célèbre that students would show others, saying, "This is what Mr. —— did to Johnny." The funny thing about project kids, or poor slum-area children, is that to them this dent symbolized "what happens to fuckups," so they needed to beware and watch their step. In short, it was a working-class deterrent for children who misbehaved at school.

Some of Bebee's best memories of his elementary school years revolve around a couple of trips he made out of the projects. Second Street Elementary, for example, took his class to a farm where Bebee was able to see animals he had never seen before. In addition, Bebee belonged to the Boy Scouts, which had a two-week program in Big Bear every summer. Bebee recalled, "I went camping with the Boy Scouts. We were in cabins, and there were counselors. There'd be two buses, and our parents were happy. I've never seen so many happy people in the projects. When I look back on it now, I can see why." Even though he was not gang affiliated at the time, he was "clique oriented," and these trips provided the kids from his project opportunities to bond with one another against kids from other projects and different cliques who also attended. In Bebee's words, "It was always territorial. . . . [T]he projects is a family." During these trips, the kids stayed in cabins and engaged in activities such as archery, boating, handicrafts, and horseback riding. "We did all the things that I'd never done in the projects," Bebee said.

Because his brothers were always in and out of jail and prison, and his sisters were much older than him, Bebee was like the little man of the house. He was responsible for doing a number of chores, which included taking out the trash, making his bed, sweeping the floor, and washing, drying, and putting away the dishes. In this respect, Bebee's household was different from those of his street friends; as he recalled, "We all did the chores, not just the females." It was also during this time that his mother met another man, Smitty, who she eventually married. Bebee grudgingly accepted this man as a stepfather because he was the only father model he had ever had. However, the stepfather disliked Bebee and his other siblings and refused to share the mother with her children. This was a constant source of friction and, as noted below, led to a very violent incident.

As Bebee's early home life suggested, his mother was a strong, central figure and influence. She provided a foundation of supervision and structure that many of the other neighborhood families lacked. Bebee attributed much of his mother's strength, conviction, and ability to provide structure to her belief in and love of God. In Bebee's words, "Religion brings structure . . . If everything else is missing, religion is your last string."

Although Bebee's mother was a strong figure, she was not able to see the signs of Bebee's increasing attraction to gang and street life. Bebee believed his mom "did the best she could with the knowledge and information and the skills that she had," but he did not think she had enough education or knowledge of parenting skills: "You got to be nosy, and if you're not, your child is going to fall through the cracks. I can't blame my mom for anything. I did it myself."

Around junior high school, Bebee began to engage in gang-related activities. However, he reached a major turning point that sealed his movement in that direction. Although he was not a particularly good student, more a mess-up than anything else, he was popular among the students for his sociability and ability to capture their attention. He was nominated for a student body office and made the final runoff. Bebee remembers this as a time when he was under a lot of pressure, for he knew that if he won, he would have to change his life and act more like a leader than a clown. He feared winning, because he did not know if he could make the grade at two levels: change a personality that had evolved from childhood, and acquire the discipline to develop leadership characteristics. Never having been in a position like this before or since, Bebee reminisced that had he won, it would have made a major difference in his life. He lost, so the path his personality had dictated required a different type of discipline, that of *la vida loca*, the crazy, volatile, and unpredictable life of a street gang member.

Because of his mother's lack of awareness of gang behavior patterns and her inability to be constantly vigilant, Bebee was able to do things "sneakily," in bits and pieces, so that his mother did not put them together "as gang-related." For example, because his mother was not aware of street styles and culture, Bebee was able to incorporate gang clothing styles into his daily wardrobe. He described his early street socialization: "We had a neighborhood really when I was in the sixth grade—we were out there banging already. It was about thirty of us from the projects. At that time, we were like a little club. We called ourselves a little social group, but we were gang affiliated. We were out looking for trouble. From that clique, that's where we turned into Cuatro."

Even as a young child, Bebee began to look up to the gang *veteranos* and consciously think about modeling himself after them. Since most of these *veteranos* just hung around the neighborhood dressed up in fastidiously starched khaki pants and sparkling white T-shirts, with a dark brown or blue plaid Pendleton shirt neatly draped over one arm, they were the few male role models that street children had contact with. When the children began to hear the near-heroic stories about the *veteranos'* exploits—gang-related or otherwise—as told by others or even by the men themselves, they were all ears. The posturing and body movements of these men, even something as simple as lighting a cigarette, were pure machismo in motion, a gestural poetry that was methodical and in control. In addition, since most of these *veteranos* had been in and out of prison and were in their late twenties or early thirties, they were all buffed out from regular weight lifting, and they sported "brushes" (thick, Pancho Villa–type mustaches) that made their appearance even more menacing. Muscles and brushes were symbols of real power, strength, and maturity that young impressionable street children viewed as requisites for street survival.

Throughout junior high at Hollenbeck, Bebee hung with Cuatro Flats, and he was initiated by being "walked" into the Chicos klika. Minor brushes with other rival gangs and with law enforcement helped build his reputation as a reliable and fearless gang member. For instance, he became very good at shoplifting and stealing from the local factories. When the police caught him one time on the Hot Wheels property, they began to berate and scare him and phoned his mother, asking her to come over to the scene. Both police officers and parent instilled the fear of God in Bebee, or so they thought. Showing remorse, Bebee was sincere at the time. He was allowed to go home with his mother and received a reprimand. Events like this are often witnessed by residents of the projects—children and adults, gang and non-gang members alike—and instead of acting as a deterrent to the observers, the dramas are likened to a celebrity event, with the culprit gaining respect and status in the eyes of the community. Among the young gang members of Bebee's clique, he rose a notch or two for receiving this attention. Minor scrapes like this characterize early gang involvement.

When Bebee arrived at Roosevelt High School, he was already a well-known member of Cuatro. In school he continued to receive barely passing grades, except in physical education, where he excelled in track and cross-country. His athletic skills could have been a stimulus and a ticket to college, but the gang was more important to Bebee, so his coaches' encouragements were for naught. Beginning in junior high, Bebee had a series of girlfriends from the projects as well as Boyle Heights in general. The most telling event associated with high school, however, was the day of the senior prom. Bebee and his friends, both gang and non-gang members, took their dates to a restaurant on the Westside of Los Angeles after the prom dinner and dance. Feeling "bad" and invincible, both as street dudes and as residents of East Los Angeles, they entered the restaurant as if they owned it. At first, no one paid attention to them, but after a while some adult white men who were gathered at another table began to become irritated with the raucous crowd. A few looks and words were exchanged, and pretty soon there was a big fistfight, with tuxedoed cholos taking on the older men. Bebee recalled that he and his friends got their asses kicked royally and received a lesson that would last for life. Ironically, this fight and beating were a type of rite of passage for the East Los Angeles group. Instead of sulking because they had been beaten, they felt that they could survive the outside world, a place far away from their own bailiwick. Graduation from high school had unexpectedly also included inauguration of their young adult lives on the street.

Bebee's gang timeline was patchy in parts but went as follows. He was born at the tail end of the zoot suit, *pachuco* era. When he was eight or nine years old, pachucos became known as cholos. One of the earliest klikas that Bebee remembered was the Apaches. There was a big gap in Bebee's memory until the Sinners arose during the mid- to late 1960s. After the Sinners, Bebee remembered the Enanos (Midgets). Bebee was part of the Enanos, who were active until the mid-1970s. Bebee explained that the older homies usually established an age-based cutoff point and required that the youngsters prove themselves by starting their own klikas. There were other klikas after that, but Bebee had an indelible image of the Peacemakers, which wasn't a klika but "a group of little bad-ass kids in the projects stealing money from the

Bebee interviewing students from the projects at Roosevelt High School

house, food stamps, and buying cigarettes and going in the back streets, smoking and having a little party and shit." Most of the Peacemakers, Bebee remembered, were only around ten years old, and some were even younger.

The Dukes and the Night Owls started up around the same time, during the mid-1970s, while Bebee was locked up. The Stoners also got started while Bebee was in prison and began as "a little party crew," going to clubs and getting high. Bebee summarized his confusing and complicated gang history up to this point:

> When we started off, we were just Cuatro Flats. There was no Enanos, no Pequeños, no Chicos, no nothing. After more youngsters started, that's when we broke off to the Pequeños. When more started coming in, they broke off into the Chicos. Then they had a dry spell for a while after the Chicos and Termites . . . and by now the Termites had faded down so much there really wasn't much of them. These dudes here just coming along, the Dukes and the Night Owls, then they got all caught up in the drugs. There became a gap between them and the Countdowns. That's when the Pico Stoners came in and filled that gap.

Bebee explained that around the late 1970s and into the 1980s—his era— the gang became more ethnically mixed, including blacks, Chicanos, and

Vietnamese. Aside from Pico Gardens, who continued recruiting, there had been only a few klikas since the 1980s.

During Bebee's increasing engagement with gangs beginning in junior high, his mother also became involved with Smitty, his stepfather. For Bebee, "that was a bad thing." Smitty was often jealous of Bebee's relationship with his mother, but she would always side with Bebee. She kicked Smitty out of the house four or five times for being abusive and coming home drunk. This was difficult for Bebee; because his own father had died and his older brother was always in and out of prison, Bebee wanted and needed a father figure. Even though Smitty was an often abusive alcoholic, Bebee wanted to be liked by him and would ask his mother to let Smitty back in after she kicked him out.

Smitty's abuse would come out most often during daily activities. For example, Bebee remembered that Smitty would hit him "upside the head" when he didn't understand his homework: "He was sadistic like that." Smitty was mean so often that Bebee lost control one day and did "the ultimate"— he stabbed Smitty. Bebee's recollection of the incident follows.

One day, Smitty came home when Bebee and a few of his nieces and nephews were eating in the kitchen. Apparently angry about the mess, Smitty went upstairs and began arguing with Bebee's mother. The children stopped eating and listened as Bebee's mother began yelling. Bebee ran upstairs and, seeing that Smitty had pushed his mother into the tub, retrieved a small ax he had gotten in Boy Scouts from his room and chased Smitty downstairs and into the kitchen. When his nieces and nephews found out, they also started chasing Smitty while Bebee's mother ran after all of them. "It's like a cartoon," Bebee recalled. His mother was eventually able to take the ax away, but Bebee grabbed a butcher knife from the kitchen and, after catching up to Smitty, stabbed him in the shoulder, breaking the knife's blade in the process. After the stabbing, one niece began hitting Smitty with a bat, while another niece hit him with a croquet stick. Bebee's nephew went through the house, putting down newspaper to soak up the blood. (In an aside to this story, Bebee lamented that this nephew had been the most peaceful one in the family but was now doing big prison time.) After the ordeal, Smitty told Bebee, "I wanted to test you, to see what you would do if someone came in here and messed with your mama." Going off like that was rare for Bebee, but every time he did so, it spelled trouble.

Bebee's relationship with Smitty was clearly volatile and complicated. "We liked him but we didn't like him," Bebee said. "He was a worker; he helped. So I'll give him that—he wasn't a freeloader. He helped; he helped big-time. He carried his weight, so I don't have anything against him like that. He was mean to me. . . . He just didn't like me, and I didn't do nothing to provoke it neither."

Smitty eventually "ended up dying of drinking." Ironically, when Smitty was in the hospital, the only person he kept asking for was Bebee. "I didn't hate him then," Bebee said. "I don't hate him today. I didn't have nothing to make peace with; he had to make peace with me." Bebee was in prison then, however, and did not see Smitty at the hospital, only at his funeral.

Bebee recalled that the stabbing was his first real act of violence: "That was my first. . . . I think that was the start of my career. . . . It felt good. That was the first time." This incident is still recounted by the participants when they get together, mostly with laughter accompanying the story because of its "cartoon" quality. Bebee also liked to tell another story about his sisters, who almost killed his brother when he attempted to slap one of them around. With the first slap, all three of the other sisters rallied to the defense of the victim and commenced to "beat the shit out of him." As Bebee described it, "They just flipped. They were busting him with the plunger. They would have killed him if he fought back. I would have one less brother. . . . Damn, I've seen my sister bust another fool upside the head with an iron. That's why I love my sisters." Domestic violence was later followed by street violence and other acts of aggression.

Bebee went to prison for murder when he was nineteen years old. The incident occurred in September 1972 and was a topic he did not enjoy discussing and therefore did not do so very often. His recollection of the incident follows.

After returning to the neighborhood from a dance at Dolores Mission with a few friends, Bebee and his girlfriend Tracy, who were high on marijuana, went to a local bar where the neighborhood wino hung out so they could get him to buy them some liquor. All the youth in the area acquired their alcohol this way, kicking back some money or liquor for the informal service. Bebee began talking to the wino just outside the bar. "He was all fucked up," Bebee remembered, "and I was talking to him to get us some alcohol, but he wanted to piss around and mess with me, so I talked real loud to him." According to Bebee, a guy he didn't know "got up and got off in my business and got off in my face while I was talking to my wino." As things began to escalate, one of the guy's friends jumped in and knocked Bebee down. From many past experiences in a predominantly Mexican neighborhood, Bebee felt that because he was black, these Mexican outsiders (not from the projects) took matters into their own hands to protect the wino from Bebee.

After getting up from the punch that had come out of nowhere, a surprised Bebee instinctively grabbed his back pocket. "I didn't even forget I was packing," he recounted, "because back then I was always packing. I had a Deuce Five, a twenty-five-caliber." Bebee chased the men through the bar, shooting both of them multiple times. One man died later from the wounds. The shooting occurred on a Friday; Bebee was arrested on the following Monday. In court, Bebee lied about his involvement. He now believed that, had he told the truth, he "wouldn't have got that time." He claimed to have received poor legal advice from his attorney, a "white boy, ol' slickster," and believed that because he had committed the murder in the heat of passion, he should have been charged with involuntary manslaughter. No one in the bar, all of whom were parents or relatives of Bebee's homies, testified against him, a fact that he was proud of and that confirmed what he and other residents felt about the projects being a haven and tight family.

Bebee was convicted of "second-degree murder, assault with a deadly weapon, and two counts with gun allegation." He did ten years in all for the charges and believed that, had his sentences been consecutive instead of concurrent, he would have done a lot more time. Overall, he did not see himself as a killer. As he put it,

> I was in a situation where I reacted by protecting myself. I don't look at myself as a killer. . . . When I went in [prison], I was innocent. They corrupted me on the inside. They say they're doing society a better deal by locking you up. Uh-uh. Oh, hell no. You keep youth out. Do something to them for what the hell they've done, but don't put them in that type of place. . . . I thought I was a killer, [but] I was in there with some killers. I wasn't no damned killer.

In prison, he learned to play the flute and saxophone and had the opportunity to join the prison track team formally. He was proud that he had run a 440-yard race in 50 seconds flat, in tennis shoes on an asphalt track. Further, showing a little entrepreneurship, he started a prison business of starching and ironing prison-issue pants, which he called Bebee's Bongaroos.

After prison, he returned to his neighborhood and family. Since then, he has kept his nose clean and taken a entirely different path. He married a community activist, and they had a son together. In addition, they adopted and raised other children from their extended families. In time, Bebee pieced together part-time work and was involved in various training programs. He never was able to secure and maintain a full-time job, however. Getting involved in a local evangelical church that caters to street people (similar to Victory Outreach), he and his wife became regular churchgoers and Bible citers. As his life course steadied, he joined the Residents Advi-

Bebee's family

sory Council of the public housing offices of Pico Gardens. Rising to the position of president of the RAC and an initiator and leader of many programs for residents, Bebee became a respected and sought-after speaker. On a trip to Washington, D.C., he spoke to more than five hundred delegates from throughout the United States and was invited to several community programs in different states thereafter. When HUD (Department of Housing and Urban Development), under Henry Cisneros' leadership, decided to raze and rebuild the Pico-Aliso public housing, Bebee was right in the middle of discussions and negotiations as to how and when it should be done. It was about this time that the formal investigation aspect of our study, in which Bebee was involved as a researcher, came to an end. However, Bebee and I continued to assist with a number of prevention and intervention initiatives that were aimed at the children of the projects. Intensive interviews and participant observation with specific individuals and at special events continued through the writing of this book.

CHAPTER SEVEN

CHOLAS IN THE WORLD OF GANGS

Young Pico Gardens females face the same social and cultural strains as their young male peers, compounded by the addition to gender strains and their own version of the psychological moratorium (Chesney-Lind and Sheldon 1992). The socialization of girls into street life not only shapes a permissive attitude toward deviant gang subcultures but also affects girls' behavior with respect to community interactions. Even so, the vast majority of gang-related crime and violence consistently originates from male gang members, who remain the focus of most researchers. Thus, there is a critical void in our knowledge of the dynamics of gender in gang life (Miranda 2003) and a relatively scarce research record on female gang members. Research suggests that anywhere from 4 to 15 percent of Chicano gang members are female (Vigil 2002a and J. Miller 2002, respectively). This chapter relates some current research on female gangs but, more importantly, uses examples from the Pico Gardens neighborhood that are culturally and contextually specific to these young women.

Most girls that are gang affiliated are less involved in the violent aspects of gang activity that captures the spotlight in public discourse as observed in Pico Gardens. In this neighborhood, most loitering and drug dealing (i.e., slanging) are male pastimes and male enterprises. Several female community researchers are responsible for most of the data gathered in this study to provide insights into the life of the chola (the feminine version of the word "cholo," which reflects marginalization and a streetwise orientation and identity). This knowledge is critical in improving our understanding of the role of females in low-income communities and how street socialization affects them.

Beth Caldwell, a student of mine at UCLA, additionally obtained more-specific ethnographic information for this study by conducting participant observation for a period of one year at a community-based violence prevention and intervention program (IMPACTO, or Imaginando Mañana: Pico-Aliso Community Teen Outreach) in East Los Angeles. This program serves and employs residents of local public housing projects in an area that is densely populated with gangs. Research was conducted in the program's office and in the community—at social events, in the local parks, and in people's homes. Further information was obtained through intensive interviews with seven girls, ranging in age from twelve to twenty-four. Attention was focused not only on girls involved in gang activity but also on male gang members, younger children, and other members of the community. This broader strategy was used to gain an understanding of the community as a whole and different perspectives on female gang involvement.

Female-affiliated gang members play important roles in the overall construction of the gang. The girlfriends, sisters, mothers, sexual partners, and homegirls of gang members are not merely passive auxiliaries to the males but in fact serve a variety of initiatory and supportive functions. In general, the relationship of females to gangs varies greatly, however, depending in part upon the ethnicity of the gang as well as the neighborhood context.

A significant number of women and girls who are involved in gangs do indeed enter the penal system. According to a prison official interviewed by one of my USC students, Diane Rodriguez (1990), an estimated 80 percent of the inmates at Sybil Brand women's correctional facility in Los Angeles are incarcerated for gang-related crimes, most of which are related to drug use or sales. Overall, incarceration experiences have had harsh and long-lasting consequences on their lives.

Even though there have always been cholas, pachucas (the 1940s street style to match the male zoot-suiter), and other street-level female participants, the recent growth in female gang activity can be attributed to a number of factors. For example, Latina immigrant groups have traditionally been resistant to street involvement and affiliation with gangs, because the culture of their home country has shielded them from the self-indulgence associated with street life. Due to the large concentration of people in certain neighborhoods today, however, acculturation has become so taxing that many more girls are now likely to join gangs. In part, gender patterns such as *marianismo* (Latino ideals for females to model themselves after the Virgin Mary, suffer in silence, and be submissive) and other Latino traditions have shifted. These transformations have allowed for first-generation females to be socialized outside the home and away from the eye of elder females. Additionally, gangs have become deep-rooted fixtures and thus have normalized gang involvement in many communities. These developments have weakened the stigma that kept large numbers of girls from participating in gangs in the past. Further, girls who are raised in families with a gang orientation often grow up to participate in the gang lifestyle or culture, and thus home socialization precedes street socialization.

Most interestingly, much research frames gang girls in terms of what male gang members say about them; the males talk boastfully about their perceptions of the girls' sexuality and promiscuity and their dominance over them. Because of societal double standards governing the sexual norms of behavior for boys and girls, girls face much greater stigmatization for their sexual activity. Promiscuity, for instance, has been presented as a character flaw in individual girls, but not as the result of a specific set of social conditions. Sexual activity is merely one aspect of the girls' social street life. Courting, dating, and partying with the homeboys at nights and/or weekends constituted the majority of their time spent in gang-related activities.

In addition, violent gang girls hold a more deviant status than males that have similar patterns of behavior. The most aggressive girls of a neighborhood are well known among the gang, law enforcement officials, and residents in the area in general. The reason for this enhanced status is that aggressive acts break with societal expectations of femininity, such as being nonconfrontational.

One day the police apprehended a chola who lived outside the projects but spent a lot of time with Cuatro. The arrest involved a major physical altercation. The incident prompted law enforcement to charge the girl with assaulting a police officer with a deadly weapon (she was carrying a knife). She was mistakenly referred to as a Cuatro Flats "shot caller" by police because she had a long arrest record of drug use and abuse and probation violations, all victimless crimes. Shot callers are usually experienced male individuals who direct drive-bys and other violent retaliations, a role the girl had never played, and the label is restricted to a type of "distinction of the streets," a primarily male status.

Structure of Female Gangs

There are three major types of female gangs: autonomous female gangs, female gangs that are auxiliaries to male gangs, and mixed-gender gangs. The majority of female gangs are auxiliaries to male gangs or are associated with a male gang in some way. Male-dominated gangs tend to emerge first, and only later do women develop their own cliques within the gang (Campbell 1991; Moore 1991). Moreover, female cliques generally last for a shorter amount of time than the male gang. Among Chicano gangs, as noted in Chapter Five, there are typically age-graded cliques into which all of the members are divided. Similarly, there are typically separate cliques for females, although some girls are included in male cliques. No females in the Pico Gardens clique were found to claim membership in both types of cliques.

In Los Angeles, where all observations for this study were conducted, one autonomous female gang was accounted for in an area already home to many old Chicano gangs, but it no longer existed at the time of the study. Although the girls who formed the gang were the girlfriends and sisters of cholos from other neighborhood gangs, they did not ally themselves exclusively with one gang. The gang had existed independently from other gangs in the area, although members would party with males from other barrio gangs. One girl who was in high school at the time of this gang explained: "Yeah, there used to be this all-girl gang—the H Girls. They knew my brother was from a gang, so they wanted to get me into their neighborhood. I'm telling you, every day when I got off the bus from school, I would have to take off running. They would be chasing me, trying to jump me so I could be from their neighborhood." The existence of an all-girl gang in the neighborhood was obviously an exception to the norm. As another girl recalled, "There used to be this neighborhood that was all girls, but they didn't last that long."

An older woman from the community opined that most girls who were involved in gangs were the girlfriends or sisters of male gang members: "We don't really ever see things like you see on TV with those gangs that only have girls. No . . . our gangs are mostly the guys and then some girls with them." The life span of the all-female gang was short; in a neighborhood that is home to gangs that have existed for generations, it lasted only a couple of years.

The situation in which a female is permitted to join a male clique is not uncommon, and it happens, more or less, during the same childhood-to-adulthood passage when a new identity is sought (the teen years). Although it is a privilege reserved only for the "downest" of homegirls, many girls tell similar stories. Even more typical, however, is that girls employ some of the same routines involving "jumping in" of other girls who want to be not only in the gang but also in the gang's female clique.

Reasons for Membership

Many of the reasons that girls join gangs are the same as those for boys, particularly when considering socioeconomic problems that affect gang mem-

Disgruntled high school students

bership, especially the related multiple marginalization that ultimately affects all gang members. The poverty and isolation within many barrios, poor educational systems that do not address the needs of minority youth, and familial problems combined with the fixture of the street gang as a socialization agent in many low-income neighborhoods cause many youth to turn to gangs to provide what is lacking within the social institutions of their lives. Many join the gang for support and friendship, particularly when such support is unavailable in the family. For both male and female youth, the gang compensates for what is missing in their lives; it serves as a surrogate family, providing friendship, companionship, protection, identity, and entertainment. What is fascinating is that Latino culture is commonly known to value the institution of the family, and gang members, both males and females, carry on this tradition, but in a warped, readapted version of the original.

Sociocultural factors such as the process of acculturation, which is particularly important in the Mexican American community, further marginalize a group of children who find themselves caught between two cultures. Many such children turn to the gang as a means of adaptation. The stress that both poverty and the acculturation process put upon families can also lead to unstable and sometimes problematic family lives. Since girls, as well as boys, are affected by these fundamental social problems, girls also look to gangs to find a substitute for society's failures. Girls are arguably more marginalized than boys because in addition to facing obstacles due to their class and race, they encounter additional gender discrimination. Such barriers show how females are devalued and dominated not only by society but also by their own homeboys. What is interesting is that cultural double standards for women also affect the psychosocial moratorium for females, making the passage to adulthood doubly difficult. Females, like males, are expected to grow up and mature, but cultural restraints reflecting gender torque this process. Hormones may abound and follow biological rules, but cultural pressures interfere and force females to adhere to different, stricter social rules than those for males.

In his classic study of Chicago gangs, Thrasher pointed out two major reasons why girls do not join gangs: cultural traditions and closer supervision. He explained, "First the social patterns for the behavior of girls, powerfully backed by the weight of tradition and custom, is contrary to the gang and its activities; and second, girls even in urban disorganized areas, are much more closely supervised and guarded than boys and are usually well incorporated into the family groups or some other social structure" (Thrasher 1927). In Latino communities, girls are fully expected to be in the home, and street involvement among females is considered extremely deviant. The gang represents a very tangible break from traditional cultural values of men and women. However, girls who become involved in gangs deviate from expected norms more than their male counterparts.

Although the traditions of many immigrant families keep many girls out of gangs, they paradoxically contribute to the reasons some girls join gangs. Traditional expectations of parents seem confining to many children of immigrants as they grow accustomed to gender norms of mainstream U.S. society. Parents' expectations seem too conservative to many girls, causing them to look elsewhere to find alternative ways to act out their gender role. Traditional expectations keep the majority of Mexican American women from participating in street life. For the minority of girls who do become involved in street life, however, those same traditional values can reinforce this lifestyle. Females are targeted for labels because of their street involvement and clothing choices, which often reflect the "street style." Traditional values protect most young women, but they increase the risk of gang involvement for girls from cholo families, because such girls are labeled before their involvement in the gang has even begun. This kind of labeling and family background can propel girls to become active in the gang. They are already socially isolated and labeled as deviant, so it is not such a large leap to join the gang.

Family life has been found to be perhaps the single most important factor in differentiating youth who join gangs from those who do not (Valdez 2007, 61). Although the family situations of both male and female gang members are often problematic, girls tend to come from even more stressed family situations than boys (Moore 1991). In immigrant families, attempts to adjust to a new culture, as well as difficulties associated with poverty, strain and stress the family structure and weaken parental control in too many cases. To compound matters, the diffusion of cholo/gang culture into Mexico has created opportunities for females to arrive in the U.S. presocialized to chola/street-like behavior. Adopting street clothing styles and values in Mexico makes the gang lifestyle in the United States a familiar and acceptable choice.

Stressful family situations can also contribute to psychological problems within an individual, in many cases resulting in low self-esteem and rebellion. The delinquent and revered "loca" behavior of a gang member is in many cases a reaction to an emotionally disturbing home life. Along with the forces and pressures of multiple marginality that destabilize a person, there are added post-traumatic stress dimensions that range from cultural to psychological (Stein et al. 2003). In many cases, gang members live under a cloud of apprehension because they do not have documents allowing them to be in the United States legally. Often there is a recurrent tension between *paisas* (Mexican-born) and "homies" (U.S.-born Mexicans) that leads to conflict. Worse yet are the domestic and street traumas stemming from extremely violent and aggressive actions that taint the mind and soul of a person, causing depression and post-traumatic stress disorder (PTSD). As noted below, these physiological stressors and traumas have a big effect on all street youth and particularly females (Herrenkohl et al. 2003), as the fight-or-flight instinct takes its toll.

Not only do girls who join gangs generally have more problematic family backgrounds than male gang members do, but like the families of male gang members, the girls' families also tend to be less traditional. In general, "gang members are more likely than non-gang members to live with a single parent" (Esbensen and Winfree 1998). One aspect of the less traditional nature of the families of girl gang members is that significantly fewer of their parents were born in Mexico, a finding similar to that for males in Chapter Five (i.e., they are mostly second-generation with a smattering of 1.5-generation). Moreover, depending on the neighborhood and home context, many girls become involved in a gang through family members who belong to gangs. Seventy-nine percent of all female gang members were found to have a family member involved in a gang, whereas only 54 percent of non-gang females had a family member previously or currently involved in a gang (J. Miller 2001). The involvement of other family members in the gang perhaps further normalizes the gang in the eyes of the family, thus making a girl's involvement seem less deviant to her family and herself.

For example, a twelve-year-old girl who already said she was from a gang began claiming the neighborhood because her two older brothers were active in the gang. She reflected about being scared as she heard gang members talk and walk by her window at night. She had participated in numerous gang-related fights that she had instigated by claiming to be from the gang. She explained that her two older brothers, both of whom were currently incarcerated, taught her "to be down for" the neighborhood. Her thirteen-year-old homegirl described a similar situation when she followed in the footsteps of her uncle. At ten years old, she had already been given a gang moniker, and later, at seventeen, she was arrested and charged with being the driver in a drive-by shooting, even though it was a spontaneous event and she had been unaware that an older male passenger in the front seat was carrying a gun, which he pulled out and used. Unwilling to divulge his name to the police, she was now doing fifteen years in prison; sticking to the code of the gang—no ratas (don't rat on fellow gang members)—she showed herself to be a "good homegirl."

Another nineteen-year-old in one of the gang families of this study described her situation this way: "My uncles, my cousins, my boyfriend, and my brothers are all gang members. It [joining the gang] was normal for me." The participation of other relatives in a gang makes it more acceptable for a female to become involved, especially in a culture that generally scorns female gang involvement.

There is another factor to consider. The majority of girls who become involved in gangs have been victims of physical, emotional, and/or sexual abuse and suffer the symptoms of PTSD; shockingly, the perpetrators of this abuse are frequently family members. The psychological trauma and repercussions of such abuse lead many to the gang for emotional support and protection. Fifty to 70 percent of delinquent girls at a Los Angeles female probation camp had been victims of physical, sexual, or emotional abuse, according to intake records (Mehren 1996). In a study conducted by Jody Miller, 52 percent of black girl gang members had been sexually assaulted or abused, whereas only 22 percent of non-gang girls had been. In addition, "two-thirds of the sexual assaults occurred within the context of the family" (J. Miller 2001). In fact, 71 percent of the victims of sexual abuse in our society as a whole are women (Daly and Chesney-Lind 1988). Thus the experience of sexual abuse is a dimension in the backgrounds of female gang members that appears to be not as great an issue for males. (A former male gang member hinted at why very little is known about sexual abuse among males, when he stated unequivocally that such episodes "would be taken to the grave.")

Tiny, a girl who defined herself as a "gangbanger," described what such abuse had been like for her:

> Finally it got so bad in my house that I just left. I couldn't take it anymore with my stepdad and everything. Now that I look back on things, that was a lot of why I was down in the projects every day, just kicking it. I never wanted to go home. So I would just be out on the streets getting shot at, getting budded out [smoking marijuana], and kicking it with my homeboys.

Despite her renowned fighting abilities and seemingly tough exterior, Mayra, a girl who was involved with gangs for years, became noticeably timid when speaking of her father:

> I was always so scared of him . . . and of what he would do to my mom. . . . My dad used to try to sexually abuse me. The first time he did it I was thirteen . . . and the last time he did it I was eighteen or nineteen. That's when I moved out . . . but I didn't want to then. He had so much power over me. I was scared of him. He still tries to tell me what to do— like he's the man in the house, but I don't even listen to him anymore because he's just freeloading. I'm the one who pays rent. . . . I'm the one who pays all the bills. It wasn't good for me—living in that house. Now that I look back at how I used to be, I regret a lot of things. . . . I was out there 'cause of my dad.

For victims of abuse, joining the gang is a way of empowering themselves. It is a pragmatic way of surviving and escaping horrid situations at home. This is particularly the case in areas where gangs flourish, places that tend to have hardly any resources. Girls who have been victimized have few places to retreat to and few close family members or friends to stay with. Already feeling rejected by mainstream social institutions, many girls look to the gang to provide the assistance they need to escape from abuse. In a sample of gang-involved youth, one-third of the boys had run away from home at least once, whereas three-quarters of the girls had done so (Moore and Hagedorn 1996). A large number of gang-involved girls had run away from home multiple times, which is one solid indicator of problematic situations in the home that they are trying to avoid. As one girl put it, "My homies will always find me a place to stay when shit gets too bad at home."

Many girls also turn to gangs for the emotional support and feelings of acceptance they provide. One such girl explained: "We're like one big family. If they do wrong to my homegirl or homeboy, it is like doing wrong to me and it hurts" (Quicker 1983, 24). Another girl said: "They were always there for me. I wouldn't have made it without my homegirls."

Members gain a sense of pride and self-esteem by linking themselves with the identity of the gang. Young women repeatedly brought up the importance of gaining respect from fellow gang members and non-gang members by belonging to the gang. According to one chola, one of the most important aspects of being in a gang was that it allowed a person "to be someone."

Some other family dimensions that can lead females to join gangs are related to drug and alcohol abuse within the home. Regular alcohol abuse occurred within the homes of 56 percent of the females involved in gangs but in only 37 percent of the homes of non-gang females. Similarly, regular drug abuse occurred in the homes of 58 percent of female gang members but in only 17 percent of the homes of non-gang females. These sorts of family problems have led many females to join a gang in order to fill some kind of "emotional void" (J. Miller 2001; see also Moore and Mata 1981). The regular alcohol and drug abuse within the females' home life precluded any type of parental supervision, as well as normal parental roles. Unlike the females from households that did not face these stresses, these girls were unable to receive guidance and support from their parent(s).

Often, living with drug-abusing family members and associating with drug-abusing gang members leads many females to experiment with drugs or become lifetime users. The proportion of female gang members who are "current and lifetime users, along with the level of polydrug use" by these women, makes them a heavier drug-using group overall than the general youth population (Hunt et al. 2000). Many female gang members, however, are able to limit their drug use to mostly recreational purposes and not become "problematic or out of control users" (ibid.). Therefore, for many female gang members, drugs do not consume their daily activities and life, but rather are used for more partying or leisure situations with their fellow gang members.

Male Dominance

Sadly, many young women who turn to the gang for protection from domestic abuse continue to be abused by homeboys in the gang. These types of verbal and sexual abuse may not be considered as such by those involved in it, but many girls accept rude and sometimes dehumanizing treatment from the guys. Gang ideals and expectations of sex roles are narrow and rigid, shaped in many ways by cultural traditions from the home country. Masculinity is defined as machismo behavior, emphasizing the dominance and assertiveness of males. Femininity is characterized by submissive behavior. Most females are afforded a subordinate status. However, male demonstrations of dominance have become increasingly important to them as women gain more independence. Because it has become socially acceptable for women to work, many women no longer depend on men for financial support as they did in previous times. Women who have children and are a single parent can also qualify for welfare and thereby maintain their independence from males. Thus, women today are in a more powerful position than they were previously, and displays of male dominance have become increasingly more desperate, almost shrill-like, as the boys attempt to gain self-respect in this way. Particularly given that machismo is defined by the assertion of power, the males feel that their identity is threatened by women's increasing power in society. Displays of male dominance reflect an insecurity that can thus be understood as reactive attempts to define and reassert their own identity and masculinity.

Gang norms are street-based and in many cases perpetuate a state of male dominance. A male's reputation is affected by his ability to "keep his lady in check"—to control her and to keep her from the streets. Stigmatizing girls who are active on the streets thus reinforces male dominance in street life. Further attempts of male domination are evident in the dehumanizing treatment of many women as mere sexual objects. Gang norms of male dominance are most likely rooted in the traditional Mexican gender ideals of marianismo and machismo. The ideal behavior for men is machismo—to be dominant. In contrast, women are expected to follow the ideal of marianismo by submitting to male dominance.

In addition, a woman is supposed to disregard her own needs and instead make the needs of her family and husband her first priority. However, many of the girls in gangs have been abandoned by men in their lives—fathers, boyfriends—and thus decide to be more independent. The abuse that many women face amid their ready acceptance of such passive roles often leads many female gang members to reject traditional ideals.

Good Girl versus Bad Girl

A female gang member's sexual identity is an important factor in deciding her role within the gang. In the eyes of many male gang members, her acceptance or rejection of traditional gender roles forms the basis for categorizing her as a "good girl" or a "bad girl." Although most male gang members are sexually active themselves, little attention is focused on this aspect of their lives. In contrast, a disproportionate amount of attention is focused on the sexual activity of girls. That sexually active girls are labeled "bad," whereas sexually active boys are considered normal, points to the double standard that is a part of both mainstream and gang ideology. The males respect girls who show their faithfulness and loyalty to a boyfriend. This type of behavior conforms to the gang members' values and expectations for women's sexual actions. For example, if one's boyfriend has a high status in the gang, the girlfriend immediately has respect and is in a position of power. As one chola explained, "I always had respect from all the guys because I was Cesar's lady. They would listen to me."

Most cholos desire to be with "good girls" as long-term girlfriends or wives. In the words of one Latina gang member from the Arizona Maravilla gang, "Cholos want girls that aren't in the gang, that are good, that will stay home and take care of the kids and not fuck around with a gang. They want pure girls" (Moore et al. 1995). The desire to have a "good girl" as a steady girlfriend or a wife is an indication of the double standard by which women are judged even by gang members. Even though it is culturally acceptable for a guy to party and be active in gang activity on the streets, it is considered the woman's responsibility to stay home and take care of her children. A cholo from Los Angeles said, "I don't want a girlfriend like those kind of girls. I want a nice girl who is smart and can talk to me and really understand my feelings. One that can take care of her family and everything. I don't want to be with one of them hoodrats." Thus, gang girls are labeled as deviant not only by outsiders but also by their own homeboys.

Sex Objects

Stigmatization and gender discrimination are prevalent even within the gang. A girl who used to be involved with gangs pointed out that many males saw the girls in their gangs only as sexual objects: "They used to tell me, 'I don't have any homegirls—just ho-girls.'" The male perception of some women as mere sexual objects is further underscored through one cholo's response to a question about the presence of prostitutes in his neighborhood: "No, we don't have any of those. But we got ones who do it for free." Despite stigmatizing these girls as "bad" and often referring to them as "hos" or "hoodrats," male gang members are generally happy to have them around because they serve a function as sexual objects. The males speak of them in derogatory words and judgmental voices but are pleased to go to parties, where girls

Young girls raising babies

who play the role of sex objects will engage in sexual relations with them willingly and frequently.

The self-destructive nature of such girls, who are both verbally and physically abused by the males, points to the low self-image and desolation of their lives. Droopy, for instance, said of his lady, "She's just a ho. I don't give a fuck about her. I'm just fucking her." Such verbal abuse occurs in front of the girls as well as when they are not around. Their acceptance of such negative treatment truly reveals how these young women view relationships with men. Female submission to this type of treatment is evidence of the self-destructive nature of gang activity. Interactions between males and females are, in a sense, a twisted enactment of the extremes of cultural gender-role definitions: male dominance and female submissiveness.

Victimization and treatment of girls as "sex objects" occur in a variety of ways. There are accounts of girls forced to have sex with one or multiple members of a gang in order to join the gang. The practice of "training" girls is particularly revealing as to the role of girls as sexual objects, as noted in Chapter Five. This term refers to a group of males having intercourse with a girl, one right after the other. It has been documented across regions and ethnicities as a fairly common practice among gangs. As one young man said, "I'm going to be honest with you. We'll bust a train every once in a while . . . Like at a party or something, we'll take a girl into a room and . . . take turns." The male view of girls as sexual objects is very much a part of the gang lifestyle, although most males do not perceive or treat tomboys or many of the "good girls" in the same way that they treat "sex objects." Many feel justified in treating the latter girls badly. As one cholo said, "They're just hos anyway. We wouldn't bust a train on a schoolgirl. That would be fucked up." Gang-involved girls who do not play the role of "sex objects" condemn girls who do and reprimand them for being sexually promiscuous. They often blame such girls for initiating the sexual encounters. It must be underscored, however, that the girls make themselves available for many reasons. Some willingly participate because of the excitement of being considered a quasi gang member and a desire to be accepted. Others value being "shared," which seems to give them a false sense of control. In fact, "control" is the operative word for girls that have been victimized. They like to think they are in control, even if events prove the opposite.

Tomboys

On the other end of the spectrum are "tomboys." These girls find and define their identities through their fighting abilities and presentations of "toughness." A chola proudly related how "down" she was for her barrio: "When my brother was locked up, I would bring him in drugs and everything. The guys he was locked up with would tell him, 'Damn—your sister's down.'" Loca, a girl with a reputation for fighting with guys and being just as tough as any of her homeboys, was described in this way: "We have this one chola who is just like a guy. She has a shaved head and everything. She dresses like a guy and has two tattoos of clowns on her neck. She's down. She'll throw it down with guys. . . . She doesn't give a fuck."

Tomboys generally have the respect of male gang members, and their behavior patterns are similar to those of males. Many girls who act in accordance with this role feel closer to the males in the gang and have adopted the role partly because of time spent with male gang members. One incarcerated girl observed, "I don't really hang around with girls, never did. I hang around with boys. I like going out a lot. I like messing around" (Mehren 1996).

Gang Girl Style

Because of their marginalized status within society, girls involved in gangs have developed their own unique styles of dress and behavior. They adopt similar patterns of dress, speech, and expression in interactions with other people, which define them as gang members.

Certain styles of dress, hair, and makeup characterize Latina gang members. Patterns of dress vary according to a girl's role or identity in the gang. For instance, girls who act more like tomboys tend to dress more like male gang members, whereas girls who are more interested in partying with male gang members dress more provocatively. Patterns of clothing tend to match one's role at a given time. For instance, when expecting a fight, some girls purposefully wear male styles of clothing. Other girls wear clothing to show that they do not belong to a gang. Provocative dress, which accents sexuality, is often the choice for late-night partying. One cholo described this style of dress: "The hoodrats wear those shorts that they cut real short so that . . . like . . . their cheeks are hanging out and everything. And they'll wear like those little shirts—I don't know what you call them." He went on to say that he enjoyed "looking at girls who dress like that" but wouldn't want to be with someone who dressed like that as a girlfriend. A girl spoke of the styles of clothing she prefers to wear: "Like if I'm going to party and get my scam on, I'll wear like a little shirt and some Daisy Dukes [very tight, very short spandex shorts]."

Even more than clothing, specific styles of makeup define the chola style. In a study by Norma Mendoza-Denton (1996), girls emphasized the importance of makeup to enhance their sense of self and their ability to fight and intimidate others. It was a way of identifying themselves as gang members. One girl advised, "If you want to know who's a chola, just look for the eyeliner" (ibid.). Makeup also gave many girls a sense of power. Another chola noted, "When I wear my eyeliner, me siento mas macha [I feel more feminine]" (ibid.). This makeup style is becoming less popular among Mexican Americans, however, but is still practiced among Mexican and 1.5-generation immigrants.

Makeup, as well as the other components of the chola style, acts as a mask, disguising a girl's individual identity and replacing it with the identity of "gang member." Cholas generally feel that they are not dressed if they lack eye makeup. By developing a style unique to cholas, these girls have expressed their feelings of separation or exclusion from mainstream American society, as well as their separation from traditional Mexican culture. Mendoza-Denton explored the importance of the chola style, explaining that it was "all focusing toward the same end: the articulation of a distinct style, different from their parents, who continually ask why their little girls must dress like this, when we have none of this in Mexico" (ibid., 51). The clothing styles, in a sense, reflect the cholas' rejection of the female aesthetic standards of mainstream society. The style affirms the gang's rejection of mainstream values.

Tattoos are an important component of the urban street scene as well as the traditional chola style. Common tattoos include three dots in the shape of a triangle, indicating "mi vida loca." Teardrops on the face are also common tattoos. Names of boyfriends artistically tattooed onto the body, as well as the name of the barrio, are common for cholas. Deceased boyfriends and close relatives, including children, also mark the backs and arms of the girls. These tattoos are mostly applied after the initiation ritual, a similar yet different affair from that of the males.

Violence

Female gang violence is not a new phenomenon. The nature of such violence and the areas in which female violence are increasing remain important considerations in the appraisal of the lifestyles of these girls. Just as fights between male gang members often originate over girls, conflicts over males spark the majority of females' fights. Jealousy or competition for boyfriends or male companions triggers many disagreements. By fighting for the barrio, girls can gain prestige and respect from the gang. Given that guns have become an important part of gang activities in recent years, many homegirls now carry guns but rarely use them, content to wield them as a threat. One girl described her response to finding out that her best male friend had been shot by a member of a rival gang: "We were driving around looking for anybody from [that neighborhood]. My homeboy was driving, and I was right there with the gun. We saw this fool from [that neighborhood]. . . . I came this close to shooting him." Another girl said, "I like to start shit sometimes—ain't nothing else to do."

Girls' involvement in violence is also a product of the intense deprivation and abuse suffered at the hands of others. Coming from abusive family situations, many girls have learned to fight and act aggressively instead of dealing with problems and emotions in more constructive ways. In a study by Esbensen and Winfree (1998), females were found to be likely to "commit the same variety of offenses as the boys, but at a slightly lower frequency." In that study, the crimes involved property, persons, drug use, and drug sales. Many girls in gangs have a great deal of anger directed both toward themselves and toward the society at large. This type of anger sometimes results in aggressive behavior and has led female gang members to be two to five times more likely to become delinquent than non-gang boys (ibid.).

Mayra, a much-respected chola, admitted that she carried a gun every day in case her homeboys needed it; they knew to find her if they needed a weapon. She would also hide their drugs and other weapons in her purse or bra when police or probation officers were near. These were not her only roles in the gang. She had used the gun herself on a few occasions and was actively involved in many other aspects of gang activity. A former Chicana gang member stated, "I used to always be out there kicking it—hiding guns for my homeboys and getting shot at. One time my best friend gave me a gun he had just killed someone with, and I'm ashamed to say it but I got rid of it for him. I even knew the guy he had killed, but I didn't want him to get in trouble."

Girls also have the unique ability to set up rival gang members. These encounters with rival gang members usually occur on the weekends at street neighborhood gatherings and parties. By talking to and flirting with a rival gang member, a girl sometimes lures him into an area where her homeboys can attack him. As a male gang member pointed out,

I don't trust girls who I just meet now because they could be one of my enemy's homegirls. My homeboy got jumped the other day because of some *jainas* [cholo slang for "girls"]. They were talking on the phone and the girl told him to cruise over to her pad. He was excited 'cause he was kind of sprung on her . . . but when he got there three guys from [another gang] were waiting there for him. They fucked him up.

Often the type of gang that female gang members are associated with can affect the amount and extent of violence that the girls are faced with. Females in auxiliary gangs encounter much more potential and actual violence than females in autonomous gangs. Those in auxiliary gangs experience violence from initiation into the gang, confrontations with male members of other gangs, fights with homegirls of rival gangs, disputes with females within their own gangs, and altercations between homegirls and homeboys within the same gang (Hunt et al. 2000).

Sexual Activity—The Double Standard

Sexual activity among gang-involved youth, both male and female, is common. This behavior has more long-term effects for women than men in that many of the women have children at a young age. Although many fathers are involved in raising their children, it is the mothers who generally take the more active role in child rearing. Becoming pregnant and raising children are an important part of the lives of most female gang members. Campbell (1990) found that 94 percent of female gang members would have kids during their gang phase, and 84 percent would raise them without husbands.

Some pregnancies are accidents, but others are planned "accidents." The reasons why many gang-involved girls wish to have children at a young age reveal a lot about their vulnerable emotions. Many girls try to get pregnant for the same reasons that they joined the gang: to counteract loneliness, to find the support they have been denied by their family and other social institutions, and to find love. In this vein, a baby becomes a focal point in fulfilling the emotional needs of the mother. When girls feel lonely and "marginalized" by their families, as well as by society in general, a baby may seem to be a cure to their loneliness—someone who will bring meaning to their lives. Having a baby seems to make life purposeful and worthwhile. A nineteen-year-old woman with a one-year-old baby confessed, "Before I had Junior, I thought he would be like a little doll to cuddle with and love me." Girls also see having a baby as a way of cementing their relationship with their boyfriends. In a "street" world, where women's relationships with men are often tenuous at best, a baby represents a lasting bond between a man and a woman. A seventeen-year-old girl confided, "If I have his baby, he'll be with me forever. It's a way to show how much we love each other. Like if he tries to use protection, I get mad because it means he doesn't want me to have his baby."

Machismo, an important part of life particularly for Chicano gang members, influences many boys' desire to have a baby as a testament to their masculinity. Thus, in this culture where girls typically try to make their boyfriends happy, a girl will become pregnant if her boyfriend wants her to. A male may show his love for a girl by wanting her to have his baby; however, the issue of pleasure is never far behind this motive, as one male stated that using condoms for protection doesn't feel as good. In the end, the resulting baby fails to reinforce the relationship between the mother and father. Sadly, having a baby can strain social and economic resources and hamper the relationship.

The culture of violence common to gangs also contributes to early parenthood. It is fairly common for gang-involved youth to grow up surrounded by violence. Given the violent nature of their lifestyles, many gang members don't expect to live to middle age. This often leads them to decide to start having children early. As a seventeen-year-old cholo said, "I'll either be dead or be doing life by this time next year." Another young man echoed: "I won't make it 'til I'm twenty-one." It follows that many young men and women in these "short-life" circumstances want to have children while they can. Given that they view their future as not very compelling and in fact as being full of despair, it is no wonder that such youth plan for death.

However, having a baby can be a turning point in the lives of girls, causing them to become less active in the gang as they focus on caring for their children. In Moore's study (1991), 43 percent of the women sampled said that having a child had been a major transformation in their lives, whereas only 19 percent of the males agreed. In a subsequent study, Moore and Hagedorn (1996) noted that "for women, but rarely for men, the new responsibility associated with child rearing may speed up the process of maturing out of the gang." Twenty-one-year-old Mayra observed: "That's when I changed—I kicked back a lot when I found out I was pregnant. Now that I have my son, I have to think about him. I don't even party anymore." Women such as these who have had a child are faced with educational problems. For most, going back to school after having a child is not an option, because they are left to raise the child on their own. This situation adds to the already very common dropout phenomenon among gang members (Vigil 2004).

Conclusion

Female gang involvement has important implications beyond the scope of the girls who are themselves gang members. Females are an important link between generations and have the power to perpetuate an intergenerational cycle of gang membership. Particularly given that many girls who are involved in gangs have children at a young age and raise them without a husband, the overall effect that women have on their children surpasses that of most fathers. It follows that the greater the number of girls and women who are involved in gangs, the greater the number of children who will become the next generation of gang members. Although females have traditionally been seen as having passive roles within the gang, the girls who are involved with gangs are far from passive. They take an active role in shaping their identities through construction of appearance and development of relationships with both girls and boys. Their decisions concerning their sexual identity and their role within the gang are not dictated to the women by others but are achieved and actively constructed by the women themselves. The role of the individual girl in shaping her identity explains the range of relationships present for girls in gangs. Many are the girlfriends and sexual partners of male gang members, as well as being sisters, cousins, and relatives through marriage.

Young girls and boys, particularly in low-income urban areas, are growing up equally deprived. Both genders are exposed to violence, and both endure many difficulties at young ages. The problems that contribute to gang membership among boys and girls are similar: a lack of jobs, poverty, the failure of traditional socialization agents, family problems, and prejudice. These combine to marginalize certain youth. Girls face further marginalization, due to gender discrimination. They turn to the gang to seek refuge from this marginalization, rejecting traditional definitions of their roles in the process.

Although seeking refuge from an alienating society by turning to the gang and denying conventional values and lifestyles, girls continue to endure discrimination based on gender by their male counterparts. Girls turn to the gang for protection or to learn survival skills, but there is a trade-off: they are abused emotionally and physically by male gang members. The girls' tacit acceptance of such treatment is a testament to the internalization of their marginalized status in society and to the essentially self-destructive nature of much gang activity. Ironically, the gang is an attempt at self-preservation for many, providing protection as well as psychological and financial support. Yet this attempt is simultaneously self-destructive, contributing to the degradation, injury, and death of its members.

CHAPTER EIGHT

WHY CHILDREN EITHER AVOID OR AFFILIATE WITH GANGS

The factors determining gang and non-gang families can be traced to macro-historical and macrostructural forces. Racism, immigration difficulties, poverty, stressed families, and other obstacles and pressures are integral to these larger-than-life dramas. Detailing the specific situations and conditions of individuals and families is another matter and comes under the rubric of micro-level research. This chapter stresses the ethnographic basis for explanations that show agent proclivities, push, pull, and interrupter effects of youth who join or avoid gangs. When these processes are examined, it is clear that no single factor is the sole motivational cause. Rather, it is a combination of factors, as suggested by the multiple-marginality framework, that leads to a better understanding of gang involvement and avoidance dynamics.

The ethnographic field notes and demographic database compiled by this study's research team provide a smaller-scale and more intimate examination of family life in a Los Angeles housing project than do other, macro-scale demographic and economic surveys, which are usually based on quantitative data. The uniqueness of qualitative information stems from the intimacy generated by ethnographic survey methods—mainly intensive interviewing and participant observation. Furthermore, the use of key informants and cultural brokers from the study community offered the opportunity to explore certain issues in-depth and helped us capture the social and family relationships to gang involvement and gang avoidance. The multiple-marginality framework used here simultaneously offers a macro-level backdrop for examining embedded social control dynamics. In this larger community context, micro-level details, such as family and personal attributes, reveal the obstacles and choices involved in joining or shunning gangs.

To organize the voluminous, complex stories relayed by this study's subjects of various events in their families' lives, an oversimplified bipolar gradient model that makes use of push, pull, agent, and interrupter conceptions of social effects is employed. This model is accompanied by brief descriptions of qualitative trends in the ethnographic surveys and an integration of these trends into coherent causal frameworks.

Conceptualization

The situation of any young person of gang age can be described in terms of his or her position on a continuum. At one end of the continuum lies the individual with no gang affiliation. He or she does not hang out with gang members and does not engage in group-organized delinquency. At the other end is the hard-core gang member who regularly interacts with other similarly committed members of his or her gang. These individuals are involved in gang-related behaviors such as (but not limited to) fighting, shooting, vandalism, and drug dealing; less we forget, however, gang members spend most of their time in normal socializing activities. Intermediate to these extremes are individuals who show mild protogangster tendencies such as the very young hyperactive and isolated child, mild drug users, and boyfriends and girlfriends of gang members. There are also those who may dress the part of a gangster without exhibiting gang behaviors and those who are part-time or peripheral gang members (see Vigil 1988a and Klein 1995 for such gang typologies).

The four classes of effects are as follows:

Agent effects are those effects that are products of the immediate and internal psychology of the person. Hyperactivity as a youngster and rebellion in the early teens are two examples. The causes of these problems are not immediately relevant to the study at hand. Their effects on predisposing family members to gang life are what is important for now.

Push effects are those effects that drive a person from one state to another. The influence of an undesirable environment pushes a person to find other outlets, making them susceptible to varying degrees of gang involvement (see Decker and Van Winkle 1996 for a detailed explanation of how loss of social control creates "threats" and pushes youth into gangs; see also Herrenkohl et al. 2003). Examples of push effects are bullying by gang members that motivates a person not to join or parental abuse that drives a child into the street and into a gang.

Pull effects are those effects that draw a person from one point on the continuum to another because of a property of the destination state. The allure of the gang mystique that leads a child into a gang is an example of this type of effect, as well as the sense of power that sometimes accompanies gang participation.

Interrupter effects are those effects arising from the interaction of one or more intervening agents, leading to the amelioration or reversal of an agent, push, or pull effect. A structured family routine and adequate parental supervision and involvement in a child's life that cut off opportunities to join a gang are examples of interrupter effects.

It is important to note that these classes of effects are not unidirectional but can operate both as safeguards against and facilitators of gang involvement.

The Ethnographic and Socioeconomic Setting

The sample of ethnographic surveys drawn from the Pico Gardens housing project for this study is primarily composed of people who identify themselves ethnically as Mexican or Mexican American. There is a smattering of black, Central American, Asian, and white self-identifiers in the sample as well. From a review and examination of the micro family ethnographies, several overarching themes become immediately apparent: unemployment, patriarchy, machismo, lack of mobility or opportunity, and denial.

Unemployment and lack of mobility or opportunity (spatial, economic, or social) go hand in hand and are regularly featured in models, such as multiple marginality, that some social researchers find useful. For example, multiple marginality starts with how place (ecology) and status (socioeconomic factors) mark a community as visually distinct and spatially separate, as well as deficits in resources and opportunities. Suffice it to say that the vast majority of adults in the Pico Gardens community, in addition to living in subsidized housing, do not have regular, full-time legitimate employment, are dependent on welfare programs, and have very few prospects for betterment. In addition to their marginal participation in the economy during good times, job prospects for the residents worsen when economic downturns or shifts occur. The transition of a manufacturing economy with plants and factories near poor areas to a service-oriented economy has left many residents without a job (Moore and Vigil 1993). In fact, both a brewery and a poultry-processing factory across the street from the projects prefer to hire newly arrived immigrant Mexicans rather than older immigrant residents. Coupled with a lack of transportation, whether personal vehicles or bus service, the dearth of nearby jobs leaves many from the Pico Gardens area trapped, willing but unable to go elsewhere for employment. A UCLA

Mariachi going to work at First and Boyle

researcher has documented this disparity, describing it as a "mismatch" syndrome in which inner-city workers are unable to easily travel to city outskirts, where more industries and jobs are located (Stole 2004).

Such economic turmoil and employment problems can be observed in Chapters Nine and Ten, where the experiences of family household heads are outlined. For example, one of the gang-family single parents, Juana, was a Mexican immigrant who discovered that her lack of education and inability to read English or Spanish relegated her to the most labor-intensive and lowest-paying jobs, which never lasted very long. Thus, she was hard-pressed to care for her children. In contrast, in a non-gang two-parent family that eked out an existence by parlaying multiple, small work activities to support the household, Sonia creatively juggled garment industry work during the day with earning extra income as a seamstress at night. Moreover, she made household crafts and gifts to be sold at the swap meet or in the projects on weekends. Her husband helped out by loading up the car with these homemade goods for the trip to the swap meet and was known in the community as the local auto mechanic, fixing cars on an irregular basis.

The vast majority of mothers in the study sample were single, having been abandoned by the fathers of their children or having kicked them out of the home for presenting a danger. In much of the political and social science discourse associated with juvenile delinquency, single motherhood is often isolated as a primary causal contributor. This goes a long way toward reifying the standard two-parent patriarchal home as the model environment for raising a child. It also has the unintended consequence of further marginalizing households headed by single, often minority females in relation to dominant cultural norms. The Pico Gardens ethnographic survey provides some interesting indicators that challenge the conventional wisdom favoring patriarchal families, in that the latter may not always be the "best practice" for some populations. This fact, not surprisingly, corresponds with Moore and Vigil's findings that "a broken family is not necessarily ineffectual" (1987, 37). As noted below, several single, female household heads in the study ran a tight ship.

In contrast, it can be safely said of the vast majority of the fathers of children in the study that they did far more harm than good. Additionally, the strict patriarchy that manifests itself in the form of machismo in the dominant culture of the projects has many dangerous consequences, as several examples below show. Coming from an impoverished background, many of the fathers had current or past drug problems, criminal records, and poor job histories and had proven themselves to be neglectful or abusive. Having them in the home proved to be a bad example at best, and a grave danger at worst, to the children and mothers of the sample. The rigid adherence of the fathers to a patriarchal worldview that designated them the sole arbiter of all family decisions thereby made them impotent in the context of changing social realities and insensitive to the expanding role of women both in the projects and in society at large.

Fathers' roles often reflect a tension that bodes instabilities for the family. A father's physical presence is not of certain benefit to the children, especially the male children. Generally, wives will tolerate emotional and ma-

Wedding party on the porch of the oldest house in the projects

terial neglect up to a point, but they often draw the line when abuse arises. In such instances, a two-parent family is better only if economic and emotional resources are pulled together, and when they are not, the couples split up. Sadly, when a marriage breakup transpires, sometimes the female head of household seeks the familiar in another neglectful and abusive mate. Such domestic developments are integral to pushing the children out into the streets, and males in particular seek another type of family, the gang.

Moreover, this desire on the part of many males to maintain strict gender hierarchy in their families has a number of disruptive effects. Adolescent males who are convinced that gang life is a sign of manhood or a rite of passage into manhood may begin to dismiss their mothers' authority over them on the basis of a macho notion that they should not be bossed around by a woman. There is still much research to be conducted over how males in female-headed households make the transition to a street socialization that is dominated by males, with or without bringing in the notion of machismo. This tangle of confusion may be responsible for improperly designed public policy programs and private interventions. Even though the men in the family may be involved in criminal activity, absent for long periods, and generally irresponsible, they may still demand a primary decision-making role in the family simply because they are men. Further, because of their poor job history and inability to care for the household, this sense of power is all they have left. In contrast, it is well known that women are the best arbiters and micro-level managers of public programs directed toward a community or a family.

As is pointed out in Moore and Vigil (1987), the underclass type of family has a strong tendency to incorporate criminal behavior into everyday life. Multiple petty criminal acts are modeled to children at an early age, usually by the males of the family. This capacity of older males to influence younger boys, coupled with more or less institutionalized unemployment, a high birth rate, and the persistence of concentrated poverty, means that there is an expanding feedback cycle whereby more and more children are born into poverty. Thus, in this context, the children are raised in a stressed family and later carry on the same sorts of influence with their own children (Mayo and Resnick 1996).

None of this is meant to imply that gangs are necessarily criminal at their core or criminogenic in nature. Moore and Vigil (1987) maintain that gangs have an oppositional character that places them in conflict with certain social institutions such as school and the police. It is maintained here that gangs in the Pico Gardens area are also oppositional institutions set up and organized by youth as an alternative set of social norms, conventions, rituals, and enforcement mechanisms that, in effect, serve as a surrogate family in the absence of a structured birth family and a functioning community structure. This sort of statement must be qualified with the obvious reality that gang membership is a very dangerous proposition. Recall that two gang members in the study sample were murdered during the course of the study. Yet gangs must also be acknowledged as important contributors to the socialization needs of the members, especially in the light of the dismal failure of the education system available to these kids and the strained nature of some, though not all, of their families.

A feature of many mothers of gang members that stands out is their tendency to claim ignorance of their sons' gang or criminal activities even in the face of overwhelming direct evidence. Rampant denial serves to stifle any remedial actions (i.e., interrupter effects) that may help divert a child from a gang or criminality. Without simple recognition of the problems that their children face, there can be no hope for an effective response.

Effects That May Influence Gang Delinquency

Among those in the study sample, agent effects that were potential motivators for gang delinquency included hyperactivity as a child, rebelliousness as a teen, a fashion predilection for gang paraphernalia such as baggy pants,

Hot summers, cool waters for kids

and personal oddities such as personal disfigurements or mental disabilities. Hyperactivity can be observed in even very young children, as the following case of a gang member's younger brother shows. The child in question was five years old, too young to be an actual gang member. He was exhibiting disruptive and destructive behavior at school and had been described by neighbors as uncontrollable. This sort of behavioral pattern could be a part of a strong predisposition for future gang trouble (Vigil 1999). It has also been underscored elsewhere in the youth delinquency literature that hyperactivity at a young age, if not channeled, is a strong indicator that the child will have behavior problems later in life (Sampson and Laub 1994).

Sara, one of the gang member mothers featured in Chapter Ten, evidenced the head-in-the-sand attitude that denied her boys were gang members and smoked marijuana, and by so doing, she was an enabler of such agent proclivities. Meanwhile, she claimed to maintain a healthy lifestyle. Denial of reality by accepting her boys' activities as normal boyhood behavior had solidified her boys' placement and permanence in the gang. Sara attempted absolutely no parental intervention to redirect the lives of her male children. Another gang mother, Juana, indignantly maintained that her boys had decided on their own to be that way, and she washed her hands of their gang involvement.

Teen rebelliousness may also be an indicator of future gang involvement as well as a part of the causal chain that leads to gang delinquency. This desire on the part of a teen to differentiate himself from his family and lose his identification with it may be represented in another case. A seventeen-year-old son of a household head was an active participant in family activities until he began to associate with gang members, especially when he got "high." He repeatedly expressed a desire to join the gang and had been kept out of the core only through his mother's vigilance and intervention. A similar case was that of a thirteen-year-old, who was too young to join. His older brother was an LAPD police officer, and he and the other older siblings helped their mother keep an eye on the youngster too.

Another story is that of an otherwise socially acceptable and family-involved sixteen-year-old boy who had a taste for gangster-style baggy pants. Although he did not show any gang activity during the course of this study, such a symbolic advertisement must certainly have drawn the attention of gang members who might have been tempted to "jump him in." He eventually steered clear of the gang but adopted some bad drinking and drug habits.

The gang member in another case was so afflicted with severe acne and generally unattractive that he was apparently teased a great deal, some peers even referring to him as "ugly." The identity derived by his gang affiliation gave him the necessary sense of peer involvement that he lacked from anyone else.

Push effects that may contribute to gang delinquency include the combined forces of the underclass and ineffective family types, which actively disrupt family structure and introduce youngsters to drugs, gang life, and criminal activity. This disruption of family structure creates a void in children's lives. Given that human beings will spontaneously set up social networks complete with social norms, rituals, and means of enforcing them, it is then no surprise that children will fill this void with their own surrogate peer social group. In the case of gangs, that peer group is multiple-aged. This not only is true for delinquent, criminal subcultures but also is a pattern evidenced by normative, benign social groups. The terms "family" and "brother," so often used by gang members and researchers to describe the relationships within gangs, take on a heightened reality when considered in this context.

Marta, separated from her husband, and her three sons, all members of Cuatro Flats, were an example of a stressed family. Her sporadic, low-paying, makeshift jobs—cleaning lady and shoe repair—were never enough to care for the children. No longer employed, she depended on a combination of AFDC, Medicare, and food stamps but still struggled. Having no car, driver's license, credit cards, or insurance, she received some babysitting help and petty loans from her brother, also a resident of the projects, but her social network ended there. With the husband away, Marta embarked on a seemingly destructive path of nightclubbing, seeking a lost love but finding only one man after another. Early on, she entertained male suitors at her home, and her boys never wanted to be at home and thus seldom received any direction or structure from their mother.

One household was a good example of a family in disarray, with the father always drunk and the mother regularly away from her home duties and mostly in church. The family spent no time together, the house was unkempt, and the children were not regularly supervised. Three of the children were already in the gang, and the other three were clearly street oriented. In another case, the abuse inflicted on the family members by the series of boyfriends the mother dated may also be an example of push effects. The children often witnessed their mother receiving a beating; the mother even reported that she told one boyfriend to hit her on the upper thigh so that her children would not see the bruises. It is this type of family environment that drives children away from home.

Pull effects present in the ethnographic data that might have contributed to gang delinquency included the combined forces of machismo and patriarchy, the desire of young people to be a part of the "gang mystique," and the desire to share in the perceived power of the gang—all of which served as a strong magnet for youth. The pull was especially strong on youths who perceived their access to legitimate sources of power to be blocked by economic or educational marginalization. The identification of gang membership with components of what it means "to be a man" might be a further attraction, given the pressures and demands of the streets.

When young gang members were unprotected on the streets, for example, they might be scared, but they had to act like they weren't and, in fact, struck a posture that showed toughness. Older gang members, the veteranos unknown to younger members, established the path to membership and periodically tested the younger novitiates for this "masculine" role by stopping them on the streets to ask them where they were from. If they didn't stand up to the veteranos by claiming their barrio, then they were sanctioned and lost face; fear of reprimands forced such youngsters to measure up very fast. Further, many of these veteranos had earned their spurs, so to speak, and were respected and looked up to as male role models, even though they no longer were active bangers or slangers. The gang's offering of a set of social norms, rituals, and rules may also be seen as attractive by potential members, given that many of them come from families where there is not much structure and what little there is is almost invariably damaged.

Almost any family in the study sample that included a male gang member provided good examples of pull effects. The draw of the gang and the peer pressure placed on young (particularly male) children is almost omnipresent and omnipotent in the projects.

Interrupter effects that may be involved in the formation of gang allegiances among youth include denial by authority figures, principally mothers, who could otherwise intervene in their children's lives and prevent gang membership and criminal behavior. The community researchers who gathered the data for the microethnographies would often describe mothers of gang members as "unaware of" or "unwilling to admit" their children's gang involvement. Some mothers would actively distance themselves from their children while in denial, even though the evidence for their children's activity was overwhelming. A mother's denial could also obstruct the efforts of others to help corral her sons. In at least one instance in the study group, a mother actively defended her son against her neighbors' charges that he was causing trouble; as a teenager, she had also been affiliated with a local female gang and was not kindly disposed to law enforcement. To underscore this interrupter notion, a non-gang mother stated: "The old have already made their lives. The children need to see good examples. If they see bad examples, they will acquire the bad examples."

Irresponsible male suitors also made for an interesting interrupter effect. In the cases cited above there were either constant streams of different boyfriends or just strange men who hung out at the households. In one case, the mother was constantly abused, and another mother spent all of her time with the strange men who were hanging about, the children seldom even learning the men's names. There is little doubt that such activities both impinged on the mother's ability to raise her children and endangered the safety of the children themselves.

What had worked for some parents, non-gang mother Elena especially, was the sense of reciprocity and respect that often transcended difficult situations. Being an authoritative child rearer, she had more knowledge, skill, resources, and physical acumen than her children but refrained from relying solely on physical punishment and blind obedience. By reasoning with her children, she explained rather than dictated, listened rather than pontificated, and maintained high standards while also remaining open to her children's point of view.

Conclusion

In sum, the following effects may contribute to gang-proofing and gang avoidance.

Agent effects that may contribute to gang avoidance include a strong personal drive and a lack of a need for peer approval—in other words, a solid image of self, or self-esteem. If a child does not feel a strong need to do anything and everything for peer approval or "popularity," then there may be a better chance that he or she will willfully avoid gang encounters.

Push effects that may contribute to gang avoidance include the bullying of "squares" by gang members. This provides negative reinforcement that results in an aversion to gang membership. The strong association of gang members with a feared and hated "other" could drive non-gang children away from membership. If the child does not have a strong and protective family setting to turn to, he or she may try to appease the gang by adopting gang practices and eventually integrating. The sons of one family were constantly bullied by gang members for being "square." But the strong family to which they could retreat contributed to their non-gang status. These youth were more afraid of their older brothers, who had successfully negotiated growing up in the projects without joining the gang and who thus made sure that the younger ones followed suit.

Pull effects on gang avoidance behavior may include a structured family and community network that can attract a child to the home and pull him or her away from a potential gang situation. It is fairly clear that much of a child's desire to be in a gang stems from push dynamics, or flight from negativity, and from the need for a social setting with norms, customs, and structure. Thus, the provision of a more easily accessible and effective social network in the form of a family and strong community network probably goes a long way to stifling gang involvement. Many of the non-gang families reported that they ate dinner together. Although this may seem to be an insignificant bit of trivia, given the important function of sharing food in most human societies, it probably merits further study. The aforementioned Sonia, a non-gang mother, brings it all home for us again: "Respect is the most important thing for children to learn. My family instilled that in me and treated me with respect in order to treat them the same." For her, the aura of respect should pervade the whole community and be valued for its own virtue.

Other pull effects involve larger social structures. Many of the successful children in the study moved on to employment in more upscale areas or joined the military. There was even one former gang member who was working for the immigration and naturalization service. A broader worldview, even one that just extends beyond the barrio, may provide the incentive for youths to leave gangs or never to join them in the first place. The prospect of better opportunities elsewhere may not be apparent to gang members who appear to be in a constricted spatial and temporal mode and cannot see beyond the narrow confines of their few square blocks.

Interrupter effects that may contribute to gang avoidance include active intervention in a child's peer group and extra time in the home environment with the mother or both parents. Many of the families with gang-aged sons who have avoided joining exhibited this sort of intervention. The community researchers reported that mothers of non-gang members would often go out of their way to keep their children from associating with gang members, even going so far as to choose their friends. Acting as escorts when their children were walking to school and as supervisors of their outdoor play, the mothers were able to abate gang influences by either removing their children from influencing situations or personally intervening in potentially influencing situations.

One single mother exemplified this sort of behavior. In addition to being heavily involved in the school and social lives of her children, she had recruited her eldest daughter to help out in the family. She was also actively involved in the broader community. There wasn't a moment when she did not know what the children were doing and who they were spending time with, and she managed all this while working on a job.

Although mothers are the primary source of this sort of intervention, some fathers and even non-family members in the projects had an exceptionally strong sense of community. An example of the latter was a mother who regularly assumed authority over other children in the neighborhood in addition to providing a steady family structure in her home. Unsurprisingly, she was also active in community and school organizations.

Overall, apart from the uneven quality of data—as some families and individuals were easier to interview and get to know—some interesting trends emerged that are addressed in subsequent chapters. In brief, important structural indicators, such as whether or not a family eats together and whether or not the children are monitored in their play, are obvious factors that help gang-proof children. I once observed a couple I was interviewing

Splashing the day away in a Doughboy pool

stop the conversation in mid-sentence to quickly check on their toddler, who had slipped around a building and out of sight. Once the child was re-tethered visually and brought back, the parents continued the exchange. Such spontaneous episodes characterized these parents, as well as a few others, on a consistent basis.

The gender scheme also showed up in that males in this community had difficulty dealing with women when they were in any role other than one of submission to male authority. Conceptions of traditional roles in the home caused serious problems when women had more employment opportunities than men. The men, in contrast, were unwilling to assume a child-rearing role and thus forced the women, in effect, to work at two jobs. Male attitudes toward violence and the important cultural value placed on "saving face" (used here to denote maintaining respect of others) also appeared to be a problem source. Since many slights or conflicts were immediately elevated to the level of violence both domestically and on the streets, and with access to firearms, it is little surprise that aggression and suicidal and homicidal behavior were rampant in the area. This propensity for violence could disrupt the home environment by making the men more prone to abuse the women and by ensuring that the surrounding areas, including play areas, remained off-limits for long periods.

The underappreciated phenomenon of denial undoubtedly has a role to play in protecting children against gang involvement. It is understandable that community leaders, many of whom are from the middle class, may want to distance themselves from the negative characterizations of Latino gangs in poor neighborhoods, a major problem that is readily exploited by sensationalistic media. However, this denial surely is not a productive strategy. Future investigations should take the phenomenology of denial into consideration while simultaneously acknowledging the sensitivity of this coping mechanism.

This chapter identified a general causal framework for gang-involved and non-gang-involved families, using an oversimplified bipolar gradient model. In the process, abstracted concepts of push, pull, agent, and interrupter effects were identified and contextualized from the present study in order to guide the reader through the next chapters.

CHAPTER NINE

FAMILIES NOT INVOLVED WITH GANGS

To transcend the one-dimensional caricatures of inner-city life that are commonplace in popular and, occasionally, academic discourse, it is important to closely examine families through methods grounded in the reality of their daily lives. It is readily apparent that these families are consumed with the typical concerns of all human beings, particularly those related to subsistence: food, clothing, and shelter. In addition to these basic needs, families must work on the promulgation of social bonds and oftentimes the desire to improve themselves and their lot in life. These concerns are equally as relevant to families with members involved in gang activity as they are for those whose members are uninvolved or only peripherally involved in gang life. To make oversimplistic distinctions between gang and non-gang families is not a useful exercise, nor is it an exercise based on reality; instead, it is instructive to look to the complex examples of how folks negotiate their existence in the face of common obstacles and less abundant opportunities.

Examining complex examples is particularly helpful in understanding and illustrating the factors that result in the wide range of gang affiliation that can be observed in Pico Gardens. Although the experiences of families with no intimate connections to gang life were not entirely distinct from those of families with strong ties to gang activities, examination of cases where gang life has been avoided allows the observer to distinguish patterns of behavior or coping that serve as a positive means of adaptation to harsh environmental and structural positioning. This chapter presents examples drawn from the life histories of families who successfully navigated the sometimes-dangerous terrain of the public housing projects in which they resided. A number of themes are elaborated upon in order to clarify the manner by which the pushes and pulls that tempt youth to walk into the open, waiting arms of a gang were rendered ineffective or weakened.

Sonia and Her Family: A Prototypical Example of a Non-Gang Family and Its Leader

Sonia is a forty-eight-year-old married mother of seven. Born in Tequila, Mexico, she moved to the United States when she was twenty-five. All of her children were born in California. On first arriving in California, Sonia lived in San Diego, and then she lived in various places throughout the Los Angeles area before settling into a five-bedroom house in Pico Gardens. At the time of the study, Sonia and her family had lived there for more than three years. None of her children had had any involvement with gangs or drugs. On the whole, Sonia liked living in Pico Gardens and stated that her family had no major problems. She did, however, wish for "more safety for the children, that's all." As she put it, "The old have already made their lives. The children need to see good examples. If they see bad examples, they will acquire the bad examples. That's up to the parents also." She and her family had experienced some minor problems with their housing, including bad plumbing as well as unwanted visitors in the form of rats and cockroaches.

Sonia and her husband were unemployed. The family survived on AFDC and food stamps. The couple owned an old car but did not have insurance for it. Sonia had a driver's license but no other identification and no credit cards or insurance. From time to time, her husband was able to find odd jobs fixing cars. Previously, Sonia had worked in the garment industry. For the past year and a half she had applied her seamstress skills to earn extra income for the family. Sonia used her innate creativity and entrepreneurialism to make household crafts and gifts such as picture frames, crocheted place mats, ornaments, and dolls to sell on the weekend both in the projects or at swap meets. In a small but supportive gesture, her husband contributed to her efforts by loading up the car with her crafts and helping her sell them.

Relations between Sonia and her husband were not without problems. He had hit her in the past, and she stated that she managed life better without him in the house. They were now semi-separated, with him coming in and out of the house: "He sometimes is out of work for long periods of time," Sonia said. "I tell him that he can't be here being lazy all the time. So he leaves for long periods of time." He came back to the house only because, according to Sonia, "he gets along well with his sons and they let him in."

Despite their economic hardships and her rocky relationship with her husband, Sonia had managed to maintain a close family unit. She loved her children and said she "would do anything for them." They all got on well with each other, largely because of the way Sonia had raised them. "If you watch out for your children," she commented, "they know that they are wanted and loved. They will respond in a positive way." Although Sonia had had a bad experience with her husband, she was sensitive to the important role he played in the development of her children: "I've never told my children not to like or love him or disrespect him. The children have seen him be mad at me and hit me—he has made himself look wrong in their eyes. I've never told them not to listen to him or talk back to him. They respect him for me [rather] than for him."

The concept of respect was very important to Sonia. "Since I was a child, my family instilled that in me—you have to respect. I think that it is very important for my children to learn that. In order to teach them about respect, I treated them with it. They saw how I would treat people, and they too would treat them the same." Thus, for this family, the value of respect was universalized beyond traditional authoritarian patriarchal relationships to include the community at large. Sonia described herself as a strict mother, adding: "It is more about teaching them to respect me because I am older and wiser and their mother. . . . My kids know how to obey me because they should respect my rules. I expect them to obey me because they respect my wisdom and that I do what is best for them, not [because] I just want my way." She believed her older children were grateful that she was strict with them, although the younger children had not yet developed a similar appreciation for her approach.

In terms of discipline, Sonia preferred to talk to her children or take away privileges if they misbehaved. She sometimes grounded them or made them do extra chores around the house, or she would not give them their allowance. She did not yell at her kids nor did she hit them. "I have set guidelines for them too," she said. "They have a little more freedom, but they still have to listen to me. I don't hit them; I just take away their privileges." She did not believe in hitting her children, because "you can have them obey you by hitting them, but they will never obey you because they love or respect you if you do, only out of fear of being hit." Despite, or maybe because of, her experiences with domestic violence, Sonia's parenting style reflected an open, affectionate exchange with her children that was guided by unambiguous boundaries.

Sonia enjoyed spending time with her children, taking care of them, laughing with them, and listening to them. She strongly believed that parents should listen to their children:

> In order to know what's going on with them you have to let them express their opinion. Lots of times kids, because they are afraid of you or

whatever, keep things from you. You have to let them talk and express their opinion, to have them open up to you. . . . It is very important for parents to show genuine interest in their children's affairs. We need to make time for them and do things that they want to do.

Sonia's physical availability and genuine interest in the concerns of her children were powerful push effects that could protect against the ever-present lure of gang life.

After school and on the weekends, the children usually stayed close to home, and the focus remained on family-centered activities. Despite Sonia's limited resources, the family did sometimes go out to eat, to the park, and to the beach. On the weekends, some went to church. Sonia had been raised Catholic but said she did not go to church often. Usually when the children all came home from school, the family ate together, and then they did their chores and cleaned their bedrooms. If the children wanted to go somewhere, they had to tell Sonia where they would be. She let them go to the playground alone and play with their friends, but she did not necessarily like all her children's friends, because some of their families used a lot of bad language and Sonia felt that her children could pick up on it. In terms of friends, she had always told her children, "Friends really don't exist. You can count friends on your fingers. If he gets into problems, are the friends going to get them out? He can go out with them, but he doesn't have to do what they do. They seem to pay attention to me." Sonia's wise instruction on the importance of self-reliance was a value in direct contradiction with street socialization experienced by gang initiates.

Also of importance to Sonia was that all of her children were aware of their cultural and linguistic heritage: "I teach them my culture and my language. While they are inside my home, they only speak Spanish. Once outside with their friends, they can speak whatever they like, but in my home it's Spanish."

Describing herself as "a strong woman," Sonia revealed an enormous sense of pride when asked about who she was and the things she'd accomplished: "I feel good. I've done a lot. . . . I believe in myself and the growth and development of my children." The main goal she had had for herself was "to raise good kids," and she felt that she had succeeded. All her children did well and behaved well in school. Her two eldest children, Jodie and Joey, were twenty years old and in military school earning degrees, after having participated in the ROTC program at their high school. To participate in the program, they had to do well academically. "Their little brothers and sisters are really proud of them," Sonia said, "and they look up to them." According to Sonia, the two had joined the ROTC "because they wanted to be somebody, and that program, since they were in the ninth grade, offered them the opportunity." She added:.

> They entered the program of ROTC. . . . They liked it and continued. . . . They send them camping; they have training outside of school, on the weekends. They liked it. But not just anyone can go in there, only the ones who have good grades and pass the tests. If they pass the tests, they qualify. If not, then they don't. They have to be intelligent and the drive to want to be somebody.

While in high school, the children participated in a variety of activities such as basketball, volleyball, football, and folkloric dancing. Jodie also participated in a choir and sports outside of school. The older children had been able to successfully translate strong family bonds to the outside world through attachment and active participation in academic achievements as well as leisure activities. Sonia hopes to extend the momentum begun by her older children to their younger siblings, who look to them as examples.

Sonia's next two children, Paula, age seventeen, and Tom, age sixteen, were following in their older siblings' footsteps by participating in the junior version of the ROTC (the JROTC). The two children differed greatly, despite their similar upbringing. Paula was more boisterous than Tom. She loved listening to loud music, whereas Tom was a quiet teenager and not too active. Despite their different dispositions, Sonia believed both children benefited from the additional structure and discipline provided by their military training, and she continued to support that path. Her three youngest children—Isabel, age nine, Richie, age eight, and Silvia, age eight—were too young to participate in such activities. Nevertheless, Sonia attempted to take advantage of any opportunities available to better their lives. She sent all of the children to Head Start, a program designed to provide preparation for youngsters before they start elementary school, and she felt that they benefited from the experience.

Another strategy that Sonia used to help her children remain on the right path was to integrate them into each other's lives. In particular, Paula, the oldest daughter, was frequently recruited to babysit and monitor the younger children. This not only afforded Sonia with convenient, reliable child care but also helped the children bond with one another as separate components of a cohesive family unit. All this intervention worked cumulatively to prevent the children from having any extended interactions with gang members. It simply removed the opportunity altogether.

Mexican immigrant couple with child

Sonia had always been involved in her children's schooling. She helped out in the school cafeteria and with school activities such as Cinco de Mayo. "Participate in your child's school activities, and encourage them to participate in them too. That's the key," she said. Thus by her own involvement in her community, Sonia's children implicitly received cues from her about how to positively interact with the community as well as how to recognize opportunities for participation. Involvement in education and community activities was a normative family affair. Without a doubt, Sonia attributed much importance to education and explained that she had emphasized this perspective to her children repeatedly:

> I always instilled in my children to have self-respect, to have education as a foundation, because I'm not rich. I don't have money to give to them; the only thing that I push them [to do is] to study. That is why I'm involved with that at school. Their foundation is to study. I tell them, "I want a college degree from you. I don't have money to leave to you or a residency, a house. The only thing I can give you is an education, and that's more than enough." They pick up on this. They know that if they don't study, they are not going to be anything—they know from the

oldest one to the youngest one. That is the goal, the foundation that I have pushed them on. That is why they say, "I'm going to study to become a doctor, a lawyer, an engineer." I tell them, "Okay. Just look out for what you are going to study."

Sonia emphasized education for her family despite her inability to continue her own. Sonia finished high school in Mexico. Her curriculum included various courses in accounting, bookkeeping, and secretarial duties. She went to college in Guadalajara for one year but had to stop because her mother did not want her to continue, and the gender roles of the time deemphasized higher education as a woman's activity. When she did attend, Sonia did well in school and participated in extracurricular activities such as volleyball, and folkloric and cowboy dancing. That past motivated her to inspire and support her children in spite of the limitations that society might want to impose on them. She stated, "I hope my children obtain a clear picture of their goals with respect to their careers. I hope to be living to see all my children fulfill their dreams."

The example of Sonia and her family illustrates the common themes that characterize the majority of the life stories of the non-gang families in this study. These include creative responses to the experience of multiple marginalization, authoritative and affectionate parenting, and an emphasis on education and extracurricular activities. Clearly no two families' experiences were identical in all respects, but non-gang families overwhelmingly shared these tactics in contrast to families heavily immersed in gang culture. An analysis of the themes with an eye to the stories of the gang families demonstrates how relationships and life circumstances are shaped by the coping strategies of family leaders.

Creative Responses to Marginalization

The non-gang families of Pico Gardens are not immune to the myriad difficulties associated with living in a public housing complex any more than the gang-involved families are. The experiences of non-gang families are those typically associated with the travails of the socioeconomically and socioculturally marginalized; their responses and outlook are nonetheless exceptional in many respects. The combination of these somewhat contradictory forces in the lives of non-gang household leaders amounts to a resiliency that affects their children, most markedly by teaching lessons related to attitude and perseverance.

Like Sonia and her family, many of the residents of Pico Gardens face

Girl watching over little brother

raising a relatively large family on a limited income, although non-gang families are on the whole smaller than gang-involved families. In addition to a lack of monetary resources, many non-gang families do not have the various forms of identification and material assets that make life immeasurably easier in all respects. Immigrants sometimes lack documentation, and others sometimes simply experience a lack of access to resources that tends to accompany life in the lower socioeconomic stratum. Nevertheless, the coping strategies of non-gang families ring of a positivity and hope that belie the difficulties inherent in their situations.

Although Sonia and her family have little financial security, due to both a lack of insurance and the means for attaining gainful employment, she and her husband have made the best of their situation by using their resourcefulness to create opportunities for themselves. They use the material resources that they do have, such as a car, along with their personal talents or abilities in areas such as cooking, crafting, and automobile repair to open up niches for themselves as entrepreneurs in the informal marketplace. This approach does not allow for huge profit making in the tradition of some entrepreneurial endeavors, but it does help pay the bills, and monies from the state supplement their earnings. Many heads of households with no gang involvement share the same general pattern of marginalized life experiences and have made similar choices in reacting to life events and constructing their own solutions to the best of their ability. Elena's experiences echoed those of Sonia's in many ways, although Elena has been able to work steadily within the formal economic structure.

Elena was a fifty-three-year-old married head of household from Sonora, Mexico. She was the third of nine children. Elena had lived with her family until she was twenty-three years old, and then she and her husband began a series of moves that eventually led from Mexicali and Tecate, Mexico, to the United States. Along the way she and her husband had gradually added to their family, and by the time they settled in Pico Gardens, after living elsewhere in Los Angeles eleven years, they had five children: two girls and three boys. Elena had lived in the housing projects for nine years at the time of the study. Three of her children had moved out and were married, while the youngest two still lived at home. Although two of the sons had problems with drug use, none of them were involved in gang activity, despite the obvious, yet often overemphasized connections between gang life and drug use.

Elena liked living in Pico Gardens because she got along with everyone and had room for her children and grandchildren to play outdoors. Nonetheless, she was concerned about the frequent shootings and the graffiti, both of which increasingly characterized her immediate environment.

As was the case for Sonia and many other women, Elena's formal education had been truncated due to cultural gender-biased expectations. Elena had dropped out of school in the seventh grade in Mexico when she got married. She had little additional educational experience except for training in housing management. Nevertheless, she had enjoyed school because she had received good grades and had a very satisfying social life as well. In addition to the marginalization that accompanied a lack of education, Elena and her family were socioeconomically disadvantaged. They had no insurance of any kind, nor did they have credit cards to rely on in emergency situations; they did, however, have a bank account. That alone distinguished Elena from less successful families in Pico Gardens. Elena did not have a driver's license, but she did have a California identification card.

Despite their precarious financial situation, Elena and her husband did not receive any type of public aid. Instead, they had managed to piece together a series of jobs that allowed them to take care of their family's needs. At the time of the study, Elena was employed at a center for the care of handicapped children and had held this position for eight years. She had also worked as an office cleaner for five years. Her husband was employed as an office cleaner and had a second job as a cook. Although Elena had a busy schedule, she was able to come home by late afternoon to spend time at home with their remaining children and to cook their evening meal and do other household tasks. Her hard work and perseverance had helped Elena and her husband not only to survive but also to ensure that their children beat the odds in the gang-ridden area in which they resided.

Authoritative and Affectionate Parenting

The aforementioned examples demonstrate the means by which many Pico Gardens residents were able to negotiate situations characterized by structural, sociocultural, and socioeconomic marginality by using their own creativity, capitalizing on their skills, and working hard. Although this was true for a number of households that had avoided gang activity, it was not always so; many mothers and fathers had not been able to make great strides in the economic realm, but their parenting skills had prevented the push of children out of the home and into the gang, as well as the pull of children to the gang because of its mystique or to the very tangible benefits of joining, such as protection from violence. In Pico Gardens, the use of effective parenting skills appears to be the primary mode of controlling an environment that was otherwise out of control in many respects. Micro-level socialization processes in the home buffered the influence of the world outside and could empower individuals to deal with the violence around them in ways that were not self-defeating. Clearly, the locus of parental control in such an environment is limited, but effective parenting can eliminate the pervasive sense of despair that can otherwise overwhelm youth in impoverished areas.

The non-gang parents in Pico Gardens often used authoritative parenting practices in contrast to overly permissive or authoritarian (overly coercive and harsh) strategies. A standard explanation of this type of parenting is provided by Cole and Cole (1989, 382).

Authoritative parents take it for granted that they have more knowledge and skill, control more resources, and have more physical power than their children, but they believe that the rights of parents and children are reciprocal. Relative to authoritarian parents, authoritative parents are less likely to use physical punishment and less likely to stress obedience to authority as a virtue in itself. Instead, authoritative parents attempt to control their children by explaining parental rules and decisions and by reasoning with the children. Such parents are willing to listen to their child's point of view, even if they do not always accept it. Authoritative parents set high standards for their children's behavior and encourage them to be individualistic and independent.

In addition to an authoritative parenting style, the non-gang-related families had parental figures who were generally warm and affectionate. These parents were comfortable expressing their emotions and their love for their children and found ways to demonstrate this daily. Once again, Sonia's example is illustrative. Although she described herself as a strict mother, Sonia clearly fell into the authoritative camp, based on her dislike for physical punishment and her emphasis on mutual respect between herself and her children. Sonia's description of her role as one based on experience and the wisdom garnered therein was the quintessential expression of an effective authoritative parent. She established appropriate limits and was open to grounding her children when necessary, but in the course of doing so, she conveyed a sense of compassion and fairness that strengthened her relationship with her children rather than damaging it. Sonia also worked to model respect for others who had personally displeased her, such as her husband, in an effort to protect her children from the fallout of marital discord and to allow them to make their own informed judgments about appropriate behaviors.

Another parent, Maria, shared a similar approach to child rearing and had had plenty of practice with her eleven children. Maria was born in Durango, Mexico; she had married and had five of her children there. She then migrated to Los Angeles, where the rest of her children were born. For more than a quarter of a century, Maria (fifty-four years old) and her husband (seventy years old) had lived in various residences in Pico Gardens; they had spent the last eighteen years in their current five-bedroom home, the largest accommodation they had inhabited in their long tenure in Pico Gardens. Maria liked where they lived; she appreciated that the rent was adjusted to income and liked the large size of her apartment. Her uncle also lived in the projects, and they saw each other daily. She also got along well with her neighbors and often chatted with them. Nevertheless, she worried about the state of the projects and crime and violence. She felt that the violence in Pico Gardens had gotten a lot worse: "The violence is so bad. The kids see all this, and it stays with them." She also believed that there was a serious problem with gangs: "I'm scared of the kids. I see them in the market; I tell them they should be in school. Some don't answer, some answer smart-mouth. They get mad, so I don't say anything."

Maria draws upon the lessons she learned from her childhood in order to

New father, mother, and son enjoy family solidarity

effectively socialize her own children to avoid gang life. Her own upbringing was problematic; her mother hit her frequently, and she was taught to fear her parents instead of truly understanding what they wanted of her. Unsurprisingly, Maria believed that the authoritarian approach was ineffectual and too strict. As a result, Maria, like Sonia, believed that parents cannot attain respect through threats and violence. Instead, Maria believed that children should be treated with respect and should learn to respect others: "We inculcated respect for us and for the elders." Thus this adult expected that her children learn to respect everybody: "It does not matter if they are big or small. We showed them how to respect one another's things."

In terms of discipline, Maria said that both she and her husband were strict. She also got her older sons to act as disciplinarian figures for the younger ones. If the children misbehaved, Maria would ground them or take away things that they liked. She tried not to hit her children and preferred to talk to them instead: "I advise them on things. They should not do things that they should not be doing. And if they do, they should take care of themselves [i.e., avoid endangering themselves]." Her refusal to use violence as a means of correcting her children's misbehavior helped maintain the legitimate respect her children had for her. Maria had been quite adamant about her expectations for her children, and because they did respect her so, they also took her position quite seriously. Her sons had been reprimanded for spending their free time with other boys Maria regarded as cholos and had learned to choose other friends. One of her son's forays into the world of "tagging" (graffiti) had been quickly terminated once Maria voiced her passionate disapproval. In addition, Maria had laid down the law in terms of potential gang membership; she had told her children that if they joined a gang, they would never be able to come back home. This kind of statement could be considered authoritarian coming from another individual, but in this particular context she had established her authority on firm ground and was seen by her family as wise rather than merely threatening.

The demonstration of affection clearly shaped children in a positive manner in Pico Gardens and reinforced the effects of the firmness that the heads of household occasionally had to display in order to protect their children from potentially dangerous affiliations. Time and time again, the non-gang heads of household stressed the value of simply "being there" for their children. In order to meaningfully share time with their children, non-gang heads of households repeatedly emphasized the necessity of forging strong bonds based on warmth and caring. The sharing of "quality time"—time in which the parent can be fully attentive to the needs of their children—can best be accomplished when youth are cognizant of the interest that a parent has in the details of their lives. As Sonia's story at the beginning of the chapter demonstrates, oftentimes the mothers in non-gang households believed that the most successful method for establishing this type of awareness in their children was to establish a two-pronged relationship involving both the traditional role of parent and that of friend. The method of establishing this dual-faceted relationship was largely based on the ability to listen to children in the same manner that a friend would and to disengage from knee-jerk reactions. To act otherwise, by appropriating the role of judge in conversations with one's children, was seen as a surefire way to alienate them and to push them into the arms of their peers, some of whom were involved in gang activities or other undesirable behaviors. In addition, non-gang heads of households often attempted to lessen the importance their children placed on problematic non-family connections. Sonia, for example, chose to tell her children that such relationships were fleeting and unreliable. Not all mothers chose to approach the issue in such a manner, but they often accentuated the permanence of blood bonds.

Maria and her husband tried to incorporate all of the aforementioned strategies into their parenting as means of keeping their children on the right track. Maria claimed that she tried to be as affectionate and nice as she possibly could toward her children, in the hopes that they would all grow up to be mature, responsible human beings. This was the goal she had held close to her heart for so many years. She explained, "I live to take care of them and hope that they do well in their lives. I believe in God and in people. . . . I tell them that I do not only want to be their mother; I want to be their friend, instead of telling someone else what they think they should tell me." This approach had been successful, and she felt that her children did tell her everything: "I try to encourage them to have confidence in me and be able to approach me with anything they want to."

Maria's family shared plenty of quality time. After school, the family would eat together and talk about school and other things, and then the children did their homework. Afterward they normally either stayed inside and watched television or played outside together. On the weekends the family spent time doing more of the same and going to social functions such as parties. Maria characterized the time spent together as time for communication that otherwise got lost in the hustle and bustle of day-to-day life. She said that her children were quite open, because of the strength of their relationship: "They talk about their problems. They talk about their girlfriends, the plans that they have in school, college. We talk about a lot of things."

Another head of a non-gang household, Raquel, used similar techniques to strengthen the bonds between herself and her four children. Unlike some of the other non-gang heads of households, Raquel was a single parent raising two daughters and two sons. The challenges she faced were substantial. She was not currently employed, although she had worked in the past as a housekeeper at UCLA Hospital and at a furniture factory. She received AFDC, Medicare, and food stamps. She had a California ID and an old automobile, but no driver's license or insurance. Raquel received no assistance from the father of her children, who lived in Mexico. Relations with him were quite strained, and he rarely communicated with the children; when he did, they usually argued.

What Raquel lacked in material assets she compensated for with emotional availability and a flair for parenting. She followed a daily routine that typically consisted of taking her kids to school and picking them up, talking to her neighbor, and doing household chores. She believed that such a routine allowed for dependability and productivity. Raquel advocated a definite setting of parameters in terms of the tasks the children must complete and the rules they must follow. After school, she brought her children home and spent time with them, mostly sitting down with them and helping them with their homework. After that task was completed, she cooked dinner, and the family ate together. Raquel heartily endorsed shared meals as one of the means by which communication was strengthened between the family members, and she found that it was the time that the children usually shared what was going on in their personal lives. After dinner she watched television with the children if they had completed their chores. Raquel believed that this simple routine was crucial to keeping her children out of trouble; their time was structured in a way that did not allow for them to be wandering the streets, and their socialization was primarily achieved through the home and the school.

An Emphasis on Extracurricular Activities and Education

Another strategy used by the parents in non-gang families, as a rule, was to get their children involved in extracurricular activities. This strategy accomplished the same goal as Raquel's use of structure at home to dissuade her children from getting involved in crime or delinquency; the hours of the day were filled with tasks the children must accomplish, and as a result there was little excess time left. When there was extra time in a day, the children were often in need of rest and did not feel like leaving the house and getting into trouble. An additional part of the rationale behind the parents' support of extracurricular activities was that participation in these activities often taught young people useful skills and provided experiences that would enrich their lives. Once youth were invested in achievement in their extracurricular activities, then that inevitably rubbed off onto their sense of investment in other pro-social behaviors. This approach paid off for Sonia; her support of military training for her eldest children had led to their increased sense of self-discipline and a desire to escape the violence of the housing projects through further military education. Maria, with her eleven children, also used this approach. The children had participated in many sports teams, such as football and basketball, and such involvement took up a great amount of time, with all of the practices and games required.

Another head of household, Alicia, depended heavily on this method also. Alicia's story was similar to the others discussed in this chapter. She had emigrated from Mexico and received a truncated education there. She and her five children had lived in Pico Gardens for seven years, and they were frightened by the violence they saw around them. Alicia was often at home, because she was unemployed. Nevertheless, she had worked periodically in the past as a seamstress in low-wage factory jobs in the garment district of Los Angeles. During those times she had enlisted the help of her oldest daughter to take care of her four younger brothers.

At the time of the study, Alicia made sure that her children were involved in activities in one of the traditional social control institutions, the church.

Family outing, family time

Church involvement has long served as a means of instilling a sense of responsibility, and commitment to something larger than oneself can provide a source of solace when everyday living gets rough. Alicia's children had made connections with others at the church to whom they turned when life in Pico Gardens got too harsh. Their belief system made it difficult for them to get pulled into gang life. Alicia hoped her children continued to go to church as they matured, because she believed that the institution was the one affordable means of keeping the children active and out of harm's way.

Despite all of the material difficulties the parents of non-gang households faced, they nonetheless displayed an overarching faith in the "American dream"—the idea that if their children took the correct route, they would be rewarded accordingly. Fundamental to this belief system is a confidence in the power of education. All of the parents emphasized their wish for their children to become educated members of society and to make the best out of the opportunities that were afforded them in the United States; most parents in Pico Gardens had not been afforded the same opportunities in their own lives and wished that they had been. As Sonia's example demonstrates, most of the parents had few material resources to give their children, but effective parents gave their time and support and aided their children in making informed choices that would likely improve their lives.

In conjunction with an emphasis on extracurricular activities, the non-gang parents simply attempted to inculcate their children with a sense that education was to be valued and taken seriously. Maria had been successful thus far with her eleven children; they all normally got good grades and on the whole behaved well in school. Maria stayed fully informed regarding their progress and believed that it was crucial to do so. She said that she called the school "every once in a while to find out how they are doing." She considered education to be important and tried to encourage her children "to look forward to school." She consistently worked with the children to help them improve their grades and always tried to prepare the children a little bit at home before each school year began. She chose to have her children enrolled in Head Start at the appropriate age, and she got involved with school groups such as the PTA to demonstrate the importance of being engaged in the educational system. Other non-gang parents also tended to be quite involved in their children's schooling and were quite aware of the happenings in their children's education. Moreover, the parents were able to intervene quickly when their children began to stray off course, and they would then remind their children of the behaviors that they had raised them to value.

In sum, it is apparent that families that have eluded the grasp of gang life in an environment that is saturated with its presence do so through the use of a number of strategies. These strategies appear deceivingly simply and are far more powerful in their impact than many would imagine.

The seeming simplicity of the protective measures that successful parents skillfully employ to mitigate the pernicious lure of gang membership is made all the more apparent by their obvious absence in gang families. The next chapter details the often diametrical contrast in resiliency, surveillance, commitment to conventional goals, communication, and parenting styles of families that are compromised by street gangs.

CHAPTER TEN

A CLOSER LOOK AT GANG-AFFILIATED FAMILIES

Some Pico Gardens residents are less capable of resisting the pushes and pulls related to the gang activity in their neighborhood and eventually succumb to gang life. This lack of resistance can be attributed to a heightened vulnerability born of repeated challenges to a healthy life—challenges that are generated both outside and within the family. Outside challenges, including the various forces of discrimination, poverty, blocked opportunities, and street socialization, are rendered more powerful when family heads are unable to direct their children effectively. Internal factors, such as single-headed households, a large family size, authoritarian or permissive parenting styles, weak or ineffectual parenting styles, and an extreme sense of disempowerment due to lack of social and financial resources cumulatively strip parents of the steadiness children need in order to follow directives.

Abuse is also present in many of the households, be it abuse of people or abuse of substances, and it further complicates the parenting efforts of heads of households. This pattern of abuse weakens families and detracts from community-level efforts at change. The life histories of the public housing residents discussed in this chapter demonstrate how youth become particularly vulnerable to the call of gang life as a result of family characteristics and processes. When parents err, the children seek other guides, and when parents aren't there, the children are up for grabs, especially when the streets become the behavioral environment. We must look at the micro and macro levels of this family/street dynamic to see why there are voids and, of course, determine when adaptation strategies show creativity and strength.

Child saddened as parents leave for work

Juana and Her Family: A Prototypical Example of a Gang-Related Family and Its Leader

Juana, who was forty years old at the time of the study, had been born in Guadalajara, Mexico. When she was a child, her parents were not around much, and she was raised primarily by her grandparents from the time she was ten years old. Although her grandparents did their best, they were older and lacked the energy to devote to raising Juana; she lamented missing the parental attention that she never experienced. As a result, she looked elsewhere for affection. Like many girls, she found that missing affection in the arms of a neighborhood boy. The relationship quickly became physical, and Juana dedicated more and more of her time to it. She had plenty of free time to give because she stopped attending school once she had completed the second grade. Her grandparents did not feel that her schooling was necessary and preferred that she help out with tasks around the house.

When she was in her late teens, Juana gave birth to her first child, a daughter, and moved in with her boyfriend. Her relationship with her boyfriend quickly deteriorated after the birth of their child—he was not interested in being saddled with the responsibilities that accompany fatherhood, and he increasingly neglected both Juana and his daughter. In an effort to experience more opportunities and to escape a hostile relationship, Juana decided to move to the United States when she was twenty-two years of age. In spite of her hopes of finding satisfying employment, she instead discovered that because of her lack of education and her inability to read English or Spanish, employers would hire her only for labor-intensive, low-paying jobs. She found it hard to maintain interest in such employment and rarely kept a job for very long.

Disillusioned and impoverished, Juana often sought the companionship of men. After living in Los Angeles for a year, she became pregnant again and gave birth to her second daughter. Once again, despite her hope for stability in her relationship with the father, she was disappointed; he was distant and wanted little to do with the baby. This pattern repeated itself time and time again. By the time that Juana was thirty-five, she had given birth to four more children, three sons and one daughter. None of the fathers stuck around for long. It got very difficult to pay for an apartment that had enough room for her large family, so when an acquaintance told her about the housing projects in Pico Gardens, she was eager to move there. After a four-month wait, her application was accepted. Juana quickly became accustomed to life in her new home and had three more children after establishing her household there. At the time of the study, she continued to be involved in tumultuous, short-term relationships with men who were emotionally and sometimes physically abusive.

Juana had had to struggle single-handedly to support her nine children. The load was lightened a bit when her two oldest children moved out of the household. She did not work outside of her home and relied solely on AFDC, food stamps and Medicare. She was not licensed to drive and did not own an automobile. Her only form of identification is a California ID card. She had no insurance of any kind, nor did she have a bank account or credit card. All of these factors made taking care of the small things in life incredibly difficult at times.

As products of erratic environments both inside and outside the home, this family's children were in peril. Juana's youngest seven children were all experiencing troubles of one degree or another. Most of them were having a hard time in school, in terms of both their academics and their behavior; they tended to be disruptive in class and were performing poorly on class tests and assignments. Her oldest son had gotten into serious trouble. He was a member of Cuatro Flats, and his gang activity had gotten him arrested on a weapons charge. He was currently incarcerated.

Juana did not think that neighborhood socialization contributed to the difficulties of her children. Instead, she looked upon Pico Gardens positively and maintained that it was a good place to live, especially because it was affordable. She recognized that there were services available to the residents, such as the 4-H Club and the field trips that were offered to children. She closed her eyes to the problems endemic to the area—she claimed that there was not a serious problem with crime in the complex and that no gang activity was present in the housing project. Juana also denied that her son was a gang member, despite evidence indicating otherwise.

Juana also believed that her children's problems were not related to her actions. She took no responsibility for her children's troubles and said that her children were the way they were because they wanted to be that way. She did not think that anything she did would change their behaviors, and she had basically given up trying. She did not keep close tabs on the children and allowed them to spend time outside after school; they spent the majority of their time playing with their peers or watching television. Juana spent most of her time cleaning the house or with her present boyfriend. She kept to herself otherwise and did not communicate with her neighbors on a regular basis, nor did she take part in any civic activities except for the occasional school meeting.

Large Families and Limited Resources

A number of themes are present in Juana's life history. First, Juana's experience is a story of a larger-than-average family living with seriously limited resources. This situation is one that characterized the majority of gang-involved families in Pico Gardens. Although all families in Pico Gardens were financially strapped, gang-involved families were even more so. The large family size hindered Juana's ability as the head of the household to creatively deal with the challenges she faced in providing for her children, simply because it was logistically difficult to take care of all of the financial and emotional demands involved. Juana's predicament was fairly serious in that she was unwilling and, for many skilled jobs, unable to keep a job for an extended period of time. The combination of these factors, paired with the lack of a stable companion to help with raising the children, made for a highly challenging scenario.

Such a situation is rendered less challenging with the presence of two parents in the home, yet it can still be highly demanding. Alejandro, one of the few male heads of household in Pico Gardens, faced similar challenges in supporting his large family.

Alejandro was sixty-three years old and married at the time of the study.

He was born in Sonora, Mexico, where he had lived with his stepmother for twenty-three years before the two of them moved to Tijuana. The years with his stepmother had been pleasant ones. He spent a lot of time helping out around the house and doing various odd jobs because he never attended school. He and his stepmother enjoyed each other's company until she died when he was thirty-five years old. The loss was a tremendous one. After grieving for a few years, Alejandro decided to start a new life by migrating to the United States.

Alejandro's first place of residence in the United States was Elena, Montana, where he worked picking potatoes. The culture shock he experienced after moving there was tremendous, and he was dissatisfied with his life. He decided that California would be more to his liking because of its diversity. Once he decided to take action, his life changed rapidly. By the time he was forty-two years old, he had moved to Los Angeles, gotten married to a woman ten years his junior, and started what would eventually be a very large family. The family had been living in L.A. when they decided to move to Pico Gardens.

Alejandro and his wife continued to have children on a consistent basis and had a total of twelve, eight boys and four girls. It had been difficult to provide for such a large family. For four years Alejandro was a self-employed handyman who painted houses and installed window and door screens. Nevertheless, at the time of the study, it had been a number of years since he or his wife had worked outside of the home. They depended on the government for their financial survival. They received AFDC, Medicare, and food stamps. Alejandro's financial resources were limited. He did have two cars, a station wagon and a truck, but both were in poor condition and were not insured. He did not have a driver's license but had a California ID. He had a savings account at an institution that allowed him to cash his checks. He had no credit cards or other forms of insurance. Sometimes he consulted his adult son about economic matters, but for the most part he struggled with the problems himself. Alejandro said that as a result of the stress and his desire to escape from it, he took to drinking. He was an alcoholic for a number of years as the children were growing up. He had been stopped for driving under the influence and incarcerated for a short time. His wife was devoutly religious and tended to leave the house during his bouts of drinking; she still spent large amounts of time in the church as a means of getting away from the stresses of the household. The children had always had a lot of unsupervised free time as a result of their parents' activities, and family activities were rarities.

Alejandro had experienced his share of what he saw as bad luck—two of his sons had passed away; one had died of cancer in 1984, and the other had been hit by a car in 1982. Six of his remaining children were members of the Cuatro Flats gang. They ranged in age from fourteen to thirty-two. Alejandro thought that neighborhood peer influence had been particularly pernicious. He appreciated the neighborhood and his spacious, affordable apartment but recognized that crime had skyrocketed. He had witnessed numerous random shootings and felt that Pico Gardens was ridiculously dangerous. Alejandro believed that there should be jobs for the children to get them off the streets. His own sons had been incarcerated for various reasons, including nonpayment of driving and traffic tickets and domestic abuse. One of his sons also had a problem with drugs; he had been hospitalized after jumping from the second floor of a building. Alejandro was thankful that his son had survived.

The experiences of Alejandro and Juana were both marked by ups and downs and can be understood as the result of the basic tension between the family structure and resource base. In both cases, the heads of households attempted to negotiate their material circumstances but ultimately were not successful in the manner that they had hoped they would be. Subsequently, their lack of material stability amounted to a deficit in the amount of emotional resources they had available to deal with their many children. Avoidance and/or ignorance of their children's behavior became standard as they grappled with their own fears and frustrations.

Material concerns often overwhelm residents of Pico Gardens, and the fear and lack of control that some household heads feel are quite serious. For example, Laura, a mother of four, suffered a back injury at work and never recovered. She had previously held assembly-line jobs, such as stuffing toys and sorting clothing, that were physically demanding and that her body could no longer handle after the injury. She received unemployment insurance immediately following the accident, but she no longer qualified as time passed. Laura's education was limited to the completion of second grade in Mexico, and finding decent work was nearly impossible. Like most other gang-related family heads, she was without sufficient financial resources, and since she did not have a car or a driver's license, she had a hard time getting around. Laura was a proud woman, and even though she had no insurance of any sort, no bank account, and no credit cards, she relied solely on herself. She had been able to inspire her eldest daughter to pursue her education and get into law school, but despite her wishes, her son had become a member of Cuatro Flats in an apparent effort to gain access to quick friends and easy money.

Laura liked Pico Gardens because the rent was reasonable. She was, however, quite put off by the vandalism and violence in the area, which had been getting worse. She was very fearful of crime, so much so that she couldn't sleep at night. She attributed these problems to the gangs. To remedy the situation, Laura suggested that the gang members simply be removed; she believed this in spite of her own son's active membership in a gang. She was becoming increasingly distanced from him as her fear and anxiety grew. Her son sensed the growing chasm and saw it simply as an exaggerated form of the inattention he felt he received earlier in his life, when his mother was preoccupied with her health and finding work.

Ineffective Parenting Strategies:
Permissive and Authoritarian Parenting

Families in which children get pushed and pulled into gangs are oftentimes characterized by parenting practices that are, modestly stated, less than ideal. The authoritative parenting style displayed by many non-gang-involved family heads was quite unusual in the case of gang-related families in this study. Instead, parenting practices in the latter families tended to be of the permissive and authoritarian varieties. These two types of practices are less effective because of their extreme nature—either the child has no sense of boundaries and appropriate behavior due to a lack of guidance, or the child reacts against rules that are too rigid and do not reflect an understanding of what a healthy parent-child relationship is about—namely, mutual respect. In either case, there is a lack of affection and respect for the child that is central to any productive approach.

As noted at the beginning of the chapter, Juana's approach to caring for her children was a permissive one. She gave her children free rein to do whatever they preferred with their free time and generally did not check up on them unless they were gone for long periods of time. They had no rules that they must follow regarding homework or chores and as a result tended to spend most of their time either staring at the television or out in the neighborhood or surrounding areas. Juana did not recognize the dangers that were present in Pico Gardens, in spite of the shootings and general violence that broke out around her. This denial of the seriousness of the situation around her had allowed her to justify the use of her time for personal interests and had contributed to the involvement of her son in Cuatro Flats. He had been easily pulled into the gang by the implicit promise of friendship and attention that otherwise was missing in his life.

Marta, another head of household in Pico Gardens, had chosen a similarly permissive parenting approach. Marta, who was forty-three years old at the time of the study, was from Guatemala and had lived in Pico Gardens for the last few years. She had three sons, ages twenty, eighteen, and thirteen; they were all members of Cuatro Flats. She had been raising them for a number of years on her own because she and her husband separated. After years of cleaning houses and doing shoe repair, Marta was no longer employed. As was common among residences in Pico Gardens, the household subsisted on a combination of AFDC, Medicare, and food stamps. Marta had no car or driver's license, no credit cards, and no insurance. She sought help with money and babysitting from her brother, who also lived in the projects. Nobody came to her for help, because she did not appear to be prepared to provide any.

After the separation from her husband, Marta started spending an enormous amount of time outside her home and inside nightclubs and bars, especially on the weekends. She now searched for new companions with seemingly reckless abandon. Marta dated a number of men twenty years her junior and had become very involved in the party scene. Her love life was now her main concern, and her children had taken a backseat as her new companions frequently stopped by and visited. Her sons had not had any structure in their lives for years. The eldest, Guillermo, had been drawn into the gang as he spent more and more time with his neighbors in an effort to get away from his house, a place that rarely had food and was not comfortable, with all the strangers coming in and out. His neighbors eventually got him involved in selling drugs. His younger brothers admired Guillermo's newly acquired financial status and set of friends—their goal was to follow in his footsteps, and they did. Guillermo had been arrested four times, and Marta had never been aware of what was going on until a significant time elapsed after the arrests. In those instances, she always retreated or disappeared without notifying anyone of her whereabouts. This same recurrent pattern of neglect and lack of awareness until after the fact had been repeated every other time her sons had gotten in trouble. Marta's children did not expect her to be around, much less to be of assistance, when they needed her. One time, Mario, the middle child, had been shot, and Marta could not be notified, because she was nowhere to be found.

Marta's example demonstrates that neglect and permissive parenting are often equivalent to a lack of concern for one's children and a desire to escape parental responsibilities, or, in another perspective, parents may be so burdened with personal emotional baggage that they are unable to care for others. Outright denial of children's involvement in gang activities can also be seen as virtual permission to engage in those activities. Repeatedly, parents of gang members claimed such ignorance. Both Juana and Marta are common examples of this parenting style and its dismal consequences. Denial, however, is not only a characteristic of permissive parenting but was also evidenced in authoritarian heads of households in this sample.

Sara was a fifty-year-old Mexican woman who had combined both permissive and authoritarian parenting approaches. She had been practicing her particular approach over a number of decades. Sara had married quite young, at age fifteen, in Mexico. Unlike many teens who marry, she and her husband were initially quite content. He made all of the major decisions in the family, and she gladly obliged. When she was about twenty years old, they moved to Tijuana, Mexico, where the first three of their sons was born. Later Sara gave birth to a daughter and another son and, at the age of thirty, moved to Los Angeles. After arriving in the United States, they had four more children. With a total of nine children, she and her husband divorced, marking the end of what had eventually evolved into a physically and emotionally abusive relationship.

As a born-again Christian, Sara spent a majority of her time in her church and being involved in church activities. She had a strong belief in the importance of the traditional, nuclear family despite her own negative experience. Sara had tried to be an authoritarian figure to her children, and the strict rules she had attempted to enforce revolved around the traditional gender roles she had been raised to uphold in Mexico. These gender roles were such that her sons had never been expected to help out with chores around the home and had been allowed to stay out much later at night than her daughters. Sara stressed that she expected her children to be completely obedient and that her word was all that mattered. When her children disagreed with her, she refused to listen to them and was of the opinion that children do not have the right to truly speak their mind until they are adults. This attitude had been especially problematic during the years of abuse that she had suffered at the hands of her husband. Her husband became abusive as more children were born to them without the concomitant resources to care for them adequately. Sara's children helplessly witnessed as their mother was beaten and emotionally battered by her husband, accepting it as if it were her fate. She did not want to hear their objections or their pleas for her to get help.

Sara's parenting approach had not been entirely successful in protecting her children from what she saw as the evils of the world. Two of her sons were involved in Cuatro Flats, and one of her daughters chose to marry someone who was active in the same gang. That daughter and her common-law husband lived in another apartment in Pico Gardens. Sara acknowledged that the public housing development was crime-ridden and that violence was

A mix of young men and little children

common. She also stated that it was not safe to go out at night and she feared for her children's well-being. She attributed much of the violence in the neighborhood to outside gangs who came from other areas to cause trouble. Yet Sara adamantly denied that the gang presence in the neighborhood was a threat, and she claimed that none of her children were in a gang. Despite her insistence on a clean-living lifestyle, her sons also smoked marijuana on a regular basis. This was yet another behavior that she denied.

Sara's persistent denial of reality, along with her belief that "boys will be boys," had essentially permitted the boys to begin and maintain an association with the gang. This association was not entirely voluntary and might have been stopped if either of the parents had intervened in time. One of her sons was forcibly jumped into the gang, and his younger brother chose to follow him in. The boys came to appreciate the social support given to them by their gang brothers. Their mother continued to replicate abusive relationships in a series of liaisons with other men, and the boys eventually lost respect for her. Her rules became empty words as they watched her betray her beliefs every time she got involved with another violent man.

Overly strict or authoritarian approaches to child rearing have been demonstrated to be ineffective in general terms and are especially so when it appears as though parents disregard their own rules. This approach on first reflection may seem diametrically opposed to that of the overly permissive parent, but they are similarly inadequate. Both shut the children out of meaningful conversations, and both help push the children out of the home and into the waiting embrace of the local gang.

Unlike the too-permissive Juana, a head of household named Brenda filled the authoritarian role. Brenda was a fifty-six-year-old resident of Pico Gardens. One of the few African-American heads of household in the housing development, she had lived there for twenty-five years. She originally moved there for the low rent and had witnessed a number of changes over the years. To protect her children and grandchildren from the escalating violence in the neighborhood, she had chosen to adopt an overly rigid and extremely strict parenting style. She was disappointed in the changes that she had observed at Pico Gardens over the years and attributed them to the rise in undocumented Mexican immigrants. Unsurprisingly, Brenda did not share her perspective with her many Mexican and Chicano neighbors who either were undocumented or knew someone who was.

Brenda had raised three children who were now adults living outside Pico Gardens. Her parenting duties were not completed, however, as she has custody of and was raising the four children of one of her daughters. Brenda treated her grandchildren as she had treated her own kids—she did not shower any special favors on them, as grandparents often do. She had a lot of time to dedicate to parenting because she had quit working in 1966. Brenda had created a number of rules that the grandchildren were to meet; she demanded that they do a number of chores around the house or else they would be harshly punished. It was not unusual, after they had completed their chores, for Brenda to complain that they did not know how to do anything right and to reprimand them at length. Serious conversations between Brenda and her grandchildren were rare; she believed that they could have their own opinions, but they had no right to express them to her. She advocated instilling fear in the children as a means of preventing them from engaging in acts of delinquency.

Nevertheless, Brenda's efforts had not prevented the children from getting into trouble. Her sixteen-year-old granddaughter was a member of the Mob Crew (TMC) and, at the time of this investigation, was pregnant. Furthermore, her fifteen-year-old granddaughter was a peripheral associate of the Black Crib gang. Brenda's fourteen-year-old grandson was affiliated with Cuatro Flats and had dropped out of school. The youngest grandchild, an eight-year-old girl, was the only one who was not connected directly to a gang. The fact that Brenda herself had been involved in a gang, the Bloodsisters, during her younger years, and her children's and grandchildren's awareness of this involvement, worked to counter any discipline she meted out or any example she attempted to set. She realized that her grandchildren stayed out late and vandalized property, and although she punished them, they simply continued where they had left off once they were allowed out of the apartment again. Brenda brutally reprimanded the children, to no avail. She did not claim any responsibility for their actions, but rather thought that her problems with her grandchildren were due to peer pressure and a lack of community investment in their lives. In order to rectify the problems of gangs and crime, she thought that the older males should impress upon the younger ones the importance of not joining a gang. This strategy becomes a problem of course when the older males are no longer around their families.

The Role of Absent or Abusive Men

As is indicated in Juana's life history and nearly all of those that have followed, abusive and neglectful males have played a major role in the trajectory of youth gang involvement in Pico Gardens. These males are often the fathers of the youth who get involved, or they can be boyfriends or other adult male figures who are an influence in their family life.

The absence of father figures can be both figurative and literal. Oftentimes the father is around but is virtually absent because he is so emotionally and materially aloof from his children's lives. Mothers may prefer to have these men around out of habit, for security, or because of a belief that two parents can sometimes be better than one if their emotional and psychological resources are pooled—a belief that is misguided when at least one of the two is responsible for serious abuse in the home. Conflict among the parents can push the children into a "family" outside the home: the gang. This type of conflict is often replicated in relationships that the heads of households have after the breakup of their marriages as they subconsciously seek the familiar. For example, Juana had gotten involved with a series of abusive boyfriends who treated her as poorly as her ex-husband had. Consequently, her children sought other male figures for companionship and to model;

in Pico Gardens these male figures frequently happen to be members of a gang.

Dahlia's story mirrors that of the others in that respect. She had gone to school in Mexico but stopped in the seventh grade because her parents did not let her continue. She had attended East Los Angeles College for two years, however, but did not finish, this time due to pregnancy.

None of Dahlia's family members had moved out of the household. However, her husband was a shadow father (technically a stepfather to her two eldest children) who repeatedly left the home for extended periods and then returned. Inevitably, his returns were accompanied by outbursts and abuse. Dahlia's four children had been negatively affected by the arrangement. Their emotional and intellectual growth had been stunted by the constant tension in the household when their father was present, and the upheaval that resulted whenever he left for any period of time. The oldest daughter, a nineteen-year-old, had not formally joined a gang but was friendly, and thus peripherally associated, with a number of gang members who lived in Pico Gardens. During times of extreme family stress, she turned to her boyfriend, who lived outside the housing complex, for emotional support; his companionship had so far prevented her from formally joining a gang. Dahlia's sixteen-year-old son, Mario, was not as lucky. When his mother and stepfather's fighting became especially intense, he had no one to vent to—at least no one versed in constructive feedback. His grades plummeted, and he began spending a lot of time outside of the house with neighbors involved in Cuatro Flats. They showed him how to forget his worries temporarily by getting high, and Mario took to the practice quite quickly. After a short time, he was jumped into the gang. Eventually he got into trouble with some of the other guys in his gang and was placed on probation. Within a short period of time he was back to drinking and smoking pot out in the neighborhood, and the parole violations resulted in his current incarceration.

Mario's behavior problems outside school were accompanied by problems inside school. He was in the eighth grade, a couple of years behind where he should have been for his age. Mario's younger brother and sister were also showing signs of learning difficulties that could largely be attributed to problems with preoccupation or concentration. They daydreamed and worried and generally lacked the energy needed to do well in school. They had problems paying attention, and when they came home to do their homework, Dahlia could not help them much. Usually they simply gave up trying to complete their assignments. The kids were all bused to a wealthy area of Los Angeles County, Pacific Palisades, and the contrast between their family's economic situation and that of their peers disturbed and depressed them.

Dahlia's own anxiety with her relationship problems had depleted her of the energy she might otherwise have expended on her children. Although she realized that she had been involved in a string of abusive relationships, she felt helpless to change her situation, because it was all she had ever known. As a parent, she oscillated between moments of extreme authoritarianism and moments of extreme permissiveness that were ultimately ineffective. Before Mario's trouble with the authorities, Dahlia noticed his withdrawal from the family, and she and his stepfather were annoyed. They decided the best thing to do was essentially to punish him by making him move to Mexico to live with relatives and to show him how rough life could really be. Once he was sent there, Dahlia and her husband basically left him to his own devices and had little contact with him. Mario grew more and more antisocial as he spent time away from California, and by the time he was allowed to return home some months later, a surly attitude was a permanent feature of his personality. His mother and stepfather took to ignoring him out of frustration and did little to encourage him to communicate the feelings he was hiding under the tough-guy facade. Mario eventually found himself in a situation in which no adult attempted to watch over him; he fended for himself, found a substitute family in the gang, and quickly wound up incarcerated.

Unlike some parents who never gain insight into their actions, Dahlia realized that the approach she had used with Mario was not effective. She had tried to make a few changes to improve her interactions with her younger children, yet struggled with her decisions. She had decided to keep her husband around now and then so that the younger children would gain something from his influence. Nevertheless, this decision came at a price, since he and Dahlia ended up at each other's throats in almost every encounter. She had gone to a few counseling classes but found it hard to make any changes to the relationship without any agreement on her husband's part.

Yvette, a forty-seven-year-old Mexican resident in Pico Gardens, shared a similar situation in her household. Although she was separated from the father of her five children, they continued to live together. This sort of situation is relatively common in Pico Gardens because of economic considerations. Many of the family heads are sensitive to the financial straits they will be in if they are forced to move out of the community into higher-rent areas. Therefore, they maintain the same residence in spite of the constant conflict that the situation invokes.

Yvette and her husband also have what can be characterized as an abusive relationship. The relationship has been rocky for years. The downhill spiral began when she and her husband moved to Los Angeles from Mexico and had their first child. At that point, relations with her husband became strained because he was never at home with the baby. Instead he was always partying or working. As she approached her early thirties, Yvette began to have more trouble with her husband because he neglected the needs of their growing family; they now had five children, and the responsibility was one that her husband preferred to avoid. He wanted to escape from it all and began gambling compulsively. The relationship continued to deteriorate, and the children were virtually without a father figure—when he was home, he was emotionally unavailable and often disagreeable. He lost his job and refused to look for work. Yvette had no patience for his behavior, and her pleas sparked screaming matches. Their children reacted to the stress at home by staying out late and getting into trouble in school.

Yvette's two boys gradually got themselves into serious trouble. Both joined gangs in order to get out of the house. Her older son, a twenty-one-year-old, joined TMC, and her younger son, a nineteen-year-old, joined Cuatro Flats, two gangs that were bitter rivals. Once Yvette and her family moved into Pico Gardens, their apartment became a place for local gang members to congregate. She tried to put a stop to that routine early on by threatening her sons, but they just laughed her efforts off and continued partying until all hours of the night. Their father did not try to put a stop to it and actually joined in a couple of times. As a result of their activities, both of her sons had been caught using drugs. Her elder one had left the state for Pennsylvania after serving time in prison for drug possession, and the younger son was currently serving time in juvenile hall for numerous drug-related violations.

As is the case with many abused individuals in Pico Gardens, the perpetual conflict they experience takes a toll on their personal energy reserves. This negatively affects both their parenting efforts and their efforts at building social and neighborhood capital outside the home. In Yvette's case, although she appreciated the low rent available in her neighborhood, she did not get along with her neighbors. Instead, she ignored them, and if provoked, she argued with them. The hostility that non-gang families have toward the gang activity of teenagers in the neighborhood had been extended to her as well, and she and her husband had been labeled as bad parents. The neighbors believed that Yvette and her husband were part of the problem because they appeared to condone the activities of the sons and their friends who hung around on the stoop outside their door. In the past, housing authorities had tried several times to evict Yvette and her husband from the complex on charges that they had a lot of loud parties and encour-

"Kicking it" with the homeboys

aged gang activity. Yvette claimed that such activities were out of her hands, and she simply gave up. Her sons had become harder and harder to control, and she was tired of trying to intervene. For example, they left firearms out in full view in the house, and when she confronted them about it, they were unfazed by her threats of discipline. The guns stayed, and Yvette was frustrated, especially in light of all the shootings that occurred around the apartment. Her husband was oblivious to what was going on with his children and did not really seem concerned.

Although Yvette was hostile toward her neighbors, she secretly agreed with many of their concerns about gang life in the complex. She was permissive at home because no other approach had worked, yet she was quite authoritarian when it came to dealing with the police. She had repeatedly told her sons that she would not defend them if they committed a crime and would demand that they be held accountable. She flushed their drugs down the toilet and turned in their firearms to the local clergyman. Yvette also turned her elder son over to the police when he violated his parole. She was comfortable with taking these kinds of actions but believed it was futile to work with others in the neighborhood to change life in Pico Gardens, and she gave little thought to such a prospect. She reasoned that she was lucky to make it through each day.

A Lack of Social Ties

One of the most striking differences that can be observed in the lives of gang-affiliated and non-gang-affiliated families is the amount of effort expended in community activities. As demonstrated in the above cases of Yvette's approach and the more common example of Juana at the beginning of this chapter, most gang-affiliated heads of household are unable or hindered in their ability to take advantage of social contact outside the home. Because so many major celebrations (i.e., musical groups, Easter and Christmas parties, Residents Advisory Council–sponsored parties or dinners) are brought to the projects, parents are often unmotivated to seek other social outlets or activities. This, in large part, may stem from the institutionalization of a type of welfare dependence where everything comes to you without anyone soliciting it. In addition, certain parents are playing out their own dramas and forget that their children also need time and attention to fashion dramas of their own.

While non-gang households' heads are stretching their time and budgets to make sure their children are involved in extracurricular activities, heads of gang households are preoccupied with other concerns. These concerns are usually ones that they find more central to their own continued existence and often are related to issues of psychological and physical survival. The benefits that result from activities outside the home thus rarely accrue to children of these households. Youth must be unusually resilient in order to combat the pushes of their home environment and the attractions of the social circle immediately outside their front door.

The importance of extensive social ties is not always salient to parents in Pico Gardens. Time and time again, parents of gang-involved children stated that to put oneself out there was a losing battle. As this pattern becomes predominant, social capital is reduced in the family and ultimately neighborhood capital is similarly destroyed. Relationships between neighbors are strained, there is less informal social control, and a sense of hopelessness prevails. One parent always had an excuse for why she never took her daughter to the library, even though her daughter had been identified as gifted and the teacher had strongly recommended that the child be given reading materials on a regular basis. There was always something better or more important to do, and thus the child went without the learning enrichment and the parent went guilt-free.

The perspective of another Pico Gardens resident, Carmela, provides another example of this phenomenon. Born in Mexico City, Carmela was fifty-four years old at the time of the study. She was the head of her household, living in an apartment with her five children. Her husband also lived with her, even though they were technically separated. Carmela saw absolutely no need to interact with others in the neighborhood or the greater community to try to create change. This remained the case even as she became increasingly disillusioned with life in her community. She witnessed the escalating violence in the neighborhood and disliked the men who loitered around her apartment, taking drugs and smoking. She was also concerned about the gangs in the area. Moreover, this concern was directly linked to her son, whom she viewed as being in immediate danger because of the gangs. She denied that the reason her son was in trouble was that he already was in a gang; he was a known member of Cuatro Flats who had been incarcerated for weapon, parole, and drug violations. He used PCP and marijuana in the neighborhood and drank alcohol excessively.

Carmela refused to open her eyes to the world around her, in fear of what she would find. Similarly, she refused to believe that social action could solve the problem. For example, she felt that the Residents Advisory Council was ineffective, and she therefore dismissed it as unimportant. Carmela was adamant in her rejection of group involvement. Her isolation from others around her who shared the same frustrations prevented her from being empowered. Additional pressure stemmed from genuine material obstacles. She felt drained by the violence in the community and spent little time participating in activities with her children. She argued with her husband, watched television, and often felt depressed. Her son continued to get into trouble.

The psychological toll that many people pay for living in a violent area results in a self-perpetuating cycle for some. Many folks in Pico Gardens simply accede to the forces around them with little resistance whatsoever, mostly because these pressures are relentless and overwhelming. The web of interconnected forces bearing down on household heads leaves the vulnerable even more vulnerable. This works in conjunction with decisions made by family heads—or sometimes their failure to make any decisions—regarding their children's activities inside and outside the home. Many of these residents deny responsibility in the face of the immense struggles they encounter, leaving their children to make important decisions when they are unequipped to do so. Juana's admission of this fact at the beginning of the chapter epitomizes a common sentiment—what children do is no reflection on the parents and simply cannot be controlled by them. When this type of attitude is combined with a lack of shared family time, a high degree of conflict in the home, and few material resources, it is predictable that youth will look outside their homes for companionship and fun. Unfortunately, for youth in Pico Gardens, outlets and fun with the local gangs often amount to violence and a devastating future.

Not all parents of gang-affiliated children simply give up hope. Many mightily struggle to keep their children safe and to make ends meet. The use of permissive and authoritarian parenting styles as complements for one another is a natural response to a lack of success with one type of parenting style or the other, yet it is ultimately less effective than authoritative parenting. The role of women in households that are often patriarchal and too often abusive attests to the gender inequality present in gang households. Victimization wears down the bodies and psyches of women trying to hold their large families together and makes it difficult for them to succeed. The lack of social networks, or social capital, that characterizes these women's lives makes them feel even more isolated and hopeless. In order to deal with the gang problems in Pico Gardens effectively, these factors must be recognized.

CHAPTER ELEVEN

GANG PREVENTION AND INTERVENTION STRATEGIES OVER TIME

The history of Pico Gardens, and, of course, Cuatro Flats as a gang, would not be complete without the history I witnessed and recorded during my life. This is especially the case with the fieldwork I conducted intensively from 1991 through 1995, with periodic visits up to the present. I have already mentioned that in the early 1950s I visited the Pico project with friends who were newspaper boys and heard countless stories about the tough, brave street youth there, particularly the future welterweight champion of the world, Don Jordan, who went by the street name "Geronimo." Back then, gang fights were mostly fisticuffs, with occasional bats and knives, and rarely involved guns.

By the time I returned to Pico Gardens in the mid-1960s, the gang had become larger and stronger and had fashioned a fearless street reputation. It was during the War on Poverty in 1966, when I became a street counselor in another neighborhood and was working with the Jardin (Garden) barrio gang of Montebello Gardens, a low-income enclave on the border between Montebello and Pico Rivera with a history going back to the 1940s. Part of my work involved meeting with other counselors and youth workers throughout the city, and I was involved in two programs, Teen Post and Neighborhood Youth Corps (NYC). Teen Post usually set up programs in low-income, ethnic-minority neighborhoods of the Greater Los Angeles area. The social and recreational programs offered by Teen Post operated on a regular basis, and a director and staff, including counselors, of which I was one, offered guidance and direction for the mostly adolescent and young adult neighborhood participants. NYC was linked to Teen Post and was like an urban version of the Civilian Conservation Corps (CCC) of the New Deal, with participants earning a modest wage working on community projects.

Operation "Clean and Green"

There were 135 such centers and programs in L.A. then, but only 5 remained by the late 1980s.

There were regular citywide meetings among Teen Post and NYC employees in which we discussed and collaborated on issues relevant to troubled youth. In addition, we often operated as crisis intervention negotiators when gang conflicts threatened to erupt, so many of the program members and associates became familiar with one another through these types of contacts. At one of these meetings I met Antonio Rodriquez and his brothers—Javier, Jorge, and Jaime—and a few other close affiliates whose names I have forgotten. Antonio and Javier also became part of an organization that I belonged to called Mexican American Action Committee (MAAC), whose members took an activist stance on local political issues. The Rodriquez brothers were working in the Pico Gardens project and ran most of the youth programs there, including Teen Post and NYC, which were located on a busy thoroughfare in the barrio/projects. They were also former members of the local Cuatro Flats gang who had matured out of the gang and were now applying their knowledge and insights to aid youngsters and hasten their maturing-out process.

The name of their center was Casa de Carnalismo, or House of Brotherhood, mentioned in Chapter One. The word *carnalismo* (from *carnal*, mean-

ing "blood brother") affirmed social ties and was used in the barrio generally but more so among gang members as an expression of the close bonds
they had. Casa de Carnalismo was a storefront building on Fourth Street,
the northern boundary of the Cuatro Flats neighborhood. Because of its
central location and the leadership and guidance provided by the Rodriquez
brothers, Casa became a center of social programs for youth. As positive as
all this might be, members still experienced obstacles on a daily basis, and
the often-hostile attitude and behavior they encountered from the Los Angeles police officers operating out of the Hollenbeck station gradually caused
the center to become politicized and embrace an activist agenda. This political orientation was born out of the constant struggles to ensure that funding would continue for the programs initiated by the War on Poverty (see
Dawley 1990).

It was a daily concern because this domestic initiative was a rather short-
lived effort, for the cold war and the fear of the spread of communism soon
took center stage. As the United States was drawn into the foreign arena
through its involvement in Vietnam, most of the government resources
were soon siphoned off, as guns won out over butter. Thus the people working in these poverty programs had to fight early on for the survival of their
activities. As for relations with law enforcement, going back to the Zoot Suit
Riots of 1943 when street youth fought it out with American servicemen,
those in the Mexican community in general always felt the police had it in
for them (Escobar 1998).

Casa de Carnalismo—amid the War on Poverty, the Chicano movement
(a civil rights struggle of its own), the anti–Vietnam War resistance, and all
that the 1960s represented in ferment and protest—went from government-
sponsored community program to community advocate and activist. While
gang membership and gang conflicts had been tempered by the social programs' prevention and intervention efforts in the early years of Casa's existence, the political radicalization of its leadership and community participants and supporters had an even stronger effect on the gangs and their
activities. The personal frustrations, aggressions, alienations, and rages that
gang members experienced were commonly expressed in destructive ways
toward other gang members or toward themselves through the use of drugs.
Activists redirected such energies, and thus aggression was partially har-
nessed and channeled toward societal authority figures—namely, political
leaders and the two institutions that most affected their community, the
police and schools. Demonstrations, boycotts, walkouts, and other acts of
resistance and civil disobedience became new ways for gang members to
demonstrate an antisocial attitude.

One of the key activist events during this period was an antidrug initiative organized by Casa leadership and many of its community adherents, including former and some active gang members. This overture was well planned but limited in its implementation because drug use and sales had become such a pervasive problem in the community. Inspired by a famous revolutionary movie of the time, *The Battle of Algiers,* Casa leaders decided to follow a theme from the film, which showed revolutionaries policing their own neighborhoods and peoples. This initiative was patterned after another Chicano movement tactic, the Community Alert Patrol, an example adapted from a black innovation in South Central Los Angeles, where community youth in automobiles would follow police patrol cars and stop a distance behind them when they were enforcing or carrying out the law. The youth who manned the cars became observers and took note of the episode to ensure that the law was being applied evenly and fairly; the Watts disturbances in 1965 were sparked by just such a police harassment incident, in which the law was unfairly applied.

The new antidrug initiative put Casa members in foot patrols of three or four to watch their neighborhood for known or suspected drug dealers. The aim, of course, was to target the drug source while simultaneously discouraging youth from partaking of drugs. Casa leaders and others involved in this initiative adhered to a very disciplined model by disavowing the use and sale of drugs of all types. As might be expected, this venture backfired for several reasons, but primarily due to its vigilante-style approach of taking the law into one's own hands. There were plenty of drug dealers in the neighborhood, both petty and big-time, but many of them were unknown to Casa members. It just so happened that one of the dealers was an undercover government agent who had penetrated the neighborhood in the hope of legally apprehending the major dope dealers. When the Casa members were informed that this person was selling drugs to some of the youth in the area, they confronted the man. The confrontation escalated to a shootout in which the agent suffered a bullet wound to the spine, an injury that paralyzed him. Within a short time the police were in the neighborhood and arrested the three Casa individuals who were responsible for the shooting. It was then that the Casa members were informed that the injured man was a government agent.

In addition to this brazen act, which undermined what on the surface appeared to be a noble cause, the policing by citizens of a neighborhood so rife with crime and drug activities was well near an impossible task anyway. The point of describing this episode here, however, is to demonstrate how Casa and many other community residents, howsoever idealistically, strove to address a serious problem that the police had shown themselves to be incapable of handling. It was a definitive act of empowerment during a highly politicized period when poor people and the gangs that are a part of them stepped forward to regain control of their own future.

As police moved into the neighborhood to show that they were the law enforcers, police repression increased as surveillance and search-and-seizure activities took an ugly turn. The three who were arrested became a cause célèbre and were soon referred to as "Los Tres," a phrase that helped bring attention and support to their cause of social justice. Rallies, protests, sloganeering, speeches, and other activities continued for a couple of years while the court case dragged on. Eventually one of Los Tres was found guilty and served ten years in prison.

When the War on Poverty ended, sometime around the early 1970s, Casa de Carnalismo was forced to secure funding from other sources. For a time it succeeded in doing so, but by the middle 1970s, support and resources ran out. The legacy of Casa, nevertheless, stands out in my mind. Parent training and counseling, Head Start, Teen Post, and NYC, as well as other social support networks and programs of the Great Society, had made a difference, an accomplishment also noted elsewhere (Dawley 1990). But perhaps the greatest outcome, albeit short-lived, is how gang members were politicized in ways that kept them from killing each other or destroying themselves with drugs and alcohol. Miracles are hard to come by, but social change can happen if the will is there.

As time went on, occasionally I would hear about different incidents in Pico Gardens or people I knew back then during the turbulent 1960s Chicano movement, incidents such as the death of Cyclone, one of the drug patrollers, who overdosed on barbiturates; Armando's arrest for drug dealing after losing his job; and the success of Beto, one of Los Tres, in securing a good job and raising a family in a home he purchased.

Aside from these mostly nostalgic stories, one stands out as significant because of the publicity it received during the O. J. Simpson trial. As was noted earlier, in 1978 there was a major police drug raid on the projects, in which doors were busted down, countless physical accosting and beatings administered, and many people arrested, young and old alike. Mark Fuhrman, made famous as the officer who discovered Simpson's glove and whose racial comments caught on tape tainted his veracity, was in on the 1978 crackdown and, according to reports, was responsible for the severe beating of a resident, a young man who had mistakenly been identified for drug dealing. Antonio Rodriquez, an activist lawyer, took the police brutality case, and the court process dragged on until Fuhrman was acquitted of all charges. Interestingly, one of the results of this near-riot affair was that housing authorities were instructed by law enforcement to cut down all the trees and shrubs (by then considerable in their height, having been planted in 1942, when the projects were founded) because they helped hide project residents and made it difficult for police to detect and arrest rioters, or protesters and dissidents, as the residents thought of them.

Contact with the Rodriquezes continued off and on during the decades ahead, as all of us moved on to different stages of our lives. In the late 1980s I had heard of a Jesuit priest working at Dolores Mission, a small community church set in the middle of the housing projects. With the help of others, he had developed a community strategy to address the rampant poverty and social problems in the area, including programs to deter and redirect the negative behaviors of gang members. Father Gregory J. Boyle was the name of this cleric, and he had already established a reputation among gang members as "G-Dog," the street tag they honored him with, making his position clear as an advocate for the youth who had become compelled to join gangs (Fremon 2004). The network of community and public servants with whom I was familiar spoke highly of Father Boyle's integrity and dedication to social justice. His main objective in ministering to the community as pastor of Dolores Mission and adviser to Proyecto Pastoral, a community-based organization, was to provide positive paths for a largely neglected and isolated youth population. At one of the programs he now heads, Homeboy Industries, the emphasis is on building a brighter future for gang members, who regularly mention that they do not expect to live very long.

I had met Father Boyle on a few occasions, but it was a conference for judges where we both spoke that really brought us together; he was familiar with my work and had read my book *Barrio Gangs* and liked it. I had made my presentation explaining how gangs came to be and why certain youth joined them, and as part of the talk I referred to gang members as night people, comparing them to *cucarachas* (cockroaches) that wait until nightfall to come out of their quarters. Although this allusion was intended to emphasize the poverty locations where gangs breed, and not the personal attributes or "insect" qualities of gang members, it was apparently lost on Father Boyle, for when he spoke, the first sentences he uttered were that gang members had souls and were not at all like soulless cockroaches. So began a close and lasting relationship with Father Boyle that continues to the present.

In 1991, a research corporation named Abt Associates contacted me to ask if I would be interested in evaluating a drug intervention program being implemented in the projects. The program was known as Pro-Force and involved housing police on bicycles in teams of twos and threes patrolling at all hours of the day, but especially during late hours, to deter the use and sales of drugs in selected locales in the housing projects. Before agreeing to take on this task, I visited and spoke to Father Boyle and asked for his help, explaining in detail what this evaluation would entail. In this meeting, he agreed to become my cultural broker and introduced me that day to the community by taking me on a walking tour of the neighborhood. He seemed to know everyone, little kids and older adults alike, and as he stopped to talk and share information with them, it was as though they were continuing a conversation, picking up where they had left off in a previous encounter. In other words, a history of personal information had been exchanged and reflected upon, creating a running dialogue on specific needs, activities, and developments between the two. During this educational tour that served as my introduction, we spotted a drug dealer at an outdoor public telephone attached to the wall of an old mom-and-pop market. Father Boyle pointed out that this type of brazen behavior was common. For example, a drug dealer from outside the community had once even brought out a couch and sat down by the curb as he conducted his business with impunity, since L.A. police patrol cars generally avoided the projects.

At the end of this tour we wound up at the home of a married couple who had been very active in the community. Father Boyle introduced me to them at the doorstep, and he proceeded to enter the house (which I thought was normal but later discovered to be significant). He explained to them what I would be doing and asked for their assistance with my research. Then he left me there to provide the couple more details about the evaluation project. Bebee and Pam McDuffie as a couple and individually were deeply involved with and familiar with the neighborhood scene in all its aspects, particularly gangs. As lifelong residents of the projects, they knew practically every gang member, not only in the Cuatro Flats gang but in the other area gangs, especially the one locked in a deadly struggle with Cuatro, the Mob Crew (TMC). The couple became both my key informants and close community researchers and friends. Soon after obtaining a cultural broker and community researchers, I contacted the research group monitoring the evaluation and agreed to carry out the work. Later, when conducting the fieldwork for this effort, after Bebee and Pam had given me complete access to information about the drug dynamics of the neighborhood, Bebee informed me that by crossing the threshold of his home that first day, Father Boyle had indicated that I was to be trusted beyond a doubt.

Throughout the early and mid-1990s, I maintained a constant presence in the community, both under the accompaniment of my community liaisons,

Eating the cupcakes before the party begins

soon to become my community research assistants, and on my own when I had made other contacts and friendships with residents and public care-takers serving the community. In addition to the drug intervention evalua-tion I was conducting, I soon was able to secure a grant from the Department of Health and Human Services, after Bebee assured me he would help with the investigation into family dynamics and gang membership, the subject of this book. We also soon hired another community researcher to assist with the research. Norma Tovar, another longtime resident of the community, was brought on board, adding a different gender perspective to our work. What follows is more or less a discussion of the many prevention and inter-vention efforts we observed and participated in during our fieldwork. Bebee played a prominent role in these activities as both an insider and outsider, for he also was the president of the Residents Advisory Council (RAC) for the Pico Gardens section of the public housing project.

Walking around the projects and being seen with the community assis-tants helped me generate a wider network for the investigation. I was in-vited to several social events, including a wedding and a birthday party in the initial phase of the fieldwork; always with a camera in hand, I took pho-tos of these events, making sure the participants received copies of their own, and soon I became the community photographer. On these as well as other occasions, I was introduced to residents to inform them of the work we were doing and to ensure the anonymity and the confidential nature of the investigation. Now even some of the young gang-affiliated males who had seemed wary of and aloof from me in the beginning recognized and acknowledged my presence when I visited the project.

Eventually I was invited to visit the regular monthly meetings of the Residents Advisory Council and learn more about the programs and activities that served the community. The RAC is a five-member elected board of residents who meet and make decisions after conferring with other residents about issues and programs that affect the community. There were prevention and intervention and some suppression programs in operation during the fieldwork period. I followed some of these over a period of time and gathered some interesting observations and opinions from the residents on how some of these programs worked, if at all.

One of the programs that received a lot of attention was a HUD-sponsored drug prevention/intervention initiative that involved drug counseling and police bike patrols. Overall, the residents, apparently believing that the counseling and personnel would be exclusively for Pico Gardens, seemed disappointed that they had to share the program's resources with other housing projects; the other projects were in East Los Angeles and South Central Los Angeles. Several residents were also unhappy with the absence of

Rappers in the summer and snowballers in the Christmas winter

youth activities that were supposed to be a part of the intervention aspect of the program. As on many other occasions, several residents strongly urged future cooperation among themselves to forge a consensus on how to increase participation, since the local social problems were so bad.

The general consensus of residents was that more monies and resources were needed to seriously combat the rampant drug and crime problems in the projects. Members of the RAC, as previously noted, generally felt that they had contributed in different ways to some aspects of the drug elimination program. However, many of these same people were so overwhelmed with other duties and responsibilities (raising troubled children, involvement in other organizations, volunteer work, and so on) that they could not consistently attend to all the details and thus had to trust the decisions of higher officials. Further, residents not involved in RAC affairs were sometimes unaware of the activities and decision-making process of the RAC. Their nonparticipation in meetings and unawareness of leadership decisions had even led some residents to bad-mouth several of the leaders.

To reiterate, most residents were so immersed in their own lives that they had little time to keep abreast of events or follow directives; thus continuity of applying pressure on housing authorities was lost. During the fieldwork period, there had been a steady increase in new residents with immigrant backgrounds who spoke mostly in Spanish, and it seemed that their unfamiliarity with American society also included no previous experience with neighborhood involvement. In fact, many showed up at community meetings only when they were well-announced affairs. From what I observed, organizational efforts were hampered when residents only chose what they considered worthy of their time and effort and ignored some of the other directives by leaders.

In short, the range of cultural variation and level of community participation found among native and foreign-born Mexicans/Latinos led to a weak, uneven support and pressure for making residents' demands clear to local housing officials. This lack of interest stemmed largely from three reasons, each related to a different subpopulation in the projects: first, those in the mostly immigrant population were kept busy preserving their home life and protecting their source of income—a job and/or some street-level entrepreneurship; second, the native Chicanos had doubts about the positive effects of intervention, because of its historical record of consistent failures; and third, those in the entrenched, marginalized cholo segment of gang members, drug users, and alcohol abusers might know they needed help but were unable to, or refused to, reach out and seek assistance.

Residents voiced other, deeper interests, even as they regularly voiced concerns about the drug counseling and bike patrolling. Sharing resources with other projects, in their opinion, was not enough to turn back habits and forces rooted in decades of neglect and isolation. Someone had to be there all the time to watch the street actions of drug users and sellers, and there also had to be a regular, full-time counselor in both Aliso Village (the neighboring project) and Pico Gardens in order to make a difference. This complaint reached a high point when even part-time counseling in Pico Gardens had been removed to Aliso Village. The years of poverty, with all the associated personal and social problems, had created a sense of apathy and ignorance in many residents, and making only a feeble public effort to combat the deep-rooted problems only added to the community's skepticism. Such a protracted arrangement, as one mother inferred in an angry voice, undermined the whole notion of whether personal counseling was helpful if the foundation for help was just as shaky as the lives of troubled community residents. The most informed residents, especially members of the RAC, were very adamant in this view; the ill-informed or uninformed residents remained rooted in the pressures and constraints of everyday life, thus displaying a wait-and-see stance.

While safety issues were a primary focus, family considerations also ranked very high. For example, parents valued education for their children, but a number of them appeared to have tacitly accepted their older children's academic failures, such as dropping out of school. Some parents, when asked about this discrepancy, reacted defensively, pointing with some justification to problems with services provided by local schools. This complaint appeared to be correct, in my estimation, given that the local Roosevelt High School had been built in the 1920s to hold approximately two thousand students but presently serviced more than five thousand students in staggered shifts, paralleling the overcrowding in the projects (Vigil 1997, 1999, 2004). Other parents admitted that they had overlooked the need for their children's education but professed to be making more effort to see that their younger children, or grandchildren, at least completed high school.

As time passed, in addition to the snowball contacts and interviews that materialized at meetings, an explosion of gang violence and shootings brought this author into a number of focused community meetings, with residents and local authorities alike, to join in concentrated efforts to stem such destructive activities. My participation in these meetings improved upon and moderately solidified my relationships with some gang members and several of the local gang experts—Community Youth Gang Services workers, Vista workers, and volunteer teachers at the Dolores Mission Alternative School. For residents, drug use was of secondary concern when violence escalated; the shooting activity and extremely antagonistic gang attitudes and interactions were seen as the primary problem. One side effect of these meetings and other interactions was the solicitation of my involvement in HUD's Technical Assistance program to serve Pico Gardens primarily and also perhaps Aliso Village. In 1997 this overture and discussion resulted in my collaboration with the Robert F. Kennedy Memorial and HUD in a ten- to fourteen-year-old intervention program known as IMPACTO (Imaginando Mañana: Pico-Aliso Community Teen Outreach).

Monitoring these developments and charting plans to address major community problems constituted a multipronged affair that involved other outlets and sources of inspiration. It became clear that several of the adults, some of whom were parents, had found some success in disabusing themselves of drugs and alcohol by affiliating with a Victory Outreach type of Pentecostal church program that was near the projects (Vigil 1983). A chola with an extensive history of street experience, in fact, slipped back and forth from a street drug life to one of an attentive and straitlaced, albeit struggling, "Bible-toting-quoting churchgoer"; this modality changed from week to week, unfortunately.

The spirits of the leaders and activists might falter occasionally, but overall they strove to stay on a positive course. When L.A. CADA (Los Angeles Centers for Alcohol and Drug Abuse) moved to the other end of the projects, anyone seeking counseling there would have to walk through enemy territory, the leaders complained. No one was insane enough to do that, although one drunken *vato* mindlessly walked, macho-style, near the boundary line and was shot in the abdomen (as noted in Chapter Four); after he was taken off the critical list, he lamented, in gallows-humor fashion, the damage done to his tattoo rather than the more-than-sixteen-inch-long scar from the middle of his chest down to his waist. It was regular incidents such as these that kept the leaders of the community off balance.

Among the continuing positive activities were the "Just Say No" workshop for children that met once a week, the VISTA (Volunteers in Service to America) members offering tutoring and other counseling services, and two parent-based groups, Neighborhood Watch and Comite por Paz (Committee for Peace). Neighborhood Watch, a community and police collaborative effort in which community members provided "warnings" to police to monitor the community, was established. This approach did not sit well with RAC leaders and other community activists, as it had a "snitch" cast to it. Comite por Paz, on the other hand, was a community-based holistic solution started by the Dolores Mission Catholic Church that attempted to create a communal, family-like umbrella where adults viewed all the children and youth as their own to guide and protect. Both of these groups, but primarily the Comite, commenced "Love Walk" efforts, hoping that the presence of adults carrying lit candles, mostly mothers, in the weekend evening hours would help calm and control the gunplay of the main shooters in the gang conflicts, especially the TMC and Cuatro Flats conflagration that had gotten out of hand. This planned activity continued in a sporadic fashion throughout the fieldwork period, and a few immigrant parents sometimes joined to contribute to a show of force and unity, even if their children were not in gangs.

Interestingly, it was not clear to me if Comite parents had more gang-affiliated children and youth than the Neighborhood Watch group, which might have provided a partial explanation for why the community had these two parent-led approaches: one linked to police because the kids were "good," and the other socially based because the kids were "bad" but not totally through their own fault. Several parents belonged to both groups, an optimistic approach that held that the more organized efforts there were to combat this gang/drug problem, the better. Generally, immigrant parents remained mostly uninvolved and appeared to be just biding their time until they could move to a better neighborhood.

As noted, RAC leaders complained about the lack of continuity in program services, but a VISTA worker reminded them to remain optimistic that eventually a consistent pattern would emerge. In her words, "New programs are always like that. You have to give it time."

One good event that buoyed RAC leaders was that fourteen people graduated from a resident management course and appeared poised to join a formal organization or start a corporation. One negative happenstance that seemed to be emerging was a minor power struggle within this group, as the RAC president was being challenged by a Mexican immigrant, but the rivalry appeared to be more a personality or racial conflict rather than one of substance, as the RAC president was black and a former Cuatro Flats gang member.

As noted, RAC members were generally more informed, aware, and involved than non-RAC members. But even within this group there was some distance between the leaders and some of the followers. The latter had built a trust in the major RAC representatives that was based on past experiences and accomplishments. However, when expectations were not met, the followers were quick to challenge the leaders. For example, the president negotiated a very equitable deal with housing officials to assure that residents would have a home in the new housing structures that were being planned. These developments were completed several years after the fieldwork I conducted, and by that time the president had lost power and the deal fell apart, leaving residents scrambling for a place to live in the new structures. The residents blamed the former president after the fact. Nevertheless, at public meetings and private interactions among RAC members during this time, no one held back their thoughts and feelings, and the voices may have been loud, but there was always respect and civility when the discussion concluded. The point to underscore, however, is that there was an even wider gap between RAC members and the remainder of the project's residents, some of whom didn't have the foggiest idea of what was going on within their communities.

Much of the discussion and disappointment noted above soon took a backseat to other developments. In July 1992, church officials made efforts to remove Father Boyle, the proactive and greatly admired and respected parish priest. In the heavily charged struggle that ensued, the Jesuit provincial of the western region of the United States was called in to meet with community leaders and other city leaders, who by that time had become avid supporters of Father Boyle. The meeting was held in the small Dolores Mission church, and the provincial addressed the overflow crowd, explaining that the authority of his office deemed that Father Boyle was to be sent elsewhere to serve another congregation. Entertaining questions and other near outbursts from the audience, the priest had homeboys crying and pleading on their knees for him to reconsider his announced decision, to no avail. The Jesuit stood fast, and as he made his exit, the crowd of people outside the church heard the news and proceeded to smash his automobile.

Many of us began to make phone calls and spread the word about this decision. I had a long phone conversation with the newly appointed provincial and discovered there was still hope. With all the networking and pressure from many different sources, the new provincial was won over and decided that Father Boyle would remain in his ministry.

This religious political brouhaha shook up the community, and simultaneously there was a tremendous eruption of gang warfare. Both of these events worked to make Pico Gardens a very unattractive place for drug suppression attempts. Drug elimination, in the thoughts and actions of the residents, had become secondary to survival, it seemed. As the wife noted during an interview with a Chicano couple in their forties with four children, "You have to watch your own back even if you know the people and what is going on."

The Big Shoot-out described in Chapter Five serves as an example of how volatile the projects could be. In the aftermath of this affair, the air was filled with accusations and recriminations involving a number of people and public institutions, and several meetings were held with residents and police officials. I was brought into the proceedings on the basis of my membership on police advisory boards and working relationships with police authorities. Residents now were even more polarized in opinion than before, as some lined up with calls for a larger and more effective police presence and strengthening of the Neighborhood Watch program, while others continued to clamor for fairer and more even-handed treatment of residents and especially the youth. Previously, it was mentioned that the police used to beat suspects before taking them to jail, but that practice had changed. As so often happens, however, an old practice had become a myth that still dominated project residents' thinking.

The drug counseling service mentioned above, L.A. CADA, was initially located in the Pico Gardens projects, but this very convenience made it difficult for Aliso Village residents because of local gang rivalries; later, as noted above, L.A. CADA moved and the situation was reversed. Other East Los Angeles counseling services had similar drawbacks, and many services to which residents might be referred were difficult to reach without a car, adding even more hindrances to what already was a problematic sell.

When L.A. CADA deployed a counselor at the housing project's center offices, the counselor spent time working through the personal problems of his clients, especially substance abuse. One afternoon I observed two young male residents waiting for their counseling sessions. One of them was accompanied by his mother. When I later questioned the counselor, he reported that most of his clients were brought to him by their mothers. He also said that he provided individual and family counseling and occasional team counseling and often made referrals to other programs. Most of his clients had drug- or alcohol-related problems.

However, the general consensus of the residents was that many persons who abused alcohol and chemical substances did not readily seek or use the services, and those individuals who went to the counselor usually were brought there by a parent or other close relation or a friend. There was a clear reluctance of substance abusers to seek help, and this was magnified when service away from the neighborhood was advised or residents were unaware of the counselor's schedule.

The interventions might have lessened the drug activities within the housing area, but several residents pointed out that the parking lot and gang hangouts across from the project continued to be centers of drug activities. Others said that drug use and sales continued at times in darker corners of the project, such as stairwells and narrow passageways between project buildings. Informants who belonged to Neighborhood Watch wanted to help the bike patrols, albeit unevenly, and expressed a continuing need to monitor foot traffic and behavior in their immediate vicinity and to report suspicious movements and/or people. Generally, however, residents wished that these patrols could be around-the-clock.

For the younger children, a "Just Say No" workshop was held every week by a volunteer associated with the school district. Residents considered this effort highly valuable because they believed that the children, reflecting the success of early education on tobacco use, would learn to appreciate the destructiveness of drugs and thus avoid experimentation and use of drugs. Unfortunately, for some of the children observed during the fieldwork, their close ties and exposure to older brothers, uncles, and other family members who used drugs diluted such workshop knowledge, since the powerful influence of these role models was a daily occurrence.

It was clear to me that the buoyed spirit of the residents in the early phase of the Pro-Force program had been replaced by disappointment and, in some instances, a feeling of betrayal. Notwithstanding these sentiments, it seemed that the drug problems were so widespread and intractable among the three housing projects that resources to combat them must, of necessity, be increased to a magnitude that many would consider impossible in this era of especially limited funding. Marijuana and beer were the two most popular mind-altering substances. The drug counselor working under the auspices of L.A. CADA explained that he could be present in the project only one day each week because his program was funded on the basis of the welfare agency's qualification of individual resident families for his services. He also pointed out that rivalries between Pico Gardens–area gangs and Aliso Village–area gangs made it unsafe for residents of other projects to visit these areas for counseling service.

All of the residents who were interviewed, and most of those with whom informal discussions were held, were well aware and supportive of the presence of the Pro-Force bike patrols. Each resident reported that the observable gang activity, drug use, and drug sales diminished almost to zero when the bikes were patrolling. However, as one resident commented, "As soon as they leave, it all comes right back." She, and most of the others, expressed a wish that the bike patrols could be there permanently. One woman noted, however, that some residents had expressed displeasure with the added patrol, and she cynically added, "But they're the same ones who yell when something happens and the police are not there." One resident questioned why none of the youth activities promised in the initial intervention had yet been set up. The 4-H Club meetings and regular activities sponsored by Los Angeles city parks were apparently not enough for all the youth in the vicinity, as the demographics for the area showed a very high number of youth. Nevertheless, at an affair celebrating the fiftieth anniversary of the

Marching during the fiftieth anniversary of the projects

projects, residents seemed to appreciate the presence and relaxed demeanor of the bike patrol officers. According to the supervising officer of the patrol, there was an expectation that in the future there would be more officers, and thus a more consistent and regular patrol pattern for the housing project. Those promises, unfortunately, never came to fruition.

Irrespective of the drug intervention developments, as I became entrenched in the neighborhood, I witnessed more drug sales and drug use. The street element in the projects became more comfortable and acted natural when I was around. Residents also began to express more displeasure with the brazen drug activities. In the absence of Pro-Force patrol officers and counseling outreach services, the drug culture had a field day.

At some RAC gatherings, it was clear that the participants wanted to bring about changes by providing additional resources for their children. However, there was a decided contrast in opinion on how this should be done. Some parents, especially from outside the projects (identifying themselves with Neighborhood Watch), emphasized more and better policing as a solution, whereas the project parents suggested that heavy-handed policing was one of the worst problems the community had. Although this intragroup strain stimulated a lively discussion, it was still apparent that all the mothers present wanted changes and wished to rid themselves of the worst effects of gangs and drugs.

Their reactions to previously noted gang-shooting incidents clarified

Preteen marchers pose for cameraman

how different the two groups are. Neighborhood Watch adherents practiced a type of community surveillance in which a resident who viewed something or someone suspicious would make a phone call that snowballed into a series of phone calls by others, thus notifying everyone in the social network to step outside their apartment and nonchalantly but collectively view the wrongdoer. A simpler method would have been to notify the police so that a squad car would appear within minutes. Comite por Paz also supported the police but preferred to work on bringing the potential culprits into the fold, so to speak, with a community-based solution. In addition, several of the members of this group had charged the police with abusive behavior toward alleged suspects in these affairs. Many residents who were united in objective (get rid of problems) but wavered regarding the means to achieve it (more police versus more community) belonged to both groups.

CHAPTER TWELVE

CONCLUSION AND RECOMMENDATIONS

In this exploration of the dynamics of family life in a low-income neighborhood, I hope that what separates gang from non-gang members has been better confirmed. Keeping the community and neighborhood effects constant, the variation in households and family members (i.e., family income, occupation, education, size of families, and even child-rearing practices) provides an indication of why some families have gang members and others do not (Gehlke-Baez 2004). Street socialization thrives when adult family members are stressed, bereft of coping skills, and unable to guide their children. The result is that untethered youth are raised in the streets by multiple-aged peer groups and thus more likely to become gang members. Much of the multilevel analysis in the present study strove to show the linkages between community and broader macro-level developments, meso-level family issues, and the individual micro details of street and gang life (Hayden 2004; Vigil 1998).

I have attempted to provide a community foundation and context for how household heads toil and raise their children. There are fairly clear reasons why some families succeed in steering their children in the conventional direction and away from gangs. This is especially so for parents who adhere to authoritative child-rearing practices. In addition, there are several explanations for the families that are unable to find their way and thus come up short for their children. Although structural problems affected all the families in this study, the families that were most lacking in resources had the most serious troubles with their children; even something as simple as automobile ownership was a problem for these families in a region such as Southern California, where cars are considered essential. Moreover, personal and emotional difficulties abounded for these families, as the adults seemed to have lost their coping skills and strategies because of early unresolved traumas and voids in their own lives. In short, in a poor neighborhood there is a range of variation of poverty and personal problems, as the influence of place and lack of status affect people differently. Some immigrants, for example, cannot adequately cope with the demands of their new environment. Adults raised in households maintained by these struggling newcomers will also be less likely to establish their own families on a firm economic and emotional footing.

Multiple marginality marks these families, as socioeconomic woes contribute to the unraveling of social control in so many ways. Parents represent lower educational and lower-income levels than those of their neighbors, even in generally low-income areas, and thus have limited access to resources. These factors, coupled with larger family size and smaller household space, result in crowded, less integrated families. Parenting efforts and skills are sharply hamstrung, and emotional baggage of the parents continues to undermine their resilience and ability to raise their children. Competition for space and stress in families crowd children out of the home and onto the streets, where other human forces begin to dominate. Yet another level of crowdedness is found in this public space, making "turf" a high priority for street gang members. In addition to macro and meso forces, micro conditions also weigh in. Sampson et al. (1997) state: "Economic stratification by race and place thus fuels the neighborhood concentration of cumulative forms of disadvantage" (919).

For example, a quick comparison of non-gang vis-à-vis gang families is highlighted in two cases. In spite of poverty and meager resources for raising her seven children, Sonia (whose non-gang family is fully described in Chapter Nine) had maintained an unsteady foothold with a mix of economic activities and assistance: AFDC, food stamps, and subsidized housing, along with garment district work, sewing for local neighbors, an entrepreneurial flair with flea markets and the like, and a husband who occasionally assisted with money from part-time auto repair work. Having finished high school and one year of college in Mexico, Sonia wisely stressed education and conventional behavior for her children, and with only symbolic help from her husband she taught self-respect and respect for the community to her children: "If you watch out for your children, they know that they are wanted and loved. They will respond in a positive way." As an authoritative parent in a very tightly centered household where all members came together daily for dinner, she occupied all her children's time with many social and recreational activities and programs.

In contrast, Juana was the matriarch of a gang family of nine children (described in Chapter Ten). Her shaky life actually began in Mexico, with errant parents and older, feeble grandparents as caretakers. Only reaching second grade in school, she never learned to read and write in Spanish, much less English when she arrived in the United States at age twenty-two to seek a better life. Early on, she found social and emotional support with boy-friends, and at age fourteen had her first child. Serial boyfriends continued in Mexico and the United States, and although having children had never resulted in a stable or permanent relation with any of the fathers, she had had nine children by the time she reached the age of thirty-four. With no education and no skills to speak of, she never had a permanent job and re-lied strictly on welfare. Always in denial about her children's behavior, she never took responsibility for them and the bad habits they were learning on the streets or at school. Instead, she spent most of her time with a series of boyfriends. One son was a member of Cuatro Flats and was incarcerated, and the others were street socialized in one way or another. With no local community ties or activities and no car or driver's license, she was isolated from most conventional routines.

A number of themes are present in these accounts and underscore the dif-ferences between non-gang and gang families. Educational background, ac-cess to economic resources, emotional and social stability, and child-rearing strategy separate the two family types. Although all families in Pico Gar-dens are financially strapped, gang-involved families are even more so. The large family size hinders the single head of household's ability to creatively deal with the challenges faced in providing for her children, simply because it is logistically difficult to take care of all of the financial and emotional demands involved. Paired with a lack of a stable companion to help with the raising of the children, a large family size makes for a highly challenging scenario.

External forces also affect attitudes and behaviors, such as a limited police presence, which invites even more criminals to the area, and overcrowded, ill-equipped schools whose teachers are overwhelmed. Where more sensi-tized police officers are needed, there are fewer; where there should be more and better-trained teachers, there are also too few. The deficiencies heighten the difficulties associated with isolated single-parent households (McLana-han and Booth 1989; McLanahan and Sandefur 1994), a significant depen-dency on outside agencies and individuals, and the crippling emotional baggage that many of the parents have carried with them since their own childhood (Loeber and Stouthamer-Loeber 1986).

In many cases, conflictual or dysfunctional home relationships that are

Showing the baby off

encumbered with domestic violence may further the allure of gang membership by pushing vulnerable youth out of the home and into the street. With
families vulnerable and schooling and policing practices tenuous at best,
it is no wonder that even concerted societal plans to counter these gang
effects fall short. Furthermore, when poverty, single parenthood, and youth
are intertwined, there is a higher risk that children will deviate from conventional paths (Farrington 1994; McLanahan and Sandefur 1994), a dynamic
that lays bare the actions and reactions of multiple marginality.

The lack of efficacy and consistency related to social control efforts can
be traced to a number of influential factors; chief among them are concentrated disadvantage, immigration concentration, and residential stability
(Sampson et al. 1997). Further, there is a lack of coordination and cooperation between various agencies and formal authorities in their attempts to
reduce gang activity. Law enforcement agencies, social service agencies, and
schools all serve interrelated functions in the community. These indispens-

able functions, as well as the overall authority of the individual agents of social control, are weakened by the pervasive lack of mutual acknowledgement and purposive organization among them. For example, why are there three separate police forces that serve the population (LAPD, housing police, and school police) yet, to an outside observer, manifest no coordination or cooperation?

Furthermore, on the rare occasion that efforts at interagency coordination are meaningfully attempted, this initiative is hampered by a lack of understanding of the origins of gang activity as they relate to family processes (see Klein and Maxson 2006 for how street gangs are misunderstood by most social caretakers). It is important for interacting agencies to agree on their conceptualization of the dynamic relationship between gang membership and family processes so that goals and interventions are in alignment. In other words, social control agencies must be both "on the same verse" and "on the right page" of the issue. For example, most caretakers lump all project residents into the same category and formulate "one size fits all" policy approaches. Moreover, the LAPD has such a guarded apprehension of the community that its absence further exacerbates the already well-entrenched criminal activities, making the neighborhood projects a free crime zone on too many occasions.

A rethinking of what constitutes gang membership—having, at once, a nuanced and comprehensive understanding of the interplay between interpersonal, familial, and community-level variables—is fundamental. Macro, meso, and micro levels are intertwined, and there are actions and reactions among them (see Sampson et al. 1997 for how the wider political economy affects poor people). In terms of gang activity in Pico Gardens, there is a tendency for social control agents to focus solely on "fixing" individuals rather than looking at the broader contexts in which the individuals are embedded (see Heath and McLaughlin 1993). While "fixing" individuals is important in its own right, we should also consider "fixing" the social and familial contexts of society as well.

A dedicated probation officer with decades of experience in the area, and who worked with many residents of Pico Gardens, was one of the few individuals I came across who recognized this common, even obvious pattern. The officer observed that there are at least two means by which families influence the production and reproduction of gang activity. The first is the tendency for siblings to become associated with gang life. Generally speaking, one child's decision to become part of a gang greatly enhances the likelihood that other siblings (and cousins, etc.) will follow suit. Although this may be the first and only instance of gang affiliation in a particular family, its long-term potential is significant. The enduring reality is that multiple siblings in a gang preclude societal interventions based on individual rationales. An approach for alleviating conditions that contribute to the problems the entire family faces must be entertained. Complex, sophisticated responses must be generated that acknowledge the significance of the family and the broader, deeper forces that mold and hold the family.

The second, and perhaps even more compelling, means by which gang-affiliated families assert influence over gang activity is in the perpetuation of gang bonds across generations. In such families, children may be encouraged by older relatives (i.e., grandparents and parents), sometimes inadvertently, to identify with a gang that the family is traditionally associated with. Because of the physical and emotional nature of these powerful influences, such models for gang involvement are impossible to avoid. Choices for youth in this context are not choices in the true sense of the word. The learning climate inside the home often determines the path and direction.

Gang culture on occasion may be learned in the household, but lest we forget, the grim material conditions that are transmitted and reproduced intergenerationally are what constitute the base. Life, for such families in these situations, is generally characterized by a cycle of poverty and lack of opportunity that thwarts social mobility aspirations. As a solution, removing a child from such families seems to ignore this incontrovertible fact, the first cause if you will, for the problem is not merely the influence of the family on the child but the influence of crushing socioeconomic forces on the family and child as well.

Yet even when the effects of family influences on gang association are acknowledged, social control authorities still fail to make the crucial connection between these influences and those of the streets. Street socialization takes on an elevated importance in the formation of gang members' personal and group identities. For the young people in the neighborhood whose families are pushing and/or pulling them into gangs, the additional influence of peers adds weight to the process, a pressure that is compounded by existing economic and cultural stressors. Efforts at controlling this situation have proven inadequate.

Understandably, it is easier for law enforcement agents to focus on removing or limiting peer group power than to identify the underlying processes that generate the level and intensity of street socialization. Since a punitive criminal justice response is increasingly the rule, such basic considerations are unintentionally overlooked or deliberately ignored. In part this is so because punishment is overused due to a lack of coordination between law enforcement and other caretaker agencies that have a less punitive, more

Three types of cops *(counterclockwise from top left):* school, housing, and LAPD

preventative focus. For this reason, the police in Pico Gardens are particularly insensitive to the causative factors contributing to gang activity. This need not be the case. A relatively recent program has shown that the police and other institutions can combine their expertise and resources to combat gangs. GREAT (Gang Resistance Education and Training) is a nationwide anti-gang program offered in middle schools in various cities. Police officers regularly conduct a series of workshops that inform and prepare young adolescents for the pressures and lures of the streets, hoping to gang-proof them during their early teen years (see Esbensen 2004; Peterson and Esbensen 2004).

The lack of cooperation between caretaker agencies can be attributed to a number of existing tensions. For example, the strain between the different law enforcement agencies that patrol Pico Gardens adversely affects the smooth coordination of related efforts. The Pico Gardens housing police and the community patrol officers working out of the Los Angeles Police Department (LAPD) have a somewhat adversarial relationship, resulting from jurisdictional (boundary) conflicts and professional jealousies. This gulf is exacerbated by their differing attitudes and contrasting styles of policing: the housing police take a more community-oriented approach while the LAPD prefers a detached, "professional" protocol that stresses formal authority, "gang sweeps," and Neighborhood Watch programs.

Consequently, the housing police have established rapport with the community that the LAPD officers have been unable and unwilling to attain. At first glance this appears beneficial to the housing authorities as well as to the community. In the long run, however, this unspoken rivalry undermines what could be a multipronged effort at limiting gang activity, especially violence. Without coordination of objectives and activities, inconsistencies result in missed opportunities for meaningful intervention. The Pro-Force bike patrols in the early 1990s show that such coordination can make a difference (see Chapter Eleven).

Other social control agencies experience similar unevenness, though to a lesser degree. Public service providers engage in mutually beneficial cooperative agreements with other agencies. Whenever established organizations with contrasting goals and perspectives begin the challenging process of coordination, however, disagreements and intransigence are likely to arise. Agencies, and their representatives, are then faced with the choice of compromising their own goals in the name of peace or maintaining their focus and thereby generating more tension.

The Los Angeles County Probation Department is facing this dilemma with respect to the Pico Gardens officers. Probation has a different mandate in that its guiding principle is to help offenders complete community-based rehabilitation, while also providing supervision sufficient to ensure safety. Consequently, probation officers enjoy a different relationship with the general public, one that is less formal, more amenable to compromise and innovation. These officers generally resort to recommending punishment only after efforts to rehabilitate have failed or there is evidence of additional offending. When clients violate the terms of their release, probation officers are often the ones who know enough about their personal life and extended social networks to apprehend them. These occasions necessitate working closely with local police and interacting in a different manner with the public.

To develop working relationships that are free of conflicts, probation officers may sometimes assume a more traditional, adversarial law enforcement stance. Temporarily changing the comportment of a few officers for the sake of these brief collaborations permits the preservation of professional relationships with other police departments. Yet, even as relationships with other police departments may be improved by the collaboration, residents ultimately suffer as the multifaceted response model promoted through rehabilitation is ignored and the less formal promising approach of probation is left by the wayside.

Continuation school in the projects

Agencies that traditionally have more preventative aims also suffer from a lack of coordination. Schools, thought by many to be the most influential preventative institutions outside of families, tend to have very loose ties with both similarly oriented agencies (such as community action or religious groups) as well as law enforcement and probation agencies. Agencies such as Hope for Youth and Community Youth Gang Services (now replaced by the city's L.A. Bridges Program) have forged connections with neighborhood schools as special intervention/prevention programs. However, limited resources make it difficult for these fledging partnerships to serve as a consistent force in the neighborhood. For example, of the $83 million allocated for gangs in the city of Los Angeles in 2005, $57 million went to suppression and the remainder to prevention and intervention combined.

Moreover, schools suffer from a tremendous lack of funding, and the local high school is overcrowded. This renders them unequipped to address the special needs or learning disabilities of youth coming from marginalized communities. Even special schools—like the Dolores Mission Alternative School started by Father Boyle, the founder of Homeboy Industries—have been unable to fill these needs. Father Boyle has moved his school to the Aliso side of the projects. However, because Cuatro Flats members cannot attend a school that is in rival gang territory for fear of losing their lives, there is still a major gap in terms of the educational avenues available to many of the gang-involved youth in Pico Gardens.

Another factor that hinders social control efforts in Pico Gardens is rampant drug abuse in the community. The effects of drug addiction and heavy drug use absorb much of the energy of folks dealing with the problem, leaving few resources to contribute to any other sort of personal change such as leaving the gang or, in the case of those with children, the acquisition of parenting skills. The young people of Pico Gardens have a variety of reasons for using drugs. Notably, the desire to escape conflict at home and in the neighborhood often motivates youth to join gangs. Such reasons often hinge on the inability to deal with deep-seated childhood trauma such as the involuntary separation from one or both parents, molestation, and neglect (see Chapter Ten).

Neglect is inherent in a number of situations and is by no means always intentional. In some cases, single parents using permissive or authoritarian parenting strategies unwittingly neglect the needs of their children, leading the children to rebel. Sometimes children are reacting to abuse suffered in the home or responding to abuse their mothers have endured at the hands of a spouse or partner. The cycle of abuse is then carried out internally through the heavy use of drugs or, in the instances of cholas, the persistence of this abusive treatment at the hands of male gang members. In other cases, the neglect is simply the result of economic exigencies that rob parents of the time and energy to adequately monitor their children. Adults who engage in petty entrepreneurship activities or hold multiple jobs tend to be away from their children in spite of their very best intentions. The children are subsequently free to roam the neighborhood, where they can easily become involved in the pervasive use of drugs that occurs in Pico Gardens and other economically distressed communities.

Despite the prevalence of drug use in Pico Gardens, there is a noticeable lack of prevention and rehabilitation information available for drug users and their families. Health and social services are scarce due, in large part, to the scandals in the 1970s when many of the drug rehabilitation centers were taken over by older, former gang members and other criminal elements. During this period, ex-offenders organized self-help groups and became somewhat active in civil rights strivings but succumbed to the temptation of making such centers money-making outlets for drug sales and distribution. Despite this history, one resource does exist for Pico Gardens residents, L.A. CADA. But as with Father Boyle's continuation school, its location in one gang's territory makes it difficult for people in the rival gang to access its services.

From the start, one of the goals of this investigation was to examine some of the key factors promoting the maintenance and expansion of gang activity at both macro and micro levels of analysis. At the macro level, a striking shift in the demographics of welfare recipients taking place at the time of the study (pre–welfare reform) and the aging of the local youth gang resulted in an increasingly large population vulnerable to the call of the streets (Venkatesh 1996). At the same time, all residents of Pico Gardens are faced with the environmental and socioeconomic conditions that are unquestionably substandard. Improving the ambient conditions of the neighborhood would alleviate, if not eradicate, the many social control problems that mark the community and resident gang.

The physical disorganization of the housing development exacerbates the many problems that social control agencies encounter on a daily basis. As noted previously, cooperation among social control agencies is rare; their efforts all too often are ineffectual. Police-community relations have historically been hostile and antagonistic (see Morales 1972 and Escobar 1998 for an account of relations between Mexicans and the police, as well as policing patterns and conflict in East Los Angeles). This antagonism has led to an unpredictable and occasionally volatile situation, in which both law enforcement and community residents harbor cynical and wary attitudes toward one another. With the exception of the actions of the public housing police, patrolling and monitoring of the housing development by law enforcement are irregular. Physical disorganization contributes to this state of affairs, allowing residents the excuse for not actively supporting the safety of their neighborhood as well as inspiring fear in the police officers assigned to it.

The LAPD has been especially reluctant to provide a continuing and visible show of force, for fear of community complaints of harassment. Based on paranoia born of reality, law enforcement officers are also hesitant to patrol Pico Gardens because of the chance that they will meet violence themselves. Regrettably, these scenarios are not uncommon. In one particular incident, a patrol car was surrounded by gang youth and the officer in the passenger seat was shot in the jaw. The LAPD, in response to this violent transgression, as noted earlier, significantly minimized its presence in the neighborhood. Moreover, on the rare occasion when officers do patrol, their apprehension, coupled with an aggressive policing style, does not cultivate positive relationships with the residents.

The ineffective or nearly absent policing is partly responsible for drug traffickers, gang members, and other criminal elements being drawn to Pico Gardens in ever-larger numbers. This has essentially transformed the area into a "free crime zone": a lawless community where anything goes and everyone is fair game to be victimized regardless of their community

Neighbors exchanging the day's events

status. In recent years, the neighborhood morphed from a "free crime zone" to a "free war zone," as violence has escalated due, in large part, to the lack of police presence and a pervasive sense of brazenness among the youth. Ironically, absent parenting, and now absent policing, along with voids in schooling, have cumulatively left children free to seek and find their own street-controlling influences (Stromquist and Vigil 1996).

The Big Shoot-out of 1993, described in Chapter Five, illustrates the gravity of this transformation. The officers' delayed arrival on the scene suggests a complicit endorsement of violence as an inevitable fact of life in the projects. Moreover, the manner in which law enforcement officers handled the immediate investigation of the crime scene can itself be interpreted as a revictimization of the residents, compounding the traumatic events they had just endured.

When the police finally did converge on the street, they did so in a typical way that flaunted their formal authority, using an assembly of dozens of vehicles and almost fifty officers. Their investigative technique consisted of knocking on every door and apprehending and patting down potential suspects, while at the same time writing tickets for lapsed automobile licenses and other minor infractions. This type of delayed but too-intensive approach, coupled with punitive enforcement of small administrative infractions, is an ineffective means of controlling gang warfare in the neighborhood. Furthermore, non-gang-affiliated residents who desire protection from the violence almost universally abhor it.

Policy Recommendations

A number of policy recommendations can be derived from the results of the present study on gangs and family life. These suggestions run the gamut in levels of analysis and breadth (Klein and Maxson 2006). To begin with, some of the implications are universal, affecting all of the families who reside in public housing developments like Pico Gardens. Two concerns are crucial: parental education and police. The remainder are also important but are much more difficult to implement.

Parental education is vital (Dinkmeyer and McKay 1976; Patterson 1975), especially addressing the parents' personal traumas. Because so many parents were very young themselves when they began parenting, they may benefit from learning about the authoritative approach successfully used in many non-gang-affiliated families. A parenting program could be designed and run by mothers within the neighborhood or by an outside entity such as a nonprofit agency. Proven strategies such as setting appropriate limits and adequately supervising children under their care can be taught. In addition, older children in the household might be involved in the program for additional reinforcement as well as preparation for the future when they may be parents or caregivers.

Broader concerns should also be considered, such as the damage that multigenerational gang involvement has on family and individual prospects (Becker 1971; Klein and Maxson 2006). Why are there emotional ties that bond individuals to a particular gang, for instance? In the event that youth will not be dissuaded from participating in gang activity, parents should remain as emotionally involved as possible in their children's lives, a practice that can be learned in parenting training. Even if they have only a modest influence, parents can begin to show their children ways of gaining respect other than through gang association (Schoor 1988).

In addition to parenting classes, various other social, behavioral, and mental health services need to be provided to the parents of Pico Gardens. Marriage counseling and general psychological services must be fashioned to address the cultural practices of the population (Alexander and Parsons 1982). More importantly, these services must be delivered in a manner that is culturally rooted in the entire neighborhood. As part of an extensive violence prevention program modeled on the adaptive principles of public health, we must unequivocally underscore the strong correlation between abuse and conflict in the home and the tendency toward violent gang activity on the streets. It became obvious to our research team that many of the female family heads are stuck in cyclical relationships in which violence or abuse commonly occurs. Although a very complicated, difficult, and sensitive issue for many abused women to discuss, such behavior must be ended, not only for the well-being of the women but also for the elimination of the negative, pathological example it sets for the children (Kruttschmitt et al. 1986). The chola life cycle is the end product of this behavior.

A key recommendation involves exposing residents to the world of possibilities that exist outside the projects. Programs and mechanisms should be developed for residents to become more mobile and experience new places, peoples, and activities outside the projects. Access to affordable transportation would open up the residents' world beyond the borders of Pico Gardens. This effort to connect with a larger society will improve psychological health, which inevitably affects all other elements of a life. Immediately after our fieldwork stay, the principal investigator was able to help formulate such a program for youth ages nine to fourteen. IMPACTO secured housing authority monies and a small grant from the Robert F. Kennedy Memorial to mentor and counsel both youth and families and to introduce the children to social and educational outings that took them to another world—even though parents wished they could be taken, too. The program has had moderate success and is still in operation as of early 2007.

As for the police, allowing a virtual war zone to evolve in Pico Gardens is an approach that not only challenges common sense but also is professionally problematic, in that police are forgoing their official duties. Social control methods of the sort employed by the LAPD disregard the stresses facing a community overwhelmed with social, economic, and personal problems. To close the gaps between the LAPD, other social service provision agencies, and the community, a proactive and positive stance needs to be adopted at the highest levels of departmental policy making so that patrol officers' routine practices are aligned with those of the housing police (Decker and Curry 2003). A community policing outreach program was indeed initiated by the LAPD at the end of this study in Pico Gardens. It has since been rescinded, however, before it could succeed in allaying the deep suspicion and mistrust that characterize resident assessments of the police. Other proactive policy changes need to be formulated and implemented to turn back the decades of resentment.

Less amenable to such straightforward, locally generated policy adaptations, the socioeconomic situation in the public housing projects needs to be given serious attention because it resounds in almost every aspect of life there (Vigil 1998). Income, employment, and other socioeconomic indicators are much lower in Pico Gardens than the national, state, and local averages (see table 2.1, page 31). Further, many household heads are immigrants and as such are subjected to additional cultural stresses and strains. Thus, social and cultural marginality complicates their adaptation to life in the United States, which is already subject to economic marginality. Cumulatively, these barriers and difficulties make their integration to life in the United States far more difficult.

Although Pico Gardens is located only a mile or two from thousands of garment factories and service-oriented industries in Los Angeles (hotels, corporate buildings, and restaurants), few residents are able to secure gainful employment there. The employment careers of the residents of Pico Gardens are fraught with fits and starts, making for an insecure and tenuous footing. As the select family case histories illustrate, education and job training of one sort or another are a common need among the household heads and other adults in our investigation. Many respondents perceptively expressed their anxiety about the entry-level jobs they were once willing to take ten to twenty years ago as newly arrived immigrants. However, these types of jobs no longer provide enough income to sustain their families.

In particular, as somewhat Americanized immigrants, they now understand what constitutes a good job in America: merit salary increases, career ladder growth, health and retirement benefits, decent working conditions, and job security. Having learned the hard way, by losing jobs, being released without cause, usually receiving wages below the minimum standard, or living in unsafe and insecure working conditions, they know when they are being exploited. After years of tacit acceptance, many have grown increasingly intolerant of the unfair treatment routinely meted out by some unethical, opportunistic employers. Unfortunately for those immigrants who demand more for themselves by reaching for the American dream, their appeals go largely unheeded.

For those willing to work, even if it means low pay without benefits, where they live is yet another barrier to successful employment. Potential employers frequently bear prejudices against people from the projects. The two examples of the chicken-processing plant and beer factory provided in Chapter Two show this reluctance to hire from the projects. Clearly, this situation needs to be rectified in order to strengthen the greater community. Especially for the young men of the neighborhood, many benefits would accrue if employment opportunities increased locally, mitigating the problem of youth having too little money and too much spare time. Partnerships need to be established with existing local organizations, as well as new businesses that could be enticed to invest in the community. Along with the logistical advantage of a large, conveniently located workforce and improved economic well-being, the overall social welfare of the community would be buoyed by such revitalization efforts.

To make ends meet, the majority of Pico Gardens residents are on public assistance. If residents had chosen to work during the years that this study took place, they would have lost most or all of this assistance. Residents are thus caught in a bind. The majority prefer to work but are aware that earnings from a low-wage job would barely equal their current meager welfare checks; anyway, few jobs are available. This choice is not an easy one for people to make; the information gathered through our investigation indicates that most residents have worked in the past and would like to work again, given moderate prospects. The preservation of dignity and self-respect in ways however small is especially meaningful for those acutely aware of their marginal status. One woman even declined to apply for the medical coverage she was eligible for after she was laid off, because she viewed the process as too demeaning; contrary to the disparaging public opinion of welfare "freeloaders," many residents try to maintain a sense of dignity in the face of want.

The cumulative effect of all of the economic forces at work in Pico Gardens is a demoralized surplus labor force held prisoner by the whims of welfare policy. To circumvent the difficulties that arise due to the low-wage ceiling requirement placed on welfare recipients, policies should be amended to temporarily allow wage-earning work and welfare to coexist. This temporary situation could have a sunset clause until the recipients finish an educational or vocational program that helps prepare them for a better-paying job; such programs still exist, even though there have been many cutbacks in social safety nets. Such simple and practical policies would pay off in the form of more economically stable households better able to address individual problems in their homes. Such a broad family strategy could incorporate the differences between structural and functional factors (Jones and Demaree 1975) or a combination of the two (Huizinga et al. 1991).

Interestingly, the passage of the 1996 Welfare Reform Act created an even more difficult situation for families on welfare. The federally mandated work requirement and five-year time limit on welfare receipt meant these opportunities have been revamped since the end of this study in the middle 1990s. "Work first" or "workfare" is the priority now, and this condition has transformed the way these families can orient their lives.

All residents in Pico Gardens suffer from their current socioeconomic positioning. Policies that provide incentives for businesses to hire public housing residents could help alleviate their problems. Nevertheless, different families cope in a variety of ways with the hand they have been dealt; some ways are much healthier than others. To stop or reduce the levels of gang activity in Pico Gardens, as noted above, a number of additional strategies can be implemented on the familial or individual level.

Similarly, drug treatment centers must offer unrestricted treatment on demand for all Pico Gardens residents, adults and youth alike, without regard to whether they are affiliated with gangs or not (Stanton and Todd 1982). As noted previously, drug use is rampant in the neighborhood and only leads to greater apathy and increased violence. If multiple flexible modalities of drug rehabilitation treatment coupled with adequate social services and support programs were offered, it is likely that some of the gang activity would be curtailed or diverted. Nonetheless, this recommendation is made with a sense that such a battle is not won easily or without serious change on other levels related to law enforcement practices, the economy, and parenting practices. For these and other reasons, its long-term success is uncertain.

All of the aforementioned policy suggestions are means of providing some hope in what often seems to be a despondent, static situation for impoverished residents. Instilling in families a genuine desire to strive for a better future is the one factor that can help them deal with their situations. But it must be a defined future with real possibilities. Time and time again, non-gang-affiliated parents stressed the possibility of a hopeful, brighter future for their children. In the meantime, they struggled against all odds to hope for something better, and this attitude helped them on occasion to improve their lot in life.

REFERENCES

Alexander, J. F., and B. V. Parsons. 1982. *Functional Family Therapy*. Monterey, CA: Brooks/Cole.

Amato, P., and B. Keith. 1991. "Parental Divorce and the Well-being of Children: A Meta Analysis." *Psychological Bulletin* 110:26–46.

Anderson, F. 1989. "Moral Leadership and Transitions in the Urban Black Community." In H. J. Bershady, ed., *Social Class and Democratic Leadership: Essays in Honor of E. Digby Balzell*, 123–146. Philadelphia: University of Pennsylvania Press.

———. 1990. *Streetwise: Race, Class, and Change in an Urban Community*. Chicago: University of Chicago Press.

———. 1999. *The Code of the Streets*. New York: W. W. Norton.

Anderson, E., and D. Massey. 2001. *Problem of the Century: Racial Stratification in the United States*. New York: Russell Sage Foundation.

Ashbury, H. 1927. *Gangs of New York: An Informal History of the Underworld*. New York: Alfred A. Knopf.

Banh, J. 1996. "A Newly Independent and Dangerous Gang: Female Southeast Asian Gangsters—Research and Public Policy." Undergraduate paper, Anthropology Department, UCLA.

Barnard, H. R. 2000. *Research Methods in Cultural Anthropology*. Thousand Oaks, CA: Sage.

Becker, R. 1971. *Parents Are Teachers: A Child Management Program*. Eugene, OR: Castalia.

Bennett, W. J., J. J. DeLulio, Jr., and J. P. Walters. 1996. *Body Count: Moral Poverty . . . and How to Win America's War against Crime and Drugs*. New York: Simon and Schuster.

Berry, M. F., and J. W. Blassingame. *Long Memory: The Black Experience in America*. New York: Oxford University Press, 1982.

Bogardus, E. 1926. *The City Boy and His Problems*. Los Angeles: House of Ralston, Rotary Club of Los Angeles.

———. 1943. "Gangs of Mexican American Youth." *Sociology and Social Research* 28:55–56.

Brody, G., X. Ge, R. Conger, F. Gibbons, V. M. Murry, M. Gerrard, and R. L. Simons. 2001. "The Influence of Neighborhood Disadvantage, Collective Socialization, and Parenting on African American Children's Affiliation with Deviant Peers." *Child Development* 72 (14): 1231–1248.

Brody, G., X. Ge, S. Kim, V. M. Murry, R. L. Simons, F. Gibbons, M. Gerrard, and R. Conger. 2003. "Neighborhood Disadvantage Moderates Associations of Parenting and Older Sibling Problem Attitudes and Behavior with Conduct Disorders in African-American Children." *Journal of Consulting and Clinical Psychology* 71 (2): 211–222.

Bronfenbrenner, U. 1979. *The Ecology of Human Development.* Cambridge, MA: Harvard University Press.

Brown, W. K. 1977. "Black Female Gangs in Philadelphia." *International Journal of Offender Therapy and Comparative Criminology* 21 (3): 221–228.

Bustillo, M. 2002. "State, Youth Sports Advocates Clash over Best Use of Parks." *Los Angeles Times,* December 22, B1, 12.

Campbell, A. 1990. "Female Participation in Gangs." In C. R. Huff, ed., *Gangs in America: Diffusion, Diversity, and Public Policy,* 163–182. Thousand Oaks, CA: Sage.

———. 1991. *The Girls in the Gang.* 2nd ed. Cambridge, MA: Blackwell Publishers.

Canada, G. 1995. *Fist Stick Knife Gun.* Boston: Beacon.

Cardenas, J. 2001. "Programs to Lower Drug Use Face Cuts." *Los Angeles Times,* June 16, B3.

Cartwright, D. S., B. Tomson, and H. Schwartz. 1975. *Gang Delinquency.* Monterey, CA: Brooks/Cole.

Chesney-Lind, M. 1993. "Girls, Gangs and Violence: Anatomy of a Backlash." *Humanity and Society* 17:321–344.

Chesney-Lind, M., and J. Hagedorn, eds. 1999. *Female Gangs in America: Essays on Girls, Gangs, and Gender.* Chicago: Lake View.

Chesney-Lind, M., and R. G. Sheldon. 1992. *Girls: Delinquency and Juvenile Justice.* Pacific Grove, CA: Brooks/Cole.

Chesney-Lind, M., R. G. Sheldon, and K. A. Joe. 1996. "Girls, Delinquency, and Gang Membership." In C. R. Huff, ed., *Gangs in America,* 2nd ed., 185–204. Thousand Oaks, CA: Sage.

Chicano Pinto Research Project (CPRP). 1979. *The Los Angeles Pinto: Background Papers and Advanced Report of the Chicano Pinto Research Project.* Los Angeles: Chicano Pinto Research Project.

Cohen, A. 1955. *Delinquent Boys: The Culture of the Gang.* Glencoe, IL: Free Press.

Cohen, J., and G. Tita. 1999. "Spatial Diffusion in Homicide: Exploring a General Method of Detecting Spatial Diffusion Processes." *Journal of Quantitative Criminology* 15 (4): 451–493.

Cohen, P., L. Robins, and C. Slomkowski. 1999. "The Relation of Community and Family Risk among Urban Poor Adolescents." In P. Cohen, L. Robins, and C. Slomkowski, eds., *Where and When: Influence of His-*

torical Time and Place on Aspects of Psychopathology, 281–299. Hillside, NJ: Lawrence Erlbaum Associates.

Cole, M., and S. Cole. 1989. *The Development of Children*. New York: W. H. Freeman.

Coleman, J. 1988. "Social Capital in the Creation of Human Capital." *American Journal of Sociology* 94 (Suppl.): 95–120.

Colvin, M., F. Cullen, and T. V. Van. 2002. "Coercion, Social Support, and Crime: An Emerging Theoretical Consensus." *Criminology* 40 (1): 19–42.

Condon, M. 1989. "Public Housing, Crime, and the Labor Market." Master's thesis, Harvard University.

Conger, R. D., X. Ge, G. Elder, F. Lorenz, and R. Simons. 1994. "Economic Stress, Coercive Family Processes, and Developmental Problems of Adolescents." *Child Development* 65:541–561.

Copeland, A. P. 1991. *Studying Families*. Thousand Oaks, CA: Sage.

Curry, G. D. 1995. "Responding to Female Gang Involvement." Paper presented at the American Society of Criminology annual meeting, November.

Daly, K., and M. Chesney-Lind. 1988. "Feminism and Criminology." *Justice Quarterly* 5 (4): 497–538.

Dawley, D. 1990. *A Nation of Lords*. Prospect Heights, IL: Waveland.

Decker, S. H. 1996. "Collective and Normative Features of Gang Violence." *Justice Quarterly* 13:243–264.

Decker, S. H., and D. Curry. 2003. "Suppression without Prevention, Prevention without Suppression: Gang Intervention in St. Louis." In S. H. Decker, ed., *Policing Gangs and Youth Violence*, 191–213. Belmont, CA: Wadsworth Thomson Learning.

Decker, S. H., and B. Van Winkle. 1996. *Life in the Gang: Family, Friends, and Violence*. New York: Cambridge University Press.

Dinkmeyer, D., and G. D. McKay. 1976. *Systematic Training for Effective Parenting*. Circle Pines, MN: American Guidance.

Dodge, K. A., G. S. Pettit, and J. E. Bates. 1994. "Socialization Mediators of the Relation between Socioeconomic Status and Child Conduct Problems." *Child Development* 65:649–665.

Dornbusch, S. N., J. M. Carlsmith, S. J. Bushwall, P. L. Ritter, H. Leiderman, A. H. Hastorf, and R. T. Gross. 1985. "Single Parents, Extended Households, and the Control of Adolescents." *Child Development* 56:326–341.

Dubrow, N., and J. Garbarino. 1989. "Living in the War Zone: Mothers and Young Children in a Public Housing Development." *Child Welfare* 68:3–20.

Dunworth, T. 1994. *Drugs and Crime in Public Housing: A Three-City Analysis*. Washington, DC: U.S. Department of Justice, National Institute of Justice.

Duran, M. 1992. *Don't Spit on My Corner*. Los Angeles: self-published.

Elder, G. H., Jr., and R. D. Conger. 2000. *Children of the Land: Adversity and Success in Rural America*. Chicago: University of Chicago Press.

Elliott, D. S., D. Huizinga, and S. Menard. 1989. *Multiple Problem Youth*. New York: Springer.

Erikson, E. 1968. "Psychosocial Identity." In D. Sills, ed., *International Encyclopedia of the Social Sciences*, vol. 7, 61–65. New York: Macmillan; Free Press.

Esbensen, F.-A. 2004. *Evaluating GREAT: A School-Based Gang Prevention Program*. Washington, DC: U.S. Department of Justice, National Institute of Justice.

Esbensen, F.-A., and L. T. Winfree. 1998. "Race and Gender Differences between Gang and Non-Gang Youth: Results from a Multisite Survey." *Justice Quarterly* 15 (3): 505–526.

Escobar, E. 1998. *Race, Police, and the Making of a Political Identity: Police-Chicano Relations in Los Angeles, 1900–1945*. Berkeley: University of California Press.

Fanon, F. 1965. *The Wretched of the Earth*. New York: Grove.

Farrington, D. P. 1994. "Early Developmental Prevention of Juvenile Delinquency." *Criminal Behaviour and Mental Health* 4:209–227.

———. 2002. "Key Results from the First Forty Years of the Cambridge Study in Delinquent Development." In T. P. Thornberry and K. Krohn, eds., *Taking Stock of Delinquent Development*, 311–335. New York: Kluwer Academic/Plenum.

Federal Bureau of Investigation (FBI). 1996. *Uniform Crime Reports*. Washington, DC: U.S. Department of Justice.

"Female Offenders in the Juvenile Justice System: Statistic Summary." 1996. Washington, DC: U.S. Department of Justice, Office of Juvenile Justice and Delinquency Prevention (OJJDP).

Fishman, L. T. 1988. "'The Vice Queens': An Ethnographic Study of Black Female Gang Behavior." Paper presented at the American Society of Criminology annual meeting, Chicago, November 11.

Fleisher, M. 1998. *Dead End Kids: Gang Girls and the Boys They Know*. Madison: University of Wisconsin Press.

Franzese, R. J., H. C. Covey, and S. Menard. 2006. *Youth Gangs*. Springfield, IL: Charles C. Thomas.

Fremon, C. 2004. *G-Dog and the Homeboys: Father Boyle and the Gangs of East Los Angeles*. Albuquerque: University of New Mexico Press.

Furstenberg, F. 1993. "How Families Manage Risk and Opportunity in Dangerous Neighborhoods." In W. J. Wilson, ed., *Sociology and the Public Agenda*, 231–258. Newbury Park, CA: Sage.

Garland, R. 1996. "Gangs and Girls in the 'Hood." *Reclaiming Children and Youth* 5 (2): 74–75.

Garrison, J. 2006. "Outspoken LAPD Critic a Gang Backer, Police Say." *Los Angeles Times*, August 6, B1, 14–15.

Gehlke-Baez, R. A. 2004. *The Relationship between Hispanic Gangs and the Structure of the Hispanic Family*. Ann Arbor, MI: UMI Dissertation Services.

Geis, G. 1965. *Juvenile Gangs*. Washington, DC: President's Committee on Juvenile Delinquency and Youth Crime.

Geisman, L., and K. Wood. 1986. *Family and Delinquency: Resocializing the Young Offender*. New York: Human Sciences Press.

"Gender and Gangs." 1994. Prepared by Gang Crime and Law Enforcement

Record Keeping. Washington DC: U.S. Department of Justice, National Institute of Justice.

Giordano, P. C. 1978. "Girls, Guys, and Gangs: The Changing Social Context of Female Delinquency." *Journal of Criminal Law and Criminology* 69 (1): 126–132.

Glueck, S., and E. Glueck. 1950. *Unraveling Juvenile Delinquency.* New York: Commonwealth Fund.

Goering, J., and M. Coulibably. 1989. "Investigating Public Housing Segregation: Conceptual and Methodological Issues." *Urban Affairs Quarterly* 25: 265–297.

Gonzalez, N. A., A. M. Cauce, R. J. Friedman, and C. A. Mason. 1996. "Family, Peer, and Neighborhood Influences on Academic Achievement among African American Adolescents: One-Year Prospective Effects." *American Journal of Community Psychology* 24 (3): 365–387.

Gorman-Smith, D., P. Tolan, R. Loeber, and D. B. Henry. 1998. "Relation of Family Problems to Patterns of Delinquent Involvement among Urban Youth." *Journal of Abnormal Child Psychology* 26 (5): 319–344.

Gorman-Smith, D., P. Tolan, and D. B. Henry. 1999. "The Relation of Community and Family Risk among Urban Poor Adolescents." In P. Cohen, L. Robins, and C. Slomkowski, eds., *Where and When: Influence of Historical Time and Place on Aspects of Psychopathology,* 217–238. Hillside, NJ: Lawrence Erlbaum Associates.

———. 2002. "A Developmental-Ecological Model of the Relation of Family Functioning to Patterns of Delinquency." *Journal of Quantitative Criminology* 16 (2): 169–198.

Greenwood, P. W., K. E. Model, C. P. Rydell, and J. Chiesa. 1996. *Diverting Children from a Life of Crime: Measuring Costs and Benefits.* Santa Monica, CA: Rand.

Haapasalo, J., and E. Pokela. 1999. "Child Rearing and Child Abuse Antecedents of Criminality." *Aggression and Violent Behavior* 4 (1): 107–127.

Hagedorn, J. 1988. *People and Folks: Gangs, Crime, and the Underclass in a Rustbelt City.* Chicago: Lake View.

———. 2002. "Gangs and the Informal Economy." In C. R. Huff, ed., *Gangs in America III,* 101–120. Thousand Oaks, CA: Sage.

Hamburg, D. 1992. *Today's Children: Creating a Future for a Generation in Crisis.* New York: Times Books.

Hannerz, U. 1969. *Soulside: Inquiries into Ghetto Culture and Community.* New York: Columbia University Press.

Hanson, K. 1964. *Rebels in the Street: The Story of New York's Girl Gangs.* Englewood Cliffs, NJ: Prentice Hall.

Harris, M. 1988. *Cholas.* New York: AMS Press.

Hayasaki, E. 2001. "A Bridge Successfully Crossed: LA Bridges Anti-Gang Program; Facts on Middle School Graduates." *Los Angeles Times,* June 26, CC, 3.

Hayden, T. 2004. *Street Wars.* New York: New Press.

Hazlehurst, K., and C. Hazlehurst, eds. 1998. *Gangs and Youth Subcultures: International Explorations.* New Brunswick, NJ: Transaction.

Heath, S. B., and M. W. McLaughlin, eds. 1993. *Identity and Inner-City Youth:*

Beyond Ethnicity and Gender. New York: Teachers College, Columbia University.

Herrenkohl, E. C., R. C. Herrenkohl, and B. P. Egolf. 2003. "The Psychological Consequences of Living Environment Instability on Maltreated Children." *American Journal of Orthopsychiatry* 73 (4): 367–380.

Hil, R., and A. McMahon. 2001. *Families, Crime, and Juvenile Justice.* New York: Peter Lang.

Hirschi, T. 1969. *Causes of Delinquency.* Berkeley: University of California Press.

———. 1995. "The Family." In J. Q. Wilson and J. Petersilia, eds., *Crime,* 121–140. San Francisco: Institute for Contemporary Studies Press.

Holzman, H. 1996. "Criminological Research on Public Housing: Towards a Better Understanding of People, Places, and Spaces." *Crime and Delinquency* 42:361–378.

Housing Authority of the City of Los Angeles. 1990. "Public Housing Drug Elimination Grant Application: Public Housing Drug Elimination Program." Application submitted to HUD, Los Angeles, California.

Huff, C. R. 1996. "The Gang in the Community." In C. R. Huff, ed., *Gangs in America,* 2nd ed., 75–102. Newbury Park, CA: Sage.

Huizinga, D., F. A. Esbensen, and A. N. Weiber. 1991. "Are There Multiple Paths to Delinquency?" *Journal of Criminal Law and Criminology* 82 (1): 83–118.

Hunt, G., and K. Joe-Laidler. 2001. "Situations of Violence in the Lives of Girl Gang Members." *Health Care for Women International* 22:363–384.

Hunt, G., K. Joe-Laidler, and K. MacKenzie. 2000. "Chillin', Being Dogged, and Getting Buzzed: Alcohol in the Lives of Female Gang Members." *Drugs: Education, Prevention, and Policy* 7:331–353.

Jarrett, R. 1990. "A Comparative Examination of Socialization Patterns among Low-Income African-Americans, Chicanos, Puerto Ricans, and Whites: A Review of the Ethnographic Literature." Unpublished manuscript. New York: Social Science Research Council.

Jencks, C., and S. C. Mayer. 1988. "The Social Consequences of Growing Up in a Poor Neighborhood." In L. Lynn Jr. and M. G. McGeary, eds., *Inner City Poverty in the United States,* 117–156. Washington, DC: National Academy Press.

Joe, K., and M. Chesney-Lind. 1995. "'Just Every Mother's Angel': An Analysis of Gender and Ethnic Variations in Youth Gang Membership." *Gender and Society* 9 (4): 408–431.

Johnson, V., and R. J. Pandina. 1991. "Effects of the Family Environment on Adolescent Substance Abuse, Delinquency, and Coping Styles." *American Journal of Drug Alcohol Abuse* 17:71–88.

Jones, A. P., and R. G. Demaree. 1975. "Family Disruption, Social Indices, and Problem Behavior: A Preliminary Study." *Marriage and the Family* 37:497–504.

Kitano, H. 1989. *Japanese Americans: The Evolution of a Subculture.* Englewood Cliffs, NJ: Prentice Hall.

Klein, M. W. 1971. *Street Gangs and Street Workers.* Englewood Cliffs, NJ: Prentice-Hall.

———. 1995. *The American Street Gang: Its Nature, Prevalence, and Control.* New York: Oxford University Press.

Klein, M. W., and C. Maxson. 2006. *Street Gang Patterns and Policies.* New York: Oxford University Press.

Knight, G. P., L. M. Virdin, and M. Roosa. 1994. "Socialization and Family Correlates of Mental Health Outcomes among Hispanic and Anglo American Children: Consideration of Cross-Ethnic Scalar Equivalence." *Child Development* 65:212–224.

Kruttschmitt, C., L. Heath, and D. Ward. 1986. "Family Violence, Television Viewing Habits, and Other Adolescent Experiences Related to Violent Criminal Behavior." *Criminology* 24 (2): 235–267.

Lauderback, D., J. Hanson, and D. Waldorf. 1992. "'Sisters Are Doin' It for Themselves': A Black Female Gang in San Francisco." *Gang Journal* 1:57–72.

Liebow, E. 1967. *Tally's Corner.* Boston: Little, Brown.

Loeber, R., and D. P. Farrington. 2001. *Child Delinquents: Development, Intervention, and Service Needs.* Thousand Oaks, CA: Sage.

Loeber, R., and M. Stouthamer-Loeber. 1986. "Family Factors as Correlates and Predictors of Juvenile Conduct Problems and Delinquency." In M. Tonry and N. Morris, eds., *Crime and Justice: An Annual Review of Research,* vol. 7, 29–149. Chicago: University of Chicago Press.

Lofland, J., and L. H. Lofland. 2005. *Analyzing Social Settings.* Belmont, CA: Wadsworth.

Maniglia, R. 1996. "New Directions for Young Women in the Juvenile Justice System." *Reclaiming Children and Youth* 5 (2): 96–101.

Mason, C. A., A. M. Cauce, N. Gonzalez, and Y. Hiraga. 1996. "Neither Too Sweet nor Too Sour: Problem Peers, Maternal Control and Problem Behavior in African American Adolescents." *Child Development* 67:2115–2130.

Massey, D., and N. Denton. 1993. *American Apartheid: Segregation and the Making of an Underclass.* Cambridge, MA: Harvard University Press.

Massey, D., and S. Kanaiaupuni. 1993. "Public Housing and the Concentration of Poverty." *Social Science Quarterly* 74:109–122.

Matsueda, R., and K. Heimer. 1987. "Race, Family Structure, and Delinquency: A Test of Differential Association and Social Control Theories." *American Sociological Review* 52 (December): 826–840.

Maxson, C., and M. L. Whitlock. 2002. "Joining the Gang: Gender Differences in Risk Factors for Gang Membership." In C. R. Huff, ed., *Gangs in America III,* 19–36. Thousand Oaks, CA: Sage.

Maynard, R. A., and E. M. Garry. 1997. "Adolescent Motherhood: Implications for the Juvenile Justice System." Office of Juvenile Justice and Delinquency Prevention Fact Sheet no. 50. Washington, DC: U.S. Department of Justice.

Mayo, Y. Q., and R. P. Resnick. 1996. "The Impact of Machismo on Women." *Journal of Women and Social Work* 11 (3): 257–277.

McCartney, A. 2002. "Theft, Disrespect Upset Graffiti Removal Workers." *Los Angeles Times,* July 13, B3.

McCord, J., C. S. Widom, and N. Crowell, eds. 2001. *Juvenile Crime, Juvenile Justice.* Washington, DC: National Academy Press.

McDonald, J. 2000. *Project Girl.* Berkeley: University of California Press.

McGloin, J. M. 2005. "Policy and Intervention Consideration of a Network Analysis of Street Gangs." *Criminology and Public Policy* 4 (3): 607–636.

McLanahan, S., and K. Booth. 1989. "Mother-Only Families: Problems, Prospects, and Politics." *Journal of Marriage and Family* 51 (August): 557–580.

McLanahan, S., and G. Sandefur. 1994. *Growing Up with a Single Parent: What Hurts, What Helps.* Cambridge: Harvard University Press.

McNulty, T., and S. Holloway. 2000. "Race, Crime, and Public Housing in Atlanta: Testing a Conditional Effect Hypothesis." *Social Forces* 79 (2): 707–726.

Mehren, E. 1996. "Jagged Justice." *Los Angeles Times,* July 9, E1.

Mendoza-Denton, N. 1996. "'Muy Macha': Gender and Ideology in Gang Girls' Discourse about Makeup." *Ethos* 61:47–63.

Miller, J. 2001. *One of the Guys: Girls, Gangs, and Gender.* New York: Oxford University Press.

———. 2002. "The Girls in the Gang: What We've Learned from Two Decades of Research." In C. R. Huff, ed., *Gangs in America III,* 175–198. Thousand Oaks, CA: Sage.

Miller, W. B. 1973. "The Molls." *Society* (2): 32–35.

Miranda, M. K. 2003. *Homegirls in the Public Sphere.* Austin: University of Texas Press.

Moore, J. W. 1978. *Homeboys: Gangs, Drugs, and Prison in the Barrios of Los Angeles.* Philadelphia: Temple University Press.

———. 1989. "Is There a Hispanic Underclass?" *Social Science Quarterly* 70 (2): 265–284.

———. 1991. *Going Down to the Barrio: Homeboys and Homegirls in Change.* Philadelphia: Temple University Press.

———. 1994. "The Chola Life Course." Unpublished paper.

Moore, J. W., and J. M. Hagedorn. 1996. "What Happens to Girls in the Gang?" In C. Ronald Huff, *Gangs in America,* 2nd ed., 205–220. Thousand Oaks, CA: Sage.

Moore, J. W., and J. M. Long. 1981. *Barrio Impact of High Incarceration Rates.* Final report for NIMH. Los Angeles: Chicano Pinto Research Project.

Moore, J. W., and A. Mata. 1981. *Women and Heroin in Chicano Communities.* Los Angeles: Chicano Pinto Research Project.

Moore, J. W., and R. Pinderhughes, eds. 1993. *In the Barrios: Latinos and the Underclass Debate.* New York: Russell Sage Foundation.

Moore, J. W., and J. D. Vigil. 1987. "Chicano Gangs: Group Norms and Individual Factors Related to Adult Criminality." *Aztlan* 18 (2): 27–44.

———. 1993. "Barrios in Transition." In J. W. Moore and R. Pinderhughes, eds., *In the Barrios: Latinos and the Underclass Debate,* 27–49. New York: Russell Sage Foundation.

Moore, J. W., J. D. Vigil, and R. Garcia. 1983. "Residence and Territoriality in Chicano Gangs." *Social Problems* 31 (2): 182–194.

Moore, J. W., J. D. Vigil, and J. Levy. 1995. "Huisas of the Street: Chicana Gang Members." *Latino Studies Journal* 6 (1): 27–48.

Morales, A. 1972. *Ando Sangrando (I Am Bleeding).* La Puente, CA.: Perspectiva.

———. 1982. "The Mexican American Gang Member: Evaluation and Treatment." In R. M. Becerra, M. Karno, and J. I. Escobar, eds., *Mental Health and Hispanic Americans,* 139–155. New York: Grune and Stratton.

Morenoff, J., R. Sampson, and S. Raudenbush. 2001. "Neighborhood Inequality, Collective Efficacy, and the Spatial Dynamics of Urban Violence." *Criminology* 39 (3): 517–559.

Park, R., and E. Burgess. 1924. *Introduction to the Science of Sociology.* 2nd ed. Chicago: University of Chicago Press.

Patterson, G. R. 1975. *Families: Applications of Social Learning to Family Life.* Champaign, IL: Research Press.

Patterson, G. R., J. B. Reid, and T. J. Dishion. 1992. *Antisocial Boys: An Interactional Approach.* Vol. 4. Eugene, OR: Castalia.

Peterson, D., and F.-A. Esbensen. 2004. "The Outlook Is GREAT: What Educators Say about School-Based Prevention and the Gang Resistance Education and Training (GREAT) Program." *Evaluation Review* 28 (3): 215–245.

Popkin, S., V. Gwiasda, L. Olson, D. Rosenbaum, and L. Buron. 2000. *The Hidden War: Crime and Tragedy of Public Housing.* New Brunswick, NJ: Rutgers University Press.

Putnam, R. 1993. "The Prosperous Community: Social Capital and Community Life." *American Prospect* (Spring): 35–42.

Quicker, J. C. 1983. *Homegirls: Characterizing Chicana Gangs.* San Pedro, CA: International Universities Press.

Rainwater, L. 1970. *Behind Ghetto Walls: Black Families in a Federal Slum.* Chicago: Aldine.

Rebellion, C. 2002. "Reconsidering the Broken Homes/Delinquency Relationship and Exploring Its Mediating Mechanism(s)." *Criminology* 40 (1): 103–135.

Reiboldt, W. 2001. "Adolescent Interactions with Gangs, Family, and Neighbors: An Ethnographic Investigation." *Journal of Family Issues* 22 (2): 211–247.

Robins, P. K. 1986. "Child Support, Welfare Dependency, and Poverty." *American Economic Review* 76 (4): 768–786.

Rodriguez, D. 1990. "Chicana Gang Member." Undergraduate paper, Culture Change and the Mexican People course, University of Southern California.

Romo, H. D., and T. Falbo. 1996. *Latino High School Graduation.* Austin: University of Texas Press.

Rosenbaum, J. L. 1989. "Family Dysfunction and Female Delinquency." *Crime and Delinquency* 35:31–44.

Rubinowitz, L., and J. E. Rosenbaum. 2000. *Cross the Class and Color Lines: From Public Housing to Suburbia.* Chicago: University of Chicago Press.

Sampson, R. J. 2002. "The Community." In J. Q. Wilson and J. Petersilia, eds.,

Crime, 193–216. San Francisco, CA: Institute for Contemporary Studies Press.

Sampson, R. J., and W. B. Groves. 1989. "Community Structures and Crime: Testing Social Disorganization Theory." *American Journal of Sociology* 94:774–802.

Sampson, R. J., and J. Laub. 1994. "Urban Poverty and the Family Context of Delinquency: A New Look at Structure and Process in a Classic Study." *Child Development* 65:523–540.

Sampson, R. J., S. Raudenbaush, and F. Earls. 1997. "Neighborhoods and Violent Crime: A Multilevel Study of Collective Efficacy." *Science* (277): 918–924.

Sampson, R. J., J. Morenoff, and F. Earls. 1999. "Beyond Social Capital: Spatial Dynamics of Collective Efficacy for Children." *American Sociological Review* 64:633–660.

Schoor, L. D. 1988. *Within Our Reach: Breaking the Cycle of Disadvantage.* New York: Doubleday.

Shaw, C., and H. McKay. 1942. *Juvenile Delinquency in Urban Areas.* Chicago: University of Chicago Press.

Shelden, R., S. Tracy, and W. Brown. 1997. *Youth Gangs in American Society.* Belmont, CA: Wadsworth.

Short, J. F., Jr. 1996. "Personal, Gang, and Community Careers." In C. R. Huff, *Gangs in America*, 2nd ed., 3–11. Thousand Oaks, CA: Sage.

————. 2001. "Youth Collectivities and Violence." In S. White, ed., *Handbook of Youth and Justice*, 237–264. New York: Kluwer Academic/Plenum.

Short, J. F., Jr., and F. L. Strodtbeck. 1965. *Group Process and Gang Delinquency.* Chicago: University of Chicago Press.

Sikes, G. 1993. *8 Ball Chicks.* New York: Anchor Books.

Smith, C.A., C. Rivera, and T. P. Thornberry. 1997. *Family Disruption and Delinquency: The Impact of Changes in Family Structure on Adolescent Development.* Washington, DC: U.S. Department of Justice, Office of Juvenile Justice and Delinquency Prevention (OJJDP).

Stanton, M. D., and T. Todd. 1982. *Principles and Techniques for Getting "Resistant" Families into Treatment. In* D. Stanton and T. Todd, eds., *The Family Therapy of Drug Abuse and Addiction*, 131–144. New York: Guilford.

Stein, B. D., S. Kataoka, L. H. Jaycox, M. Wong, A. Fink, P. Escudero, and C. Zaragoza. 2003. "Theoretical Basis and Program Design of a School-Based Mental Health Intervention for Traumatized Immigrant Children: A Collaborative Research Partnership." *Journal of Behavioral Health Services and Research* 29 (3): 603–611.

Steinberg, L., S. D. Lamborn, N. Darling, N. S. Mounts, and S. M. Dornbusch. 1994. "Over-Time Changes in Adjustment and Competence among Adolescents from Authoritative, Authoritarian, Indulgent, and Neglectful Families." *Child Development* 65:754–770.

Stole, M. 2004. *African Americans and the Color Line.* New York: Russell Sage Foundation.

Streeter, K. 2005. "Gangs on Back Burner at the Homegirl Café." *Los Angeles Times*, September 5, B1, 12.

Stromquist, N., and J. D. Vigil. 1996. "Violence in Schools in the United States of America: Trends, Causes, and Responses." In J. C. Tedesco, ed., "Violence in the School," special issue, *Prospects* 27 (2): 361–383. Paris: UNESCO, International Bureau of Education.

Stuewig, J., and L. A. McCloskey. 2005. "The Relation of Child Maltreatment to Shame and Guilt among Adolescents: Psychological Routes to Depression and Delinquency." *Child Maltreatment* 10 (4): 324–336.

Suarez-Orozco, C., and M. Suarez-Orozco. 1995. "Migration: Generational Discontinuities and the Making of Latino Identities." In L. Romanucci-Ross and G. De Vos, eds., *Ethnic Identity: Creation, Conflict, and Accommodation*, 321–348. London: Altamira Press.

Sullivan, M. 1989. *"Getting Paid": Youth Crime and Work in the Inner City.* Ithaca, NY: Cornell University Press.

Suttles, G. 1968. *The Social Order of the Slum: Ethnicity and Territory in the Inner City.* Chicago: University of Chicago Press.

Thornberry, T. 1987. "Toward an Interactional Theory of Delinquency." *Criminology* 251:863–892.

Thornberry, T., and M. Krohn. 2001. "The Development of Delinquency: An Interactionist Perspective." In S. White, ed., *Handbook of Youth and Justice*, 289–305. New York: Kluwer Academic/Plenum.

Thornberry, T., C. Smith, C. Rivera, D. Huizinga, and M. Stouthamer-Loeber. 1999. *Family Disruption and Delinquency.* Washington, DC: U.S. Department of Justice, Office of Juvenile Justice and Delinquency Prevention.

Thrasher, F. M. 1927. *The Gang: A Study of 1,313 Gangs in Chicago.* Chicago: University of Chicago Press.

Tiet, Q., H. Bird, M. Davies, C. Hoven, P. Cohen, P. Jensen, and S. Goodman. 1998. "Adverse Life Events and Resilience." *Journal of the American Academy of Child and Adolescent Psychiatry* 37 (11): 1191–1201.

U.S. Census Bureau. 2000. United States Census 2000. http://www.census.gov/main/www/cen2000.html.

Valdez, Avelardo. 2007. *Mexican American Girls and Gang Violence.* New York: Palgrave.

Vale, L. 2000. *From the Puritans to the Projects: Public Housing and Public Neighborhoods.* Cambridge, MA: Harvard University Press.

Venkatesh, S. A. 1996. "The Gang in the Community." In C. R. Huff, ed., *Gangs in America*, 2nd ed., 241–256. Thousand Oaks, CA.: Sage.

———. 2000. *American Project: The Rise and Fall of a Modern Ghetto.* Cambridge, MA: Harvard University Press.

Vigil, J. D. 1983. "Chicano Gangs: One Response to Mexican Urban Adaptation in the Los Angeles Area." *Urban Anthropology* 12 (1): 45–75.

———. 1988a. *Barrio Gangs: Street Life and Identity in Southern California.* Austin: University of Texas Press.

———. 1988b. "Group Processes and Street Identity: Adolescent Chicano Gang Members." *Ethos* 16 (4): 421–445.

———. 1993. "Gangs, Social Control, and Ethnicity: Ways to Redirect Youth." In S. B. Heath and M. W. McLaughlin, eds., *Identity and Inner City Youth: Beyond Ethnicity and Gender*, 94–119. New York: Columbia University Press.

———. 1996. "Street Baptism: Chicano Gang Initiation." *Human Organization* 55 (2): 149–153.

———. 1997. *Personas Mexicanas: Chicano Highschoolers in a Changing Los Angeles*. Fort Worth: Harcourt Brace College Publishers.

———. 1998. *From Indians to Chicanos: The Dynamics of Mexican American Culture*. 2nd ed. Prospect Heights, IL: Waveland. (1st ed., 1980; reprint, 1984.)

———. 1999. "Streets and Schools: How Educators Can Help Chicano Marginalized Gang Youth." *Harvard Educational Review* 69 (3): 270–288.

———. 2002a. "Community Dynamics and the Rise of Street Gangs." In M. Suarez-Orozco and M. M. Paez, eds., *Latinos! Remaking America*, David Rockefeller Center for Latin American Studies, Harvard University, 97–109. Berkeley: University of California Press.

———. 2002b. *A Rainbow of Gangs: Street Cultures in the Mega-City*. Austin: University of Texas Press.

———. 2003a [1997]. *Personas Mexicanas: Chicano High Schoolers in a Changing Los Angeles*. Belmont, CA: Tomson.

———. 2003b. "Urban Violence and Street Gangs." *Annual Review of Anthropology* 32:225–242.

———. 2004. "Gangs and Group Membership: Implications for Schooling." In M. Gibson, P. Gandara, and J. Koyama, eds., *Peers, Schools, and the Educational Achievement of U.S.-Mexican Youth*, 87–106. New York: Columbia Teachers College Press.

Vigil, J. D., and B. Caldwell. N.d. "Chicana Street Youth: Lives of East L.A." Unpublished manuscript.

Vigil, J. D., and J. M. Long. 1990. "Emic and Etic Perspectives of Gang Culture: The Chicano Case." In C. R. Huff, ed., *Gangs in America: Diffusion, Diversity, and Public Policy*, 55–68. Thousand Oaks, CA: Sage.

Vigil, J. D., and S. C. Yun. 1996. "Southern California Gangs: Comparative Ethnicity and Social Control." In C. R. Huff, ed., *Gangs in America*, 2nd ed., 139–156. Thousand Oaks, CA: Sage.

———. 2001. "A Cross-Cultural Framework for Understanding Gangs: Multiple Marginality and Los Angeles." In C. R. Huff, ed., *Gangs in America III*, 161–174. Newbury Park, CA: Sage.

Walker-Barnes, C., and C. A. Mason. 2001. "Ethnic Differences in the Effect of Parenting on Gang Involvement and Gang Delinquency: A Longitudinal, Hierarchical Linear Modeling Perspective." *Child Development* 72 (6): 1814–1832.

Waters, T. 1999. *Crime and Immigrant Youth*. Thousand Oaks, CA: Sage.

Weatherburn, D., and B. Lind. 2001. *Delinquent-Prone Communities*. Cambridge: Cambridge University Press.

Websdale, N. 2001. *Policing the Poor: From Slave Plantation to Public Housing*. Boston: Northeastern University Press.

Weisner, T. S. 1997. "The Ecocultural Project of Human Development: Why Ethnography and Its Findings Matter." *Ethos* 25 (2): 177–190.

Weppner, R. S., ed. 1977. *Street Ethnography*. Beverly Hills, CA: Sage.

Wilson, J. Q., and J. Petersilia. 1995. "The Family." In J. Q. Wilson and J. Petersilia, eds., 121–140. *Crime*. San Francisco: Institute for Contemporary Studies.

Wilson, W. J. 1987. *The Truly Disadvantaged: The Inner-City, the Underclass, and Public Policy*. Chicago: University of Chicago Press.

———. 1991. "Studying Inner-City Social Dislocation." *American Sociological Review* 56:1–14.

———. 1996. *When Work Disappears: The World of the New Urban Poor*. New York: Knopf.

Wright, J. P., and F. Cullen. 2001. "Parental Efficacy and Delinquent Behavior: Do Control and Support Matter?" *Criminology* 39 (3): 677–706.

Young, P. 1929. "The Russian Molokan Community in Los Angeles." *American Journal of Sociology* 35 (3): 393–402.

INDEX

abuse. *See* alcohol use; drug use; physical abuse; sexual abuse
acculturation, 29, 82, 107, 110–111
AFDC, xi, 20, 22, 30–31, 33, 35, 135, 142, 154, 160, 162, 165, 196
African Americans: in gangs, 44–45, 49, 51–52, 68, 85, 101; music of, 67; and parenting styles, 15; in Pico Gardens, 128, 168–169. *See also* McDuffie, Bebee
agent effects, 127, 132–134, 137
Aid to Families with Dependent Children. *See* AFDC
alcohol use: of Bebee's stepfather, 102–103; in gang families, 102–103, 115, 135, 158, 162; by gang members, 63, 64, 74, 170, 175; in non-gang families, 35, 37, 115
Alejandro (gang father), 161–164
Alexander, J. F., 207
Alicia (non-gang mother), 155–156
Aliso Village, 22, 39–40, 44, 187, 188, 191–192
Amato, P., 17
American Me, 69
Anderson, E., 2, 9, 14, 16
Apaches clique, 1–2, 66, 100
authoritarian parenting, 14–15, 152, 164, 166–169, 171, 176, 204. *See also* parenting

authoritative and competent parenting, 15–16, 36–37, 136–137, 142–147, 150–155, 195, 196. *See also* parenting
automobile ownership, 31, 35, 47, 142, 154, 162, 195

Bad Boy (gang member), 71–72
Barnard, H. R., 6
Battle of Algiers, The, 180
Becker, R., 207
Bennett, W. J., 43
bike patrols, 183, 192–193, 201, 202
blacks. *See* African Americans
Bogardus, E., 43, 56
Booth, K., 197
boyfriends of single mothers, 35, 135, 136, 160, 165, 168, 169–171, 197
Boyle, Father Gregory, xiii, xiv, 28, 78, 79, 93, 182–183, 190, 203, 204
Boyle Heights, 28, 30, 31, 40, 56, 85
Brenda (gang mother), 168–169
Briggs, Xavier, xi
Brody, G., 14, 15
Bronfenbrenner, U., 8
bullying by gang members, 137
Burgess, E., 14

Caldwell, Beth, 107
California Youth Authority (CYA), 62
calo (Spanish slang), 69

Campbell, A., 108, 123
Canada, G., 42
Carmela (gang mother), 174–175
Cartwright, D. S., 38
Casa de Carnalismo (House of the Brotherhood), 2, 178–181
Catholic church, 11, 42, 43, 144, 155–156, 162, 166, 182–183, 188–190, 203
Catholic Youth Organization (CYO), 42, 43, 66
CETA (Comprehensive Employment and Training Act), 52
Chesney-Lind, M., 106, 113
Chicago, 10–12, 111
Chicano civil rights movement, 2, 67, 179
Chicano Pinto Research Project (CPRP), xiii, xiv, 4, 28, 42
Chicos clique, 66, 67, 69, 79, 99–101
child-rearing strategy. See parenting
cholas. See female gangs
choloismo, 69
Church. See Catholic church; Pentecostal church
Cisneros, Henry, 105
Clarence Street Locals (CSL), 48, 49
Clarence Street Stoners (CSS), 45, 46
Clinton, Bill, 10
cliques: of Cuatro Flats gang, 64–93, 100–101, 109; female cliques, 108–109; females in male cliques, 109, 168–169
clothing and physical appearance: as agent effect, 132–133, 134; of Cuatro Flats gang members, 67, 71–72, 74, 99; of female gang members, 111, 112, 120–121; and tattoos, 41, 64, 71, 121
Cohen, A., 38
Cole, M., 150
Cole, S., 150
Coleman, J., 16
collective efficacy, 12–13
Comite por Paz (Committee for Peace), 11, 12, 49, 188–189, 194
Community Alert Patrol, 180
community groups. See extracurricular activities; prevention and intervention programs; Residents Advisory Council (RAC)
Community Youth Gang Services, 49, 187, 203
Condon, M., 22
Conger, R. D., 15
Continental era, 67
Copeland, A. P., 25
cora (empathy, heart), 55, 62
Countdowns clique, 66, 69, 74, 79, 101
CPRP. See Chicano Pinto Research Project (CPRP)
crime: drive-by shootings, 46–47, 63–65, 78, 108; of female gang members, 106, 107; petty criminal acts within underclass families, 132; in Pico Gardens, 11, 23, 28, 46, 151, 155, 163, 164, 166–167, 205–206; statistics on arrests, 23; by youth in non-gang families, 37. See also drug-related crime; violence
CSL (Clarence Street Locals), 48, 49
CSS (Clarence Street Stoners), 45, 46
Cuatro Flats gang: Bebee as member of, 94–105; and Big Shoot-out (1993), 79–80, 190–191, 206–207; black members of, 68, 101; and cholo signs and symbols, 47, 59, 62, 167; cliques of, 64–93, 100–101, 109; clothing and physical appearance of, 67, 71–72, 74, 99; and Continental era, 67; drug and alcohol use by, 63, 64, 69, 163, 170, 172, 175; and drug-related crime, 44–47, 50, 52–53, 58, 69; egalitarian nature of, 61–62; ethnicity of, 101–102; and fatherhood, 123–124; first-generation immigrants in, 24, 70; and gang-as-family, 62, 110, 132, 134–135, 167–168; and gang banging, 57–58, 62, 78–81, 84, 89–90; and gang slangers, 62, 89–90, 106; girlfriends of, 48, 71–72, 117, 125; and guns, 44–47, 52–53, 69, 173; history of, 23–24, 39–53, 56–57, 66–69,

100–104, 177; initiation into, 58, 99;
and inter-gang rivalries, 43, 44–45,
48–49, 57–58, 60–61, 64, 79–80,
172, 183, 189; and *locura* (manly
mind-set), 63–64, 72–73, 78–81, 89–
90; loyalty to, 61; and machismo,
116, 123–124, 130–132, 135–136; and
marginalization, 69–70; and mediation of inter-gang rivalries, 49–50;
and Mexican Mafia, 69; photographs of, 41, 47, 51, 63, 68, 167; and
police, 21, 28; and power of "gang
mystique," 135–136; pre-initiation
behavior for, 37, 58–59; and prison
experience, 62–63, 78, 94, 103, 104,
160, 163, 170, 172, 197; protection
function of, 57–58; reasons for
membership in, 48, 51, 125, 135–136,
167–168; and school, 58–61, 82–83,
169, 170; self-image of members of,
59; and sexual activities, 74, 76, 108,
117, 119, 123–124; siblings and other
relatives belonging to, 83–84, 165–
168, 199–200; and street socialization, 58, 59–60; subculture of, 44,
54–93; values and norms of, 47–48,
50, 61–64, 113, 116; veteranos of, 43,
45–46, 51, 61–62, 99, 135–136. *See
also* female gangs; gang families;
Pico Gardens; Pico Gardens (P.G.)
clique
Cullen, F., 16
Curry, D., 208
CYA. *See* California Youth Authority
(CYA)
CYO. *See* Catholic Youth Organization
(CYO)

Dahlia (gang mother), 170–171
Daly, K., 113
DAP (Deputy Auxiliary Police), 66
Dawley, D., 179, 181
Decker, S. H., 127, 208
delinquency, 8–9, 13–17, 37, 130. *See
also* Cuatro Flats gang; female
gangs; gangs
Demaree, R. G., 210

denial, xi, 132, 133–134, 136, 140, 161,
164, 165–168, 175, 197
Denton, N., 9
Deputy Auxiliary Police (DAP), 66
Dinkmeyer, D., 207
divorce, 13, 17, 166
DL belief (staying "down low"), 74, 76
Dolores Mission Catholic Church,
182–183, 188–190, 203
domestic violence. *See* physical abuse
drive-by shootings, 46–47, 63–65, 78,
108
Droopy (gang member), 119
dropping out of school, 59, 169. *See
also* education
drug intervention programs, xiii, xiv,
2, 180–188, 191–193, 204
drug-related crime: and crack cocaine,
40; by Cuatro Flats gang, 44–47, 50,
52–53, 58, 69, 172; and guns, 44, 76,
77–78; and informers, 77–78; and
lack of police presence in Pico Gardens, 205–206; and Mexican Mafia
(EME), 50, 69, 83–84; and PCP, 44,
47; by Pico Gardens (P.G.) clique,
69, 76–78, 85, 89–91; police arrests
for, 23, 181–182; prices of drugs, 75;
and rock cocaine, 76; statistics on,
23; and young children, 50
drug treatment centers, 211
drug use: citizen activism against,
180–181; and crack cocaine, 40; by
Cuatro Flats gang, 63, 64, 69, 163,
170, 175; and drive-by shootings, 47;
as factor hindering social control,
20; by female gang members, 115; in
gang families, 115, 158; in non-gang
families, 37, 115; by parents, 50; and
PCP, 44, 47; by Pico Gardens (P.G.)
clique, 74, 75, 76, 84–85; police
arrests for, 23, 181–182; and rock
cocaine, 76; by Stoners, 68. *See also*
drug intervention programs
Dubrow, N., 13
Dukes clique, 66, 67–68, 101
Dunworth, T., 23
Duran, M., 66

East Coast Crips gang, 44–45, 49, 68
eating habits, 16, 137, 144, 154–155, 196
economy. *See* employment; poverty
education: and alternative schools, 203, 204; Bebee's school experiences, 95–100; corporal punishment in school, 97; and dropping out, 59, 169; funding for, 203; and gang families, 160, 163; and gang members generally, 38; gangs and gang rivalries in schools, 60–61; high school walkout (1968), 67; of household heads, 34, 82, 147, 149, 159, 162, 163, 170, 196, 197; learning difficulties of gang members, 58–59, 170; and non-gang families, 144–147, 157, 196; and overcrowded schools, 187, 197, 203; parents' concerns about, 187; school problems of Pico Gardens (P.G.) clique members, 82–83; and truancy, 37
Elder, G. H., Jr., 15
Elena (non-gang mother), 136–137, 149–150
El Hoyo Maravilla gang, xiii, 65, 69
Elliott, D. S., 8
EME. *See* Mexican Mafia (EME)
employment: and biases of employers, 33; and CETA, 52; and entrepreneurialism, 130, 142, 148–149, 196, 204; of former gang members, 138; and gang families, 129–130, 162, 163; of immigrants, 82, 129–130, 148–150, 155, 160, 163; and informal "underground economy," 31, 32, 33, 34–35; and non-gang families, 130; for Pico Gardens residents, 22, 54, 82, 128–130, 138, 142, 148–149, 207–209; policy recommendations on, 207–209; of single mothers, 129–130, 154, 155, 160, 163; and unemployment, 31, 40, 128, 132, 142, 163; of women, 129–130, 139, 142, 154, 155, 160, 163
Enanos (Midgets) clique, 66, 67, 100
enculturation, 29

Erikson, Erik, 59
Esbensen, F.-A., 112, 122, 201
Escobar, E., 179, 205
extracurricular activities, 145, 155–156, 174, 196

Falbo, T., 24
families: and divorce, 13, 17, 166; and family-functioning variables, 13; and family-structural variables, 13; father's role in, 130–132, 139, 143, 169, 171; needs and problems of generally, 141, 195–196; and parent education, 207; petty criminal acts within, 132; physical and emotional abuse in, 98, 102–103, 130, 131, 135, 158, 160, 166, 168, 169–172, 176, 197–198, 204, 210; push effects of underclass and ineffective family types, 134–135; research on connection between poverty, delinquency, and, 13–16; traditional immigrant families, 111–112; types of, in barrios, 6, 8, 13; underclass type of, 6, 132, 134–135. *See also* fathers; gang families; mothers; non-gang families; parenting; single parents; size of households
Fanon, Franz, 67
Farrington, D. P., 8, 13, 198
fathers: absent fathers in gang families, 159–160, 169–170, 172–173, 197; alcohol use by, 35, 37, 102–103, 135; gambling by, 172; in gang families, 161–164; gang members as, 123–124; and machismo, 130–132, 139; in non-gang families, 130, 142–143, 149–154; physical and emotional abuse by, 98, 102–103, 130, 131, 139, 142, 143, 166, 169–172, 197–198, 204; role of, within family, 130–132, 139, 143, 169, 171; and sense of community, 138; as "shadow" spouses, 35, 136, 170. *See also* gang families; non-gang families; parenting
fear: and authoritarian parenting,

168; of gang members, 63, 135–136; of Pico Gardens residents, 151, 155, 163, 164, 167

female gangs: arrest of member of, 108; and attraction to "bad boys," 48, 74; clothing, makeup, and physical appearance of, 111, 112, 120–121; and dances and social gatherings of gang members, 74–76; drug use by, 115; emotional support by, 115; families of females in, 112–115, 122; and females as sex objects, 117, 119; first- and second-generation immigrants in, 112; and gang-as-family, 110; and "good girl" versus "bad girl" role, 116–117; and guns, 121–122; Hang Out Girls as, 49; male dominance of females in, 115–116, 125; male gang members' view of, 108, 117, 119; and multiple marginality, 110–111, 123, 125; physical, emotional, and sexual abuse of females in, 74, 113–116, 119, 125; pregnancy and motherhood of females in, 118, 123–125, 169; and prison experience, 107; psychological problems of females in, 112, 113–114; reasons for membership in, 109–115, 125; reasons for recent growth of, 107–108; relationship of, with male gangs, 48, 71–72, 74–76, 107, 108, 116–119, 122–125; and relatives belonging to gangs, 112–113, 168–169; research on, 106–108; running away by females in, 114–115; and self-esteem, 115; sexual activities of females, 74, 76, 108, 117, 119, 123–124; statistics on, 106; and street socialization, 106; structure of, 108–109; and tomboys, 119–120; violence by, 108, 121–123

females: and attraction to "bad boys," 48, 74; and dances and social gatherings of gang members, 74–76; double standard for, 110; employment of, 129–130, 139, 142, 154, 155, 160, 163, 196; as girlfriends of Cua-

tro Flats gang, 48, 71–72, 117, 125; and intergenerational cycle of gang membership, 124–125; marginalization of, 110–111, 123; and *marianismo*, 107; and motherhood, 118, 123–125; physical and emotional abuse of, 98, 102–103, 113–114, 125, 130, 131, 135, 136, 139, 142, 143, 160, 166, 168, 169–172, 176, 197–198, 204; and reasons for not joining gangs, 111; relationship of, with male gang members, 48, 71–72, 74–76, 107, 108, 116–119, 122–125; sexual abuse of, 74, 113–116, 119; and sexual activities, 74, 76, 108, 117, 119, 123–124; and "training" by male gang members, 74, 119. *See also* female gangs; mothers

food stamps, 31, 33, 135, 142, 154, 162, 165

Franzese, R. J., 4

Fremon, C., 78, 182

Fuhrman, Mark, 23, 67, 181–182

Furstenberg, Frank, 33–34, 36

gambling, 172

gang banging, 57–58, 62, 78–81, 84, 89–90

gang families: and absent fathers, 159–160, 169–170, 172–173, 197; alcohol and drug abuse in, 102–103, 115, 135, 158, 162; automobile ownership by, 35, 162; Bebee's family, 94–105; case histories of, 129–130, 133–135, 159–175, 197; challenges of, 158; characteristics of, x; childhood of parents in, 36, 159, 160, 162; denial of gang membership of children in, xi, 132, 133–134, 136, 161, 164, 165–168, 175, 197; denial of responsibility by parents in, 161, 169, 175, 197; eating habits in, 16; educational level of household heads of, 34, 82, 159, 162, 163, 170, 197; education of children in, 160, 163; and employment, 129–130, 162, 163; and family-functioning variables, 13;

and family-structural variables, 13; of female gang members, 112–115, 122; and guns, 173; heads of households as active gang members, 34; and health problems, 163; hostility of non-gang families against, 172–173; income of, 34–35; and lack of social ties, 36, 174–176; number of, in sample, 34; number of gang members per family, 34; overview of differences between non-gang families and, 33–38, 196–198; parenting in, 14–15, 35–37, 132–136, 158, 161, 164–169, 171–173, 176, 197; parents as former gang members in, 34, 169, 200; photographs of, 159, 167, 173; physical and emotional abuse in, 98, 102–103, 135, 158, 160, 166, 168, 169–172, 176, 197–198, 204; of Pico Gardens (P.G.) clique members, 81–82; and push effects, 134–135; siblings and other relatives of, as gang members, 83–84, 112–113, 165–169, 172, 199; and single female-headed households, 34, 129–130, 135, 159–161, 163–175, 197; and size of household, 14, 34, 82, 161–164, 197; and social services, 36; and street socialization, 38; and types of families in barrios, 6, 8, 13; welfare benefits for, 35, 160, 162, 165

gang prevention. *See* prevention and intervention programs

gangs: in Chicago, 10–11, 111; continuum of involvement with, 127; definition of, 20; females' relationships with, 48, 71–72, 74–76, 107, 108, 116–119, 122–125; life expectancy of members of, xi; and marginalization, 8; multigenerational gang involvement, 34, 169, 200; as peer family, x, 62, 110, 132, 132–134, 167–168; in Pico Gardens area generally, 23–24, 48–49, 60, 183; policy recommendations on, 207–211; and poverty, 9–11, 51, 110–111, 125; as

predators, xi, 11; pre-initiation behavior for, 37; protection function of, xi, 11, 37, 38, 51–52, 55–58, 125; research on, xiii, xiv–xv; in schools, 60–61; siblings and other relatives belonging to, 83–84, 112–113, 165–169, 172, 199; social roles of members of, 12, 38; territory of, 49, 196. *See also* Cuatro Flats gang; female gangs; gang families

gang slanging, 62, 89 90, 106
gang violence. *See* violence
Garbarino, J., 13
Garcia, Robert ("Viejo"), 42
Garrison, J., 79
Gehlke-Baez, R. A., 195
Geisman, L., 13
gender. *See* fathers; female gangs; females; machismo and patriarchy; *marianismo*; mothers
Geronimo (gang leader), 1–2, 66, 177
gestures, signs, and symbols of gangs, 47, 59, 62, 167
Ghetto Boys, 46, 68
girl gangs. *See* female gangs
Glueck, E., xiv, 13, 14
Glueck, S., xiv, 13, 14
Gonzales, N. A., 15
Gorman-Smith, D., 14, 15
graffiti, 37, 65, 75, 149, 153
GREAT (Gang Resistance Education and Training), 201
Green, Norman, 95
Groves, W. B., 14
guns, 44–47, 52–53, 69, 76–80, 121–122, 139, 173, 188. *See also* violence

Haapasalo, J., 14–15
Hagedorn, J. M., 9, 114, 124
Hamburg, David, 36
Hannerz, U., 2
Harmon, Tom, 43
Hayden, T., 53, 195
Head Start, 58, 157, 181
Heath, S. B., 199
Heimer, K., 16

Herrenkohl, E. C., 112, 127
Hil, R., 13
Hirschi, T., 13
Holloway, S., 9, 13
Homeboy Industries, 182, 203
homicides. *See* violence
Hope for Youth, 203
housing. *See* public housing
Housing and Urban Development
   Department (HUD), 105, 188
housing police, 201, 202, 205, 208
HUD (Department of Housing and
   Urban Development), 105, 188
Huizinga, D., 210
Hunt, G., 115
hyperactivity, 127, 132, 133

immigrants: acculturation of, 82, 107;
   in Cuatro Flats gang, 24, 70; in East
   Los Angeles, 56; employment of,
   82, 129–130, 148–150, 155, 160, 163,
   207–211; expectations of, for daughters, 111; and multiple marginality,
   57; obstacles for, 82, 112, 148, 149;
   in Pico Gardens generally, 56, 70,
   186; in Pico Gardens (P.G.) clique,
   89, 90; policy recommendations
   on, 207–211. *See also* fathers; gang
   families; mothers; non-gang families; Pico Gardens; single parents
IMPACTO (Imaginando Mañana: Pico-
   Aliso Community Teen Outreach),
   107, 188, 208
income: of Boyle Heights residents,
   31; of Pico Gardens households, 22,
   33, 34–35. *See also* poverty
informal "underground economy," 31,
   32, 33, 34–35
initiation into gang, 58, 99
inter-gang rivalries: and Big Shoot-out
   (1993), 79–80, 190–191, 206–207;
   and gang banging, 57–58, 78–81, 84;
   history of, 43, 44–45, 48–49; mediation of, 49–50; in school, 60–61;
   TMC-Cuatro Flats rivalry, 64, 65, 78,
   79–80, 172, 183, 189

interrupter effects, 128, 136–137,
   138–139
intervention programs. *See* prevention and intervention programs

Jencks, C., 22
jobs. *see* employment
Johnson, V., 14
Jones, A. P., 210
Jordan, Don, 2, 66, 177
Juana (gang mother), 129–130, 134,
   159–161, 163, 165–166, 169–170, 174,
   175, 197
juvenile delinquency. *See* delinquency; gangs

Kanaiaupuni, S., 9
Keith, B., 17
Kitano, H., 56
Klein, M. W., 34, 38, 127, 199, 207
klika. See cliques
Kling, Jeffrey, xi
Kruttschmitt, C., 208

L.A. Bridges Program, 203
L.A. CADA (Los Angeles Centers for
   Alcohol and Drug Abuse), 188,
   191–192, 204
LAPD. *See* Los Angeles Police Depart-
   ment (LAPD)
Laub, J., 14, 133
Laura (gang mother), 163–164
law enforcement. *See* bike patrols;
   housing police; Los Angeles Police
   Department (LAPD)
leva (sanctioned), 62
Leventhal, Tama, xi
Liebow, E., 2
Lind, B., 9, 13, 15
loco, locura (manly mind-set), 63–64,
   72–74, 78–81, 89–90
Loco (veterano), 78–79
Loeber, R., 5, 8, 13, 197
Lofland, J., 27
Lofland, L. H., 27
Long, J. M., 4, 28, 42, 43, 90

Los Angeles County, statistics on, 31
Los Angeles County Probation Department, 202
Los Angeles Housing Authority, xiii, 22, 23, 24, 29
Los Angeles Police Department (LAPD): and Big Shoot-out (1993), 80, 190–191; brutality and abuse by, 21, 28, 181–182, 191, 194; and Casa de Carnalismo (House of the Brotherhood), 179; and causative factors for gang activity, 200–201; citizen monitoring of, 180–181; and DAP (Deputy Auxiliary Police), 66; and death of Loco, 78–79; drug arrests by, 23, 181–182; and female gang members, 108; and Neighborhood Watch, 11, 12, 76, 188–189, 191–194, 202; in Pico Gardens, 11, 20–21, 23, 28, 76, 183, 192–193, 197, 201–202, 208; policy recommendations on, 208; relationship between other law enforcement agencies and, in Pico Gardens, 199, 201–202, 208; violence between police and residents in Pico Gardens, 11, 23, 28, 89, 205
"Los Tres," 181

MAAC. See Mexican American Action Committee (MAAC)
machismo and patriarchy, 116, 123–124, 130–132, 135–136, 139
Maravilla gang, xiii, 45, 65, 69
marginalization: and Cuatro Flats gang, 69–70; and female gangs, 110–111, 123, 125; and gangs generally, 8; multiple marginality, 4–6, 8, 14, 57, 92, 110–111, 123, 125, 126, 128
Maria (non-gang mother), 151–154, 155, 157
marianismo, 107
Marta (gang mother), 135, 164–166
Más chingón (baddest dude), 43
Mason, C. A., 14, 15
Massey, D., 9
Mata, A., 115
matones (killers or bad dudes), 44

Matsueda, R., 16
Maxson, C., 199, 207
Mayer, S. C., 22
Mayo, Y. Q., 132
Mayra (gang member), 122, 124
McCord, J., 13
McDuffie, Bebee, xiv, 25, 62, 72–75, 94–105, 183, 184
McDuffie, Pam, xiv, 183
MCF (Michigan Criminal Force), 46
McKay, G. D., 207
McKay, H., 14
McLanahan, S., 5, 16–17, 197, 198
McLaughlin, M., 199
McMahon, A., 13
McNulty, T., 9, 13
mediation of inter-gang rivalries, 49–50
Medicaid, 33
Medicare, 135, 154, 162, 165
Mehren, E., 113
Mendoza-Denton, Norma, 120–121
Mexican American Action Committee (MAAC), 178
Mexican Mafia (EME), 50, 69, 83–84
Michigan Criminal Force (MCF), 46
Miller, Jody, 106, 113, 115
Miranda, M. K., 106
Mob Crew (TMC), 45–49, 64, 65, 78, 169, 172, 183, 189
momos (parties), 74
Montebello Gardens, 177
Moore, Joan W., xiii, 4, 6, 9, 13, 21, 22, 23, 27, 28, 42, 65–66, 84, 108, 115, 117, 124, 128, 130, 132
Morales, A., 84, 205
Morenoff, J., 12–13
mothers: boyfriends of single mothers, 35, 135, 136, 160, 165, 168, 169–171, 197; and denial of gang membership of children, 132, 133–134, 136, 161, 164, 165–168, 175, 197; female gang members as, 118, 123–125; in gang families, 129–130, 133–135, 159–161, 163–175, 197; in non-gang families, 130, 137–138, 142–147, 149–157, 196; physical and

emotional abuse against, 98, 102–
103, 130, 131, 135, 136, 139, 142, 143,
160, 166, 168, 169–172, 176, 197–
198, 204. *See also* gang families;
non-gang families; parenting; single
parents
multiple marginality: and female
gangs, 110–111, 123, 125; as framework for Pico Gardens research,
4–6, 8, 14, 126, 128; and immigrant
families, 57; and Pico Gardens (P.G.)
clique, 92
murders. *See* violence
Myra (gang member), 114

National Youth Survey, 17
Neighborhood Watch, 11, 12, 76, 188,
189, 191–194, 202
Neighborhood Youth Corps (NYC),
177–178, 181
Night Owls clique, 66, 68, 101
non-gang families: and active monitoring of children and extra time in
home environment, 138–139, 144,
153–155; alcohol and drug use in, 35,
37, 115; and "American dream," 156;
automobile ownership by, 35, 142,
154; case histories of, 130, 137–138,
142–147, 149–157, 196; characteristics of, x; childhood of parents in,
36, 152; and community groups, 36;
and creative responses to marginalization, 147–150; delinquency of
children in, 37; discipline in, 143,
150–153; eating habits in, 16, 137,
144, 154–155, 196; and education,
144–147, 157, 196; educational level
of household heads of, 34, 147, 149,
196; and employment, 130, 148–
150; and extracurricular activities,
145, 155–156, 174, 196; hostility
of, toward gang families, 172–173;
income of, 34–35; and listening to
children, 143–144, 151; on need for
children to see good examples, 136;
overview of differences between
gang families and, 33–38, 196–198;

and parental efficacy, 16; parenting
in, 14, 16, 35–37, 36–37, 130, 136–
138, 142–147, 150–155, 196; photographs of, 146, 148, 152, 156; and
respect, 137–138, 143, 151, 152, 196;
and single parents, 138, 154–155;
and size of household, 14, 34, 148;
and social services, 36; and types of
families in barrios, 6, 8, 13; welfare
benefits for, 35, 142, 196
norms of gangs, 47–48, 50, 61–64, 113,
116
NYC. *See* Neighborhood Youth Corps
(NYC)

OGS (original gangsters), 43, 45, 46
One Strike rule, 10, 29
Operation "Clean and Green," 178
overcrowding. *See* size of households

pachuco (zoot suit) era, 100, 107
paisas (Mexican-born), 112
palabra (keeping your word), 62
Pandina, R. J., 14
parenting: affectionate and nurturing
parenting, 14, 16, 142–144, 150–155,
196; alcohol problem of father in
non-gang families, 35, 37; authoritarian parenting, 14–15, 152, 164,
166–169, 171, 176, 204; authoritative
and competent parenting, 15–16,
36–37, 136–137, 142–147, 150–155,
195, 196; and childhood of parents,
36, 152, 159, 160; and denial of gang
membership of children, xi, 132,
133–134, 136, 161, 164, 165–168,
175, 197; education for, 207; in
gang families, 35–37, 132–136, 158,
164–169, 171, 197; lack of, and street
socialization, 38; and multigenerational gang involvement, 34, 169,
200, 210; in non-gang families, 35–
37, 130, 136–138, 142–147, 150–155,
196; and parental efficacy, 16; permissive parenting, 15, 161, 164–168,
171, 172–173, 176, 204; precision
parenting, 15; by "shadow" spouses,

35, 136, 170; and social capital, 36;
types of, 14–16, 150. *See also* families; fathers; mothers; single parents
Park, R., 14
Parsons, B. V., 207
patriarchy. *See* machismo and
patriarchy
Patterson, G. R., 15, 207
Peacemakers clique, 66, 67, 100–101
Penguins clique, 66, 67
Pentecostal church, 104, 188
permissive parenting, 15, 161, 164–
168, 171, 172–173, 176, 204. *See also*
parenting
Peterson, D., 201
P.G. (Pico Gardens) clique, 65, 66, 69,
71–93
physical abuse: of female gang members, 113–114, 125, 204; in gang
families, 98, 102–103, 135, 158, 160,
166, 168, 169–171, 176, 197–198,
204; of mothers by fathers, 98,
102–103, 130, 131, 139, 142, 143, 166,
169–170, 197–198, 204; of single
mothers by boyfriends, 135, 136,
160, 168, 169–171
physical appearance. *See* clothing and
physical appearance
Pico Gardens: age of residents of, 30,
31; demographic statistics on, 30–
31; deteriorating infrastructure of,
23; ethnicity of, 128; gangs in generally, 23–24, 48–49, 60, 183; history
of, 23, 39–40, 56–57; household size
in, 30, 31; immigrants in generally,
56, 70, 186; income per household
in, 22, 33, 34–35; lack of trees and
shrubbery in, 23; location of, xiii–
xiv, 4, 5, 21–23, 56, 57; photographs
of, 10, 15, 22, 24, 25, 32, 206; policy
recommendations on, 207–211;
population statistics on, 22; renova-
tion of, 29, 105; social connections
in, 55, 184–185; Vigil's experiences
in, 1–2, 177–185. *See also* Cuatro
Flats gang; employment; female
gangs; gang families; Los Angeles

Police Department (LAPD); non-
gang families; Pico Gardens (P.G.)
clique; poverty; prevention and
intervention programs; violence
Pico Gardens (P.G.) clique: active
members of, 88–90; age of joining
gang, 84; ages of members of, 72,
85–87; alcohol and drug use by, 74,
75, 76, 84–85; dances and social
gatherings of, 74–76; demographic
information on, 81–85, 91–92; and
drug sales, 69, 76–78, 85, 89–91;
ethnicity of members of, 72, 85, 88,
90; as first- and second-generation
immigrants, 82, 89, 90; and guns,
69, 76–78; and hanging out, 76–78;
home life of members of, 81–82;
locura and gang banging by, 78–81,
84, 89–90; and multiple marginality, 92; nicknames of members
of, 85–87; number of members of,
72, 81, 85, 91; peripheral members
of, 90–91; photographs of, 73, 77;
and positive perception of gangs
and gang life, 84; relations of, with
Vigil, 72–74; and relatives belonging to gangs, 83–84; school problems of members of, 82–83; and
street life, 84; violence by, 89–90;
years in existence, 65, 66, 69, 91
Pico Gardens research: and anthropological perspective, 92; collaborative research strategy for,
28; collateral data collection for,
27–28; community researchers for,
27, 57, 184; and demographic and
employment characteristics of Pico
Gardens, 30–33, 128–132, 205; and
ethnographic survey, 126, 128–132;
and family variables, 6–9; four-step
plan for, 25–28; funding for, 2, 184;
goals of, 204–205; individual and
family histories for, 25–27, 29; as
longitudinal study, 26–27, 30; methodological deviations from plan for,
28–30; multiple marginality framework for, 4–6, 8, 14, 126, 128; obser-

vation of families in, 26; overview of, 3; overview of differences between gang families and non-gang families in, 33–38, 196–198; rationale and methods of, 20–38; reasons for site selection for, 4, 20–24; and research on economy and public housing, 9–13; and research on family, 13–16; samples for, 25–26; and single parents, 13, 16–17, 34; social control analysis for, 4–6
Pico Stoners, 46, 66, 68, 101
Pinderhughes, R., 27
Pokela, E., 14–15
police. See Los Angeles Police Department (LAPD)
policy recommendations, 207–211
Popkin, Susan, xi, 9, 11–12, 16
post-traumatic stress disorder (PTSD), 112, 113
poverty: of Bebee's family, 96; in Boyle Heights, 31; and gangs, 9–11, 51, 110–111, 125; income of Pico Gardens households, 22, 33, 34–35; in Pico Gardens, 5–6, 20, 21, 22, 30–31, 33, 40, 110–111, 125, 132, 195–196; and public housing, 9, 22; research on, 2–3. See also War on Poverty
pregnancy of female gang members, 118, 123–125, 169
prevention and intervention programs: Casa de Carnalismo (House of the Brotherhood), 2, 178–181; Comite por Paz (Committee for Peace), 11, 12, 49, 188–189, 194; Community Youth Gang Services, 203; and Dolores Mission Catholic Church, 182–183, 188–189; drug intervention programs, xiii, xiv, 2, 180–188, 191–193, 204; and factors hindering social control, 198–207; funding for, 203; gang-proofing and gang avoidance, 137–139; and gang violence, 187; GREAT (Gang Resistance Education and Training), 201; Homeboy Industries, 182, 203; Hope for Youth, 203; IMPACTO (Imaginando

Mañana: Pico-Aliso Community Teen Outreach), 107, 188, 208; L.A. Bridges Program, 203; in Montebello Gardens, 177–178; and Neighborhood Watch, 188, 189, 191–194; Neighborhood Youth Corps (NYC), 177–178, 181; Operation "Clean and Green," 178; policy recommendations on, 207–211; Pro-Force, 182–183, 192–193, 202; Proyecto Pastoral, 182; Teen Post, 177–178, 181
Primera Flats gang, 23–24, 42, 44, 45
prisons: for female gang members, 107; for male gang members, 62–63, 68, 75, 78, 94, 98, 103, 104, 160, 163, 170, 172, 197; and Mexican Mafia (EME), 50, 69, 83–84
probation agencies, 202
Pro-Force program, 182–183, 192–193, 202
protection function of gangs, xi, 11, 37, 38, 51–52, 55–58, 125
Proyecto Pastoral, 182
PTSD (post-traumatic stress disorder), 112, 113
public housing, 9–13, 22, 55. See also Pico Gardens
pull effects, 127–128, 135–138
push effects, 127, 134–135, 137
Putnam, R., 12

Quicker, J. C., 115

RAC. See Residents Advisory Council (RAC)
Rainwater, L., 3
Raquel (non-gang mother), 154–155
Rebellion, C., 17
rebelliousness as teen, 127, 132, 134
research on Pico Gardens. See Pico Gardens research
Residents Advisory Council (RAC), 94, 104–105, 174, 175, 184–187, 189–190, 193
Resnick, R. P., 132
respect, 137–138, 143, 151, 152, 164, 196

Rodriguez, Antonio, 178, 181–182
Rodriguez, Diane, 107
Rodriguez, Javier, 178
Rodriguez brothers, 2, 178–179,
    181–182
Romo, H. D., 24
Rosenbaum, J. E., 9
Rubinowitz, L., 9
runaways, 114–115

Sad Boy (gang member), 78
safety issues, 55, 187, 205. *See also* Los
    Angeles Police Department (LAPD)
Sampson, R. J., 14, 16, 133, 196, 198,
    199
Sandefur, G., 5, 16–17, 197, 198
Sara (gang mother), 133–134, 166–168
schools. *See* education
Schoor, L. D., 207
self-esteem, 59, 115, 137
sexual abuse, 74, 113–116, 119
sexual activities, 74, 76, 108, 117, 119,
    123–124
"shadow" spouses, 35, 136, 170
Shaw, C., 14
Shelden, R., 13
Sheldon, R. G., 106
Short, J. F., Jr., 13, 16, 91
shot callers, 108
Simpson, O. J., 23, 67, 181
single parents: and adolescent male
    children, 131–132; and Bebee's
    family, 94–99; boyfriends of single
    mothers, 35, 135, 136, 160, 165, 168,
    169–171, 197; childhood of, 36, 159;
    employment of, 129–130, 154, 160,
    163; in gang families, 34, 129–130,
    135, 159–161, 163–175, 197; in non-
    gang families, 138, 154–155; physical
    and emotional abuse of mother by
    boyfriend, 135, 136, 160, 168, 169–
    171; in Pico Gardens, 20, 34; of Pico
    Gardens (P.G.) clique members, 81;
    research on delinquency and, 13,
    16–17, 130; and "shadow" spouses,
    35, 136, 170
Sinners clique, 67, 100

size of households: of gang families,
    14, 34, 82, 161–164, 197; of non-gang
    families, 14, 34, 148; and overcrowd-
    ing, 196; in Pico Gardens, 30, 31
social capital, 12, 16, 36, 174
social control: analysis of, 4–6; break-
    down of, 8, 9, 11, 13; diagram of, 7;
    factors hindering, 198–207; and
    "mamas' mafias," 11; policy recom-
    mendations on, 207–211; and street
    socialization, 200. *See also* educa-
    tion; families; Los Angeles Police
    Department (LAPD)
social services, 36, 211. *See also* food
    stamps; Medicare; prevention and
    intervention programs; welfare
    benefits
Sonia (non-gang mother), 130, 137–
    138, 142–147, 151, 155, 156, 196
sports, 2, 42, 43, 45, 75, 145, 155
Stanton, M. D., 211
Stein, B. D., 112
Stole, M., 129
Stoners, 45, 46, 68–69, 101
Stouthamer-Loeber, M., 5, 13, 197
street ethnography, 28
street socialization, 7, 9, 38, 58–60,
    84, 106, 131, 195, 200
Stromquist, N., 206
Suarez-Orozco, C., 24
Suarez-Orozco, M., 24
substance abuse. *See* alcohol use; drug
    use
Sullivan, M., 16
Suttles, G., 3

tagging. *See* graffiti
tattoos, 41, 64, 71, 121
Teen Post, 177–178, 181
Termites clique, 66, 67, 101
Thornberry, T., 8
Thrasher, F. M., xiv, 38, 111
Thumper (gang member), 64, 65
Tiet, Q., 15
Tiger (veterano), 72–74
Tiny (gang member), 114
Tiny Wino (gang member), 64

TMC (Mob Crew), 45–49, 64, 65, 78, 169, 172, 183
Todd, T., 211
Triste (gang member), 63

"underground economy," 31, 32, 33, 34–35
unemployment, 31, 40, 128, 132, 142, 163

Valdez, Avelardo, 112
Vale, L., 9
values of gangs, 47–48, 50, 61–64, 113, 116
Van Winkle, B., 127
Venkatesh, S. A., 9, 10–11, 16, 23, 205
veteranos, 43, 45–46, 51, 61–62, 73–75, 78, 99, 135–136
Victory Outreach, 104, 188
Vietnamese, 72, 85, 90, 102
Vietnam War, 67, 179
Vigil, James Diego: *Barrio Gangs* by, 182; encounters of, with Pico Gardens, 1–2, 177–185; evaluation of drug intervention program by, xiii, xiv, 2, 182–184; photograph of, 57; references to writings by, xiii, 4–6, 9, 13, 14, 21–25, 28, 34, 37, 43, 56, 58, 59, 83, 84, 90, 106, 124, 127, 128, 130, 132, 133, 187, 188, 195, 206, 209; and War on Poverty, 177–178
violence: and Big Shoot-out (1993), 79–80, 190–191, 206–207; changes in, from 1930 to present, 42–49; community concerns about, 187–188; by Cuatro Flats gang, 11, 23, 28, 37, 42–50; deaths of gang members, 63, 78, 79, 89–90, 132; drive-by shootings, 46–47, 63–65, 78, 108; and drug deals, 77–78; by female gangs, 108, 121–123; between gang members and police in Pico Gardens, 11, 23, 28; and guns, 44–47, 52–53, 69, 76–80, 121–122, 139, 173, 188; and lack of police presence in Pico Gardens, 206–207; and *locura*

and gang banging, 57–58, 62–64, 72–73, 78–81, 84, 89–90, 188; male attitudes toward, 139; murder by Bebee, 103–104; by Pico Gardens (P.G.) clique, 89–90; police abuse and brutality, 21, 28, 181–182, 191, 194; street-level shootings with participants on foot, 78; and TMC-Cuatro Flats rivalry, 64, 65, 78, 79–80, 169, 172, 183, 189. *See also* crime; physical abuse
VISTA workers, 187, 188, 189

Walker-Barnes, C., 14, 15
War on Poverty, 44, 45, 52, 67, 177–181
Waters, T., 56
weapons. *See* guns
Weatherburn, D., 9, 13, 15
Websdale, N., 20
Weismann, Gretchen, xi
Weisner, Thomas S., ix xii, 27
welfare benefits: and AFDC, xi, 20, 22, 30–31, 33, 35, 135, 142, 154, 160, 162, 165, 196; for gang families, 35, 160, 162, 165; for non-gang families, 35, 142, 196; and Welfare Reform Act (1996), 210. *See also* food stamps
Welfare Reform Act (1996), 210
Weppner, R. S., 28
White Fence gang, xiii, 42, 45, 60, 61, 65
Wilson, W. J., 9, 16, 27
Winfree, L. T., 112, 122
women. *See* female gangs; females; mothers
Wood, K., 13
Wright, J. P., 16

Young, P., 56
Yun, S. C., 9
Yvette (gang mother), 171–173, 174

zoot suit (*pachuco*) era, 100, 107
Zoot Suit Riots, 43, 179